ARCHBISHOP HOWLEY, 1828–1848

The Archbishops of Canterbury Series

Series Editor: Andrew Chandler, University of Chichester, UK

Developed in association with Lambeth Palace Library archives, this series presents authoritative studies on the Archbishops of Canterbury. Each book combines biographical, historical, theological, social and political analysis within each archiepiscopacy, with original source material drawn from the Archbishop's correspondence, speeches and published and unpublished writings. The *Archbishops of Canterbury* series offers a vital source of reference, of lasting importance to scholars, students and all readers interested in the history of the international Church.

Other titles in this series:

Archbishop Pole
John Edwards

Archbishops Ralph d'Escures, William of Corbeil and Theobald of Bec
Heirs of Anselm and Ancestors of Becket
Jean Truax

Archbishop Anselm 1093–1109
Bec Missionary, Canterbury Primate, Patriarch of Another World
Sally N. Vaughn

Archbishop Fisher, 1945–1961
Church, State and World
Andrew Chandler and David Hein

Archbishop Howley, 1828–1848

JAMES GARRARD
Ely Cathedral, UK

Routledge
Taylor & Francis Group
LONDON AND NEW YORK

First published 2015 by Ashgate Publishing

2 Park Square, Milton Park, Abingdon, Oxon OX14 4RN
711 Third Avenue, New York, NY 10017, USA

Routledge is an imprint of the Taylor & Francis Group, an informa business

First issued in paperback 2017

British Library Cataloguing in Publication Data
A catalogue record for this book is available from the British Library

Library of Congress Cataloging-in-Publication Data
Garrard, James, 1965–
Archbishop Howley, 1828–1848 / by James Garrard.
pages cm. – (The Archbishops of Canterbury series)
Includes index.
ISBN 978-1-4724-5133-0 (hardcover : alk. paper)
1. Howley, William, 1766–1848. 2. Church of England–Bishops–Biography. 3. Bishops–Great Britain–Biography. I. Title.
BX5199.H873G37 2015
283.092–dc23
[B]

2014045779

ISBN 978-1-4724-5133-0 (hbk)
ISBN 978-1-138-05307-6 (pbk)

William Howley, Archbishop of Canterbury 1828-1848, led the Church of England during the beginning and expansion of the Oxford Movement, at a time when the precursor to the Church Commissioners was established, and during the momentous debates and decisions in Parliament which saw the final retreat from the myth of an all Anglican legislature. Howley's chairmanship of the commissions of the 1830s and 1840s which began the gargantuan task of reforming the Church's practices and re-arranging its finances, made him an object of fury and scorn to some of those who benefited from things as they were, most especially in the cathedrals.

Exploring the central events and debates within the Church of England in the first half of the nineteenth century, this book draws on primary and secondary evidence about Howley's career and influence. A section of original sources, including his Charges and other public documents, correspondence and speeches in the House of Lords, places Howley's achievements in proper context and illustrates his prevailing concerns in education, the establishment and political reform, relationships with the Tractarians, and in the early stages of Church reform. Dealing thematically with many of the issues faced by Howley, and exploring his own High Church theological views in historical context, James Garrard offers a fruitful re-appraisal of the intellectual, spiritual and 'party' context in which Howley moved.

Contents

About the Author

James Garrard is Canon Precentor of Ely. He was Denyer and Johnson Student of the University of Oxford from 1991–92 and was awarded a doctorate in 1992 for a thesis on Archbishop Howley. He was ordained in 1994. He has published several articles and reviews in the areas of Church history and Liturgy and contributed to the 3rd edition of the *Oxford Dictionary of the Christian Church*.

Preface and Acknowledgements

My initial research on William Howley was as a doctoral student at Keble College, Oxford and my supervisor was Geoffrey Rowell who was Chaplain of the College then. I owe Geoffrey a great debt of gratitude for his support of my studies and in many other ways over the last twenty-five years; amongst other contemporaries I am grateful to Peter Nockles and to Arthur Burns (who kindly read the whole manuscript as it approached publication more recently) for their very generous support and advice.

During my time as a research student I had financial and other help from Pusey House, Oxford, the British Academy, Keble College and the Faculty of Theology which elected me Denyer and Johnson Student for 1991–92. I received a scholarship from St Deiniol's Library, Hawarden which allowed me to begin the process of revising my text, and the kind support of my colleagues at Ely Cathedral at a later stage of study. I express my warm gratitude to all these institutions and to the staff of all the archives and libraries in which I have worked. I thank the staff of Ashgate warmly for all they have done to bring the book to publication.

My thesis was originally dedicated to my parents, and I expand that dedication to my whole family for this book.

James Garrard

Abbreviations

BL	British Library
Bodl Lib	Bodleian Library, Oxford
Ch Ch	Christ Church Library, Oxford
DNB	*Dictionary of National Biography*
EHR	*English Historical Review*
FP	Fulham Papers [Lambeth Palace Library]
HJ	*Historical Journal*
HP	Howley Papers [Lambeth Palace Library]
JEH	*Journal of Ecclesiastical History*
KCL	Keble College Library, Oxford
LD	*The Letters and Diaries of John Henry Newman*, vols iv and v, eds Ian Ker, Gerard Tracey and Thomas Gornall, S.J. (Oxford, 1980–84); vols xxi and xxiv, eds C.S. Dessain, E. Kelly and Thomas Gornall, S.J. (London and Oxford, 1971–73)
LPL	Lambeth Palace Library
PH	Pusey House, Oxford
PRO	Public Record Office, Kew
TRHS	*Transactions of the Royal Historical Society*

Introduction

In the last thirty years it has been widely accepted that the eighteenth century and early nineteenth century saw far more dynamism in all areas – political, religious, social, economic, cultural and intellectual – than was ever previously allowed. Nowhere had the torpor which supposedly afflicted the nation's life and institutions been identified with such confidence as in the Church of England. There is no dissent amongst historians of religion that William Howley was the last Archbishop of Canterbury of this 'long eighteenth century'.[1] However, since he held office from 1828 until his death in 1848, Howley led the Church of England not only during the momentous debates and decisions in Parliament which saw the final retreat from the myth of an all Anglican legislature but also at the beginning and expansion of the Oxford Movement and whilst the precursor to the Church Commissioners was established. Howley's reputation has certainly suffered from the general caricature of the age but if the long eighteenth century is to be radically reassessed, then the leaders of its institutions must be due similar reassessment. In this spirit W.M. Jacob holds up the Church of England in this period as a case study of how an institution can adapt well to change without recourse to radical change or legislation.[2]

The Tractarians' fabled ambiguous attitude towards bishops, their reverence for the office and their disobedience to those who held it has coloured many impressions of Howley and other bishops of the same period. I was fortunate to undertake my original research at the same time as several important studies of the Church of England's theological tradition and diocesan and parochial life were published, all of which undergirded a positive re-appraisal of many long established nostrums about the intellectual, spiritual and High Church 'party' context in which Howley moved. Nearly thirty years after Howley's death, when Dr Pusey himself preached at the opening of the chapel at Keble College, Oxford

---

1 See, for example, Jeremy Gregory and John Stevenson, *The Routledge Companion to Britain in the Eighteenth Century 1688–1820* (London and New York, 2007), ix, 201 and, more generally, John Walsh, Colin Haydon and Stephen Taylor (eds), *The Church of England c.1689–c.1833: From Toleration to Tractarianism* (Cambridge, 1993).

2 W.M. Jacob, *The Clerical Profession in the Long Eighteenth Century, 1680–1840* (Oxford, 2007), 18.

he described Howley with a certain amount of rhetorical hyperbole as 'the only bishop who understood us, alone never censured us'.[3] The renewed appreciation of the strength and quality of the 'long eighteenth century' inheritors of the High Church tradition has very much encouraged me in my own estimate of such a long-standing and powerful figure.[4]

This re-assessment of the individual who held the Church's most significant office for twenty years can be yet more broadly conceived by taking account of what Arthur Burns describes as the enduring historiographical construction of the nineteenth-century Church through narratives of reform which cast the eighteenth-century Church in the role of the 'unreformed' object of that reform. He notes specifically that historians of the Hanoverian Church 'have shown little interest in integrating the major reforms of the mid-1830s into their accounts'.[5] It was, as noted above, under Howley's chairmanship that the various commissions of the 1830s and 1840s began the gargantuan task of reforming the Church's practices and re-arranging its finances and made him an object of fury and scorn to some of those who benefited most from things as they were (most especially in the cathedrals) and who believed that he had betrayed their interests comprehensively.

More recent attention to Howley by scholars has been spread throughout a large selection of different kinds of writing: general histories, biographies of other ecclesiastical or political leaders, specialist articles and theses, histories of the Oxford Movement, of parliamentary or Church Reform, and so on. Despite certain absences from Howley's papers, there is still a wide variety of source material. First, a considerable quantity of his private and family papers remains in Lambeth Palace Library. Correspondence with the Royal Family has survived. Financial and domestic arrangements as Bishop of London and Archbishop of Canterbury are well documented. Howley's correspondence as Bishop of London (the Fulham Papers) has survived in full. There are over fifty volumes of correspondence which deal with all aspects of diocesan administration and a full set of visitation returns for 1815. In addition there is a large amount of correspondence with fellow bishops and clergy, politicians and courtiers. The papers of various Prime Ministers – Liverpool, Peel and Gladstone at the British

3 E.B. Pusey, *'Blessed are the Meek'. A Sermon Preached at the Opening of the Chapel of Keble College on St Mark's Day, 1876* (London, 1876), 25.

4 See the copious published writings of Peter Nockles and especially his *The Oxford Movement in Context: Anglican High Churchmanship, 1760–1857* (Cambridge, 1994).

5 Arthur Burns, 'English "Church Reform" Revisited, 1780–1840', in *Rethinking the Age of Reform: Britain 1780–1850*, ed. Arthur Burns and Joanna Innes (Cambridge: Cambridge University Press, 2003), 136–62 at 138.

Library; Russell and Grey at the Public Record Office, Kew – have been the cornerstone of the research into Howley's primacy. The archives of Pusey House and Keble College, Oxford have been invaluable for work on the Tractarians and various collections in the Bodleian Library contain correspondence between Howley and major figures. Other correspondence is identified in the text.

Chapter 1
Winchester and Oxford

Education and Early Preferment

William Howley was born on 12 February 1766, the first child of another William Howley, vicar of the parish of Bishop's Sutton with Ropley in the County of Hampshire. His mother, Mary, was the eighth child of a prosperous wine merchant's family, the Gauntletts, from Winchester.[1] He had a younger sister, Mary, and the family lived in Ropley where his father served from 1757 until his death in 1796. The medieval Bishops of Winchester had had a residence there, and Winchester College still owned land. Howley was therefore given one of the first chances after any Founder's Kin to be examined for a scholarship under rules drawn up by William of Wykeham, the fourteenth-century Bishop and Chancellor of England who founded the College. He was elected to a scholarship tenth in the order of merit in 1779 at the age of 12.[2] The seventy scholars lived separately from the rest of the school's pupils and followed classical and literary studies which had been designed by Wykeham to be the outstanding example of a Christian education which would inculcate 'Godliness and Good Learning'.[3] At least fifteen hours in the week was given to Latin composition and modern languages were not taught at all until 1821.[4]

Wykeham had also established New College, Oxford as a sister foundation – 'Sainte Marie College of Wynchester in Oxenford'.[5] Elections were made at the same time as the scholarships to Winchester, but a scholar could easily fail to get into New College whatever his ability or industry. The number of places available fluctuated every year so junior scholars were nominated for election two or three years before they were expected to move to Oxford. Howley was

1 Will of Mary Gauntlett, widow of John, 2 January 1770, LPL MS 2201, no. 18.

2 T.A. Trollope, *What I Remember* (London, 1887), i, 97; C.W. Holgate and H. Chitty, *Winchester Long Rolls 1723–1812* (Winchester, 1904), 148.

3 Holgate and Chitty, *Winchester Long Rolls 1723–1812*, 148; David Newsome, *Godliness and Good Learning: Four Studies on a Victorian Ideal* (London, 1961).

4 A.K. Cook, *About Winchester College* (London, 1917), 287–88; W. Tuckwell, *The Ancient Ways: Winchester Fifty Years Ago* (London, 1893), 95.

5 A.F. Leach, *A History of Winchester College* (London, 1899), 69.

elected after two years, in 1782, in sixth place.[6] He entered in 1783, essentially as a probationer Fellow, although still called a scholar.[7] Like Winchester, New College had seventy scholars, which was almost as many as the scholars of all the other colleges of the university combined. Letters survive between Howley and Thomas Burgess, a scholar of Winchester 1768–75, later Bishop of Salisbury. They give a rare glimpse of Howley's interests at this time which unsurprisingly mostly concerned classical scholarship. Howley assisted Burgess in translating and revising Lessing's comments on Aristotle for publication. He evidently learned German, Italian and Spanish well and also studied Hebrew.[8] This is the earliest remaining evidence both of his command of languages and of his delicate health. He spoke of a nervous fever and severe headaches which he blamed on overwork both to Burgess and to others from time to time.[9]

In 1787, like all Oxford students intending to be ordained, Howley attended the lectures of the Regius Professor of Divinity, John Randolph. A certificate of attendance was required by all bishops before ordination after 1790 but it was already all but universal practice.[10] Howley was ordained deacon on the title of his fellowship of New College by William Cleaver, Bishop of Chester in Christ Church Cathedral on 20 December 1789, and priest by Edward Smallwell, Bishop of Oxford on 19 December the following year.[11] The Warden of New College throughout Howley's time was his uncle Samuel Gauntlett who had attended Winchester and New College in the same way as Howley. Although he was originally chosen as a compromise by two rival factions, he became 'the beau-ideal of a Warden' who managed the college estates so well that there was a great improvement in the fellows' income.

Howley received his MA degree in December 1790. New College held its own internal examinations for degrees, a situation which was only regularised after 1822.[12] Fellows were under no obligation to teach or study. The teaching of undergraduates was done by tutors drafted in from outside the college. Some

---

6 Holgate and Chitty, *Winchester Long Rolls 1723–1812*, xli, 151, 154, 156.

7 Cook, *About Winchester College*, 113.

8 Benjamin Harrison, *The Remembrance of a Departed Guide and Ruler in the Church of God: A Charge Delivered to the Clergy of the Archdeaconry of Maidstone* (London, 1848), 42; Margaret Sparks, 'Archbishop William Howley and his Books', *Canterbury Cathedral Chronicle* (2004), 35.

9 Howley to Burgess, 14 April 1788, Bodl Lib MS Eng Lett c 136, ff. 48–49; Howley to Aberdeen, 12 July 1809, BL, Add MS 43195, f. 3; Howley to William Sotheby, 22 January [?1796], Beinecke Library, Yale University, USA.

10 Jacob, *Clerical Profession*, 53.

11 See LPL MS 2201, ff. 1–2 for the letters of orders.

12 G.V. Cox, *Recollections of Oxford* (London, 1868), 173–76.

of the more dramatic accounts of the poor state of the university's tuition and scholarship at that time are overplayed, but there was malaise. Although the pastoral care offered throughout the university was better than the caricature, discipline could remain lax – as James Woodforde (who became a scholar at New College in 1759) said himself.[13] The Warden and the thirteen senior fellows of the college had a dining table and a common room separate from the junior fellows who were in turn separate from the newly arrived scholars. Any fellow who became incumbent of a parish that paid more than a set income (which had been reckoned at £120 a year in 1764) or any fellow who got married, had to give up his fellowship after a year. As the eighteenth century progressed fewer and fewer fellows left the college and as a result the number of new elections sank to an average of four or five a year. Howley did become a senior fellow, but resigned in 1794 when elected a Fellow of Winchester, since his income then greatly exceeded £120. As late as 1860, the Warden of Winchester received £1,750 a year and the ten Fellows divided £6,598 between them.[14]

Howley's appointment as the Marquess of Abercorn's Domestic Chaplain in 1792 was highly significant for his future. Abercorn's first wife, Catherine, bore his heir, James, Viscount Hamilton, and two daughters. As John James Hamilton, Abercorn had occupied a distinguished place in the Court of George III and had used his huge wealth to help a poverty-stricken Pitt.[15] Like many domestic chaplains Howley was also a tutor, to Abercorn's son.[16] He made a particular friend of the fourth Earl of Aberdeen who married Hamilton's sister, Katharine, in 1805. A future cabinet minister, Foreign Secretary (1841–46) and Prime Minister (1852–55), Aberdeen relied heavily on Howley, particularly during Katherine's final illness in 1811, for consolation and religious assurance. Howley was popular and a peacemaker 'from the drawing room to the scullery'.[17] In 1796 he was appointed to succeed his father as Vicar of Bishop's Sutton and Ropley by the private patron of whom nothing is known beyond his name, the Revd W. Ralph. After Howley's resignation in 1811 the advowson (the right

13 W.N. Hargreaves-Mawdsley (ed.), *Woodforde at Oxford 1759–1776*, [Oxford Historical Society, n.s. vol. xxi] (Oxford, 1969), xiii–xv. Jacob, *Clerical Profession*, 49.

14 Cook, *About Winchester College*, 207.

15 Vicary Gibbs (ed.), *The Complete Peerage ... of England, Scotland, Ireland, Great Britain and the United Kingdom* (London, 1910), i, 7–8; N.W. Wraxall, *Posthumous Memoirs of his Own Time* (London, 1836), i, 61–65.

16 William Gibson, *A Social History of the Domestic Chaplain, 1530–1840* (London and Washington, 1997), 88; Jacob, *Clerical Profession*, 10.

17 Howley to Aberdeen, 4 November 1811, BL, Add MS 43195, ff. 5–6; Shute Barrington to Howley, 3 September 1813, LPL, MS 2184, ff. 158–59.

to appoint his successor) was sold to Abercorn, who appointed two further incumbents before selling the patronage himself.[18]

In 1802, Howley was also appointed Vicar of Andover. It was one of Winchester College's most significant parishes and the incumbent was nearly always a Fellow. Samuel Gauntlett had been the incumbent from 1778 until 1788. The 13 acres of a former Priory and two other gifts of land had been made to the College by Cardinal Beaufort in 1413. Howley paid the curate he appointed to act in his place about £100, a good salary of its kind from the income of around £400. Howley resigned from Andover in 1811 to take on another Winchester living, Bradford Peverell in Dorset.[19] In 1805, shortly after his appointment to Christ Church, he married Mary Frances Belli, the daughter of John Belli, a former Private Secretary to Warren Hastings when Governor-General of India.[20] He was 39, she 22.

Christ Church

Howley was appointed Canon of Christ Church by the Crown on 27 April 1804 after the promotion of Robert Holmes to the Deanery of Winchester. No correspondence survives but Abercorn's closeness to Pitt must be surmised as the most influential factor. The Dean and Chapter administered Christ Church's huge estates and regulated its internal economy. They exercised a large ecclesiastical patronage by electing Students and by appointing to parishes in the College's gift. The canons were by long tradition accorded the status of Heads of Houses and as such did not teach undergraduates. They were not formally concerned with educational policy which was the preserve of the Dean. From 1783 until his retirement in 1809 this was the formidable Cyril Jackson. He had made the college system of Collections into a real test of study.[21] Howley did do some examining of undergraduates by virtue of being Treasurer from 1808 to 1812.[22]

---

18 Will of Rev. William Howley, 22 October 1796, LPL MS 2212; *The Victoria History of Hampshire and the Isle of Wight*, ed. W. Page (London, 1908), iii, 45.

19 Hampshire Record Office 60M67/ PB 1: Vicarage of Andover 1811; Sheila Himsworth, *Winchester College Muniments* (Winchester, 1984), ii, 42.

20 See Clive Dewey, *The Passing of Barchester* (London and Rio Grande, 1991), 50–56 on the Belli family. Michael Edwardes, *Warren Hastings: King of the Nabobs* (London, 1976), 171.

21 Ch Ch MS D.P. i b 3.

22 E.G.W. Bill, *Education at Christ Church, 1660–1800* (Oxford, 1988), 88.

Christ Church appointed 'Students': something of a cross between a privileged undergraduate and a junior fellow. The majority were Westminster Students (the school stood in a somewhat similar relation to Christ Church as Winchester did to New College) who were elected by the Dean and the Master of Trinity College, Cambridge. There were also Canoneer Students, positions in the gift of the Dean and individual canons, but there were not enough vacancies to allow a regular annual election so the Dean, Sub-Dean and canons filled up a list of candidates in their order of seniority. Howley only ever made four nominations in nine years. Cyril Jackson was responsible for some improvements to the system, enforcing residence and giving most of his studentships on merit.[23]

As Treasurer, Howley was responsible both for domestic outgoings (he personally checked off individual payments to scouts, porters and kitchen staff) and for the college's vast estates.[24] The income from the 'fines' on leases of Christ Church estates ran into thousands of pounds every month. A fine was the term for a payment for renewal or on a new lease after the death of the previous holder. The system was unsatisfactory because income fluctuated wildly from year to year based as it was in the main on nothing more predictable than a tenant's mortality. For that reason, it became increasingly common to issue leases for periods of years rather than for life.[25] In one month in 1809 the college's income was £4,475. 9s. 8¼d.; in December 1811 £7,760. 13s. 6d. and in January 1812 £14,679. 10s. 1d.[26] The canons' income came from these sources and so they themselves received very erratic instalments of income, sometimes every five weeks and sometimes with a three-month gap. The payments varied greatly in amount. For example, in a thirteen-month period from January 1810 to January 1811 Howley received income in January, February, May, twice in August, October and January 1811. Sometimes he received as little as £5, mostly £100–£200 with one bumper payment of £500.[27] Such a system's shortcomings were of course far more troublesome to an incumbent existing on an annual salary of £100 than for a Canon of Christ Church who received over £1,300 in thirteen months.

Howley was painfully shy. G.R. Chinnery, in regular letters between himself and his mother throughout his time at Christ Church as commoner and Student

23 Bill, *Education at Christ Church*, 118–19.

24 Ch Ch MS, VII A 7.

25 For further details on clerical and episcopal incomes, see, for example, Peter Virgin, *The Church in an Age of Negligence: Ecclesiastical Structure and Problems of Church Reform* (Cambridge, 1989), 33–43 and *passim*.

26 Treasurer's Accounts 1802–1812, Ch Ch MS, iv a 5: 81, 118v, 119.

27 Ch Ch MS xxxviii b 3.

(1808–11), spoke of several dinners he attended with the Howleys. Howley's conversation was full of 'dreadful breaks and pauses' and his wife's was barely any better.[28] Howley acted as tutor to the Hereditary Prince of Orange, later King William II of the future kingdom of Holland. The Duke of Portland, the Prime Minister, consulted John Parsons, the Master of Balliol, and Cyril Jackson, who both recommended Howley as a senior member of the university community to take overall charge of the Prince's education.[29] The job was felt particularly important because the Prince was very likely to marry Princess Charlotte Augusta, the only child of George IV and Queen Caroline, and therefore heir to the throne. Her father had almost nothing to do with her after his separation from her mother. Charlotte Augusta and Orange were indeed eventually engaged in 1813 but she broke off the arrangement the next year and married Prince Leopold of Saxe-Coburg in 1816, and died in childbirth in 1817.[30] Howley controlled the Prince's social life. Only the Vice-Chancellor, Howley and the Bishop of Oxford were to entertain him. The Prince could entertain guests himself with the approval of his *chaperon* Baron de Constant. Both the Prime Minister and the Duke of York expressed their pleasure even though neither knew Howley, proof that his name was becoming more widely known.[31]

Regius Professor of Divinity

Howley was offered the Regius Professorship of Divinity in 1809; nine years after the new Examination Statute had been introduced. This statute had been pioneered by Jackson, Parsons and John Eveleigh, Provost of Oriel, though it owed most to Jackson's driving personality. It introduced classification of degrees for the first time. If not the cause, it was a symbol of the renaissance of studies throughout the university. There were only thirteen candidates for honours between 1802 and 1806 and the vast majority of degrees continued to be unclassified. An examination for the MA existed briefly from 1800, but was abolished in 1807, the same year that candidates began to be classified in 'Greats' and mathematics: ten in 1807 and thirty-two in 1808. In some ways Jackson achieved a tightening of the grip of religion for a while since under the

28 Chinnery to Mrs Chinnery, 25 February 1808 and 23 March 1808, Ch Ch MS Estates xlviii a 42a, 43.

29 Memorandum by John Parsons and Cyril Jackson, 3 July 1809, LPL MS 2184, ff. 25–26.

30 *Illustrated London News*, 19 February 1848, 96.

31 Portland to Howley, 8 July 1809, LPL MS 2184, ff. 27–28; The Duke of York to Howley, 8 July 1809, LPL MS 2184, f. 31.

new regulations one could not graduate without knowledge of the Gospels in Greek, the Thirty-Nine Articles and Joseph Butler's *Analogy of Religion*.[32]

Howley could not decide whether to accept. Jackson thought that he might sentence himself to a long period in office since it was so difficult to find suitable candidates for the position.[33] Spencer Perceval, the Evangelical Prime Minister, thought Howley the best man for the job and also wanted someone with plum preferment to vacate. For Howley this involved exchanging the seventh for the fifth stall at Christ Church. Jackson thought that Howley would probably pick up a small bishopric later on, which could be held with the professorship since no other *commendam* (a term for an appointment held in conjunction with a poorly paid bishopric, which boosted a bishop's salary) would be required.[34] This was a very common situation for Regius Professors of Divinity at Oxford and Cambridge. John Randolph had been Regius Professor whilst Bishop of Oxford and later of Bangor; Howley's successor, William Van Mildert, held it as Bishop of Llandaff.

The Regius Professors of Divinity had lectured regularly since the 1770s whereas neither of the two Regius Professors of Greek gave a single lecture in the same period. The obligation on those who wished to be ordained to have attended the lectures meant that they drew a large audience however variable their quality. There were neither personal questions nor inspection of note books. All that students really took away from these lectures were the copious reading lists.[35] Jackson thought that the lectures of past professors were nearly all too long. Howley intended to abolish lectures on Natural Religion, and Jackson advised giving half the course to a sweeping survey of 'ecclesiastical history' from the Fathers to Luther.[36]

The rarity of theological lectures and education for those wishing to be ordained was lost neither on Howley nor on Jackson, and they discussed endlessly how to make best use of the brief time available and the best way to handle sensitive subjects.[37] Like many leading churchmen they thought that Herbert Marsh, the Lady Margaret Professor at Cambridge, had ploughed not only an

32 Cox, *Recollections of Oxford*, 46, 57 (2nd edn), 63; M.C. Curthoys, 'The Examination System', in *The History of the University of Oxford*, vol. VI: *Nineteenth Century Oxford, Part I*, ed. M.G. Brock and M.C. Curthoys (Oxford, 1997), 339–44, 347–48; Jacob, *Clerical Profession*, 26.

33 Jackson to Howley, 20 October 1809, LPL MS 2186, ff. 1–3.

34 Jackson to Howley, 24 October 1809, LPL MS 2186, ff. 4–5.

35 William Ince, *The Past History and Present Duties of the Faculty of Theology in Oxford* (London, 1878), 24; Cox, *Recollections of Oxford*, 140–41.

36 Jackson to Howley, 4 July 1811, LPL MS 2186, ff. 32–38.

37 Howley to Aberdeen, 1 June 1812, BL Add MS 43195, ff. 18–22.

undesirable but a positively dangerous furrow in giving detailed lectures on biblical criticism, but neither could the subject be avoided altogether. Marsh had caused much consternation by promoting the unpopular discipline in England.[38] There was wide disparity in undergraduates' ability to use the New Testament in Greek. This was so pronounced that Westminster scholars in their first year at Christ Church were encouraged to study Hebrew to allow others to catch up with their superior knowledge of Greek.[39] Howley's recollections twenty years later were that he had not in fact abandoned lectures on Natural Religion and had used that subject to launch into lectures on the inspiration of scripture. He did not lecture on the Thirty-Nine Articles (since the Lady Margaret Professor did) and he never extended his course on ecclesiastical history because his final preparations to give six new lectures were thwarted when he became a bishop. When Edward Burton became Regius Professor in 1829 Howley encouraged him to do exactly what Jackson had told him – to concentrate on a broad sweep of historical studies from the Fathers to the Reformation.[40]

---

[38] Jackson to Howley, 6 December 1810, LPL MS 2186, ff. 26–31. R.K. Braine, *The Life and Writings of Herbert Marsh (1757–1839)* (Univ. of Cambridge unpubl. PhD, 1989), 195–243.

[39] R.W. Greaves, 'Religion in the University 1715–1800', in *The History of the University of Oxford*, vol. v: *The Eighteenth Century*, ed. L. Sutherland and L.G. Mitchell (Oxford, 1986), 401–24, at 404. Cf. M.G. Brock, 'The Oxford of Peel and Gladstone 1800–1833', in Brock and Curthoys, *History of the University of Oxford*, 13: 35 per cent of undergraduates were from nine schools: Winchester, Eton, St Paul's, Shrewsbury, Westminster, Merchant Taylors', Rugby, Harrow and Charterhouse.

[40] Howley to Burton, 3 July 1829, Ch Ch Microfilm Box 91.

Chapter 2

The Diocese of London

Appointment

John Randolph died on 28 July 1813 after four years as Bishop of London. He had preceded Howley as Regius Professor of Divinity at Christ Church from 1783 until his translation from the bishopric of Oxford to Bangor in 1807. He was tainted by a reputation for nepotism and identified with the 'High and Dry' wing of the old High Church.[1] Howley was a well-established candidate for a bishopric. The Prime Minister Lord Liverpool's long-standing desire was to appoint able and learned bishops, with a few bishops 'of Rank and Family' – enough to make the bishops who had been appointed on their own merits feel appreciated and important. Liverpool also committed himself never to promote a 'man of Rank' unless he had the right character.[2] Bishops who were sons of clergy were normally sons of parochial incumbents, not of Church dignitaries.[3] Howley's academic strength was entirely typical of many of those elevated to the bench at this time despite the fact that he did not publish editions of Greek plays in the same way as did men like Charles James Blomfield (his successor at London) or J.H. Monk (Regius Professor of Greek at Cambridge from 1809 and Bishop of Gloucester from 1830). Classical scholarship was rarely

1 *Gentleman's Magazine*, ii (1813), 187.

2 Liverpool to Lord Talbot, 19 September 1819, BL Add MS 38279, f. 323, quoted in William Gibson, 'The Tories and Church Patronage: 1812–30', *JEH*, 41 (1990), 266–74 at 268.

3 Viviane Barrie-Curien, 'The Clergy in the Diocese of London in the Eighteenth Century', in *The Church of England c.1689–c.1833: From Toleration to Tractarianism*, ed. John Walsh, Colin Haydon and Stephen Taylor (Cambridge, 1993), at 87–88. Her analysis shows 1.2 per cent sons of nobility, over 38 per cent sons of gentry (only 2.6 per cent of them sons of knights or baronets), over 35 per cent clergy sons (only 6.2 per cent with a father a canon or more senior) and 19 per cent sons of plebeians: traders and so on. See also Viviane Barrie-Curien, 'Clerical Recruitment and Career Patterns in the Church of England during the Eighteenth Century', in *Crown and Mitre: Religion and Society in Northern Europe since the Reformation*, ed. W.M. Jacob and Nigel Yates (Woodbridge, 1993), 93–104 at 98.

advertised as reason for elevation, neither was ability in that area alone regarded as qualification to become a bishop, but it was significant.[4]

A year before Randolph's death, Liverpool told Aberdeen's brother (which Aberdeen repeated to Howley) that his predecessor Spencer Perceval had been unable to decide whether to appoint Howley or Edward Legge to the next vacancy on the bench of bishops. Aspiring bishops were interviewed personally by the Prime Minister and it was during such an interview with Liverpool that Howley was, to all intents and purposes, promised such a job.[5] Howley's nerves made him imagine that Liverpool was going to fob him off with a deanery, until the Prime Minister reassured him.[6] When Randolph did die Howley knew that, if passed over, he would have to wait for the next vacancy but one, since there was a rarely breached tradition that the Prime Minister alternated between an Oxford and Cambridge graduate in filling vacant sees.[7] Liverpool acted exactly according to his expressed principles and chose the learned over the aristocratic candidate. Legge, who was the son of the Earl of Dartford and had been Dean of Windsor since 1805, eventually became Bishop of Oxford after a tussle about having to give up all his other preferment.[8] Liverpool gave Aberdeen the satisfaction of confirming that Howley would be selected – where, would depend on who succeeded Randolph at London.[9] Howley wrote several letters informing people that he was going to be a bishop. All including him assumed it would be a diocese like Rochester or Oxford.

Howley was the fourth person offered London. The Bishop of Lincoln refused it in the same week that Randolph died – he wanted 'ease and comfort' after twenty-six years at Lincoln. The Bishop of Worcester next refused.[10] The Prince Regent offered it in person to Cyril Jackson, retired to Sussex. It is a safe assumption that Jackson suggested giving it to Howley after he himself had declined it at that meeting, since the Prince indicated his consent to the idea immediately afterwards to Lord Liverpool.[11] The appointment caused

4 See Arthur Burns and Christopher Stray, 'The Greek-play Bishop: Polemic, Prosopography and Nineteenth Century Prelates', *HJ*, 54 (2011), 1013–38 *passim* – especially 1022.

5 Aberdeen to Howley, 15 June 1812, LPL MS 2186A, ff. 42–43.

6 Aberdeen to Howley, 22 June 1812, LPL MS 2186A, ff. 44–45; Howley to Aberdeen, 15 June 1812, BL Add MS 43195, ff. 27–28.

7 Howley to Aberdeen, 30 July 1813, BL Add MS 43195, f. 47.

8 Aberdeen to Howley, 2 June 1812, LPL MS 2186A, ff. 38–41. Gibson, 'Tories and Church Patronage', 270.

9 Aberdeen to Howley, [28] July 1813, LPL MS 2184, f. 77.

10 Tomline to Liverpool, 31 July 1813, BL Add MS 38253, f. 371.

11 Liverpool to Manners Sutton, 7 August 1813, LPL MS 3274, f. 59; Prince Regent to Liverpool, 10 August 1813, BL Add MS 38190, f. 25; *Gentleman's Magazine*, lxxxix (1819), 461.

astonishment to some other bishops and even Aberdeen feared that Howley had too little of the 'assurance, activity and worldliness' needed by a Bishop of London.[12] Shute Barrington, Bishop of Durham, gave him £2,000 for his immediate expenses and advised him never to promise or hint at appointments to parishes in his gift, even if encouraged to do so by 'family, friends, the great, ministers and Royalty itself'.[13] Howley was consecrated on 3 October 1813 in the chapel of Lambeth Palace by Archbishop Manners Sutton and other bishops. Queen Charlotte was curious to see such a ceremony for the first time and attended with two of her daughters.[14]

Clerical Residence and the Wright Case

Howley's new diocese was, in many ways, ungovernable. Immensely large, it extended north as far as Hertfordshire, east into Essex and was met at the Thames by the equally unwieldy diocese of Winchester which included all of South London. In addition, the Bishop of London was charged in some vague sense with the episcopal oversight of Europe. Yet another responsibility was the provision and oversight of clergy to the colonies. No one could deal with these three tasks adequately. The most pressing issue was requests for patronage, and Howley was inundated by requests for appointments, financial assistance and recommendations of all kinds. These issues and non-residence formed the greater part of his daily correspondence.

Sir William Scott had sponsored an Act of Parliament in 1803 to regulate the conditions under which incumbents could organise their ministry in a parish. Anyone absent from his living for three months in a year without being resident in another was liable to lose a third of his income. Scott did not intend to abolish non-residence but to regulate it. Bishops could keep their *commendams*. Certificates of non-residence could be granted under certain other conditions and these were in the hands of the bishops, which made their own exemption seem invidious.[15] Scott's Act allowed dispensations for holding pluralities (i.e. more than one parish at a time), but based on valuations made in the day of

12 W.S. Goddard to Howley, 16 August 1813, LPL MS 2184, f. 127; Howley to Liverpool, 16 August 1813, BL Add MS 38254, f. 85; Copy Aberdeen to Lord Harrowby, 23 September 1813, BL Add MS 43230, f. 180.

13 Barrington to Howley, 13 August 1813, LPL MS 2184, ff. 121–22; Barrington to Howley, 16 August 1813, LPL MS 2184, f. 124.

14 *The Times*, 12 February 1848.

15 W.L. Mathieson, *English Church Reform 1815–1840* (London, 1932), 47 and *passim*.

Thomas Cromwell's *Liber Valorum*, which therefore often bore no relation to their real income.[16] Because of the exemptions, Bishop Porteus (Randolph's immediate predecessor) had considered the legislation an inadequate watering down of Henrician prohibitions on non-residence. He objected to giving curacies in large towns to those who were incumbents of small benefices.[17]

Amendments to Scott's Act by Manners Sutton and Lord Sidmouth attempted to deal with this issue but managed rather to resurrect the spectre of the ruinous penalties for non-residence unchanged since the days of Henry VIII. Prosecutions could take place if clergy failed to renew their licences for non-residence and many of the clergy were technically in breach of the law. In London these fell into three broad categories. First, there were those non-resident without permission, a tiny number; second, those who had claimed ill health but were now recovered, again very few; and third, those who had received permission from previous bishops and were living near the church but not within the parish boundaries. By mid-century half of all parishes in the diocese had an incumbent who had another parish elsewhere and vicars often served curacies elsewhere as well, though the technicalities of non-residence and pluralism often mask effective pastoral ministry.[18]

The Secretary to Bishop Randolph, William Wright, convinced that he had been cheated out of his fees, had taken advantage of Randolph's failing health to thwart the issuing of licences for curates so that he could institute proceedings under the Act. The complaint of Henry Owen, Vicar of St Olave's, Hart Street in the City of London could stand for many others. Owen had fallen ill and agreed to Bishop Randolph's direction that a curate should be appointed. When the curate was duly found, Wright delayed sending out the licence until Randolph's death and three months later issued a writ against Owen for wilfully absenting himself from duty.[19] Wright challenged vicars who had licences of non-residence as to why they did not reside in their vicarages, when their fully paid curates were occupying one and they were resident in the vicarage of their other parish. The real difficulty was that Wright stood to gain financially from every case where he could prove infringement of the law, since Manners Sutton's amendments to Scott's Act had given an inducement to informers. The Archdeacon of Essex

16 Johnson Grant, *A Summary of the History of the English Church, and of the Sects Which Have Departed from its Communion* (London, 1825), iv, 251–55.

17 [Robert Hodson], *The Life of the Right Reverend Beilby Porteus, D.D., late Lord Bishop of London* (London, 1811), 181–82.

18 Barrie-Curien, 'Clergy in the Diocese of London', 91. See Jacob, *Clerical Profession*, 101–12 *passim*.

19 Henry Owen to Howley, LPL FP (HP) 32, ff. 72–85 *passim*.

added that there was not even a regular return brought before the bishop at his visitation with all the details of non- and partial residence, so that he and his fellow archdeacons did not have robust information with which to combat Wright.[20] The lawyers were gloomy about the possibility of a Bill of Indemnity to protect those without licences because the legislation was hopelessly flawed.[21]

Wright published his own complaints of clerical unwillingness to renew licences, pay fees and their 'sham illnesses' alongside his own statistics of the extent of non-residence and how many churches had only one instead of the regulation two services on a Sunday. He claimed that as the clergy's income had increased so their frequency in taking services and their rate of residence in the parish had decreased.[22] John Wade's *Extraordinary Black Book*, the most well known of all the attacks on the worldliness and corruption of the Church of England, reprinted all of his claims in 1831.[23] It was only in 1814 that Parliament agreed to stall the legislation until the financial incentive to inform was removed.[24] Howley's own investigations showed that most clergy whom Wright described as 'non-resident' actually did have legal permission – such as an annual fifty-day absence by an archdeacon who was also prebendary of another cathedral.[25]

Howley's new secretary, Christopher Hodgson, published *Instructions for the Use of Candidates for Holy Orders, and for the Parochial Clergy, as to Ordination, Licences, Institutions, Collations, Induction and Dispensations* in 1817. This was an exhaustive survey of all the legal requirements to which a clergyman might ever have to conform. It devoted seventy-four pages to Scott's Bill so even without Wright the issue would have come to a head. Howley was made a member of a committee of the Privy Council concerned with the residence of the clergy alongside Manners Sutton, Lord Liverpool and the Chancellor of the Exchequer. But they had only received complete returns for residence in 1811 by early 1814 and even then they had not agreed to tell the bishops to send out an identical return form to the clergy so that they could have a standardised picture

20 F. Wollaston, Archdeacon of Essex – Statement, LPL FP (HP) 32, f. 122

21 Sion College Report on Non-Residence, LPL FP (HP) 32, ff. 135–37.

22 *Morning Chronicle*: 21 January 1814 (Letter V); 16 February 1814 (Letter VI); 4 March 1814 (Letter VII); see Wright to Manners Sutton, 1 November 1813, LPL Manners-Sutton Ps, i, f. 62.

23 [John Wade], *The Extraordinary Black Book: An Exposition of the United Church of England and Ireland; Civil List and Crown Revenues...* (London, 1831), 30–35.

24 *Hansard*, xxvi (1814), col. 129.

25 'A correct list ... of the clergy of Middx., the Deanery of Braughing, Herts. and the Archdeaconry of St Albans', LPL FP (HP) 32, ff. 152–53.

of the Church.[26] Howley therefore had a battery of statistics to hand concerning non-residence. Nationally, between 1810 and 1815 approximately 1,000 fewer clergy became non-resident and there was an increase in residence of 800. In that period the total number of benefices increased by 240.[27]

Clerical Education, Patronage and Income

No one could be ordained unless he had been nominated to a curacy or other 'title' (like Howley's own ordination as a Fellow of New College). A college certificate of suitability was also expected. A degree was not an absolute necessity and 'literates' (non-graduates who nevertheless had proven academic ability) had been ordained for many years. In London during Howley's time as bishop most literates were ordained to serve in the colonies but the ordination register shows that this was not their only destination, at least up to 1824.[28] Howley accepted neither a Scottish MA nor attendance on Divinity lectures at Scottish universities as a qualification for ordination in his diocese.[29] He began an attack on lax academic qualifications in 1825, and took aim at the 'ten-year men' at Cambridge. There was a clause in the University of Cambridge's Elizabethan Code which allowed those over the age of 24 when they began their studies to read Theology and take a Bachelor of Divinity degree after ten years without first graduating in Arts. A few did so during the eighteenth century, but between 1803 and 1825 the numbers registered rose from 33 to 230.[30] Howley denied ordination to Samuel Perry, who was a ten-year man, despite his having certificates from college and the Regius Professor of Divinity. Perry criticised Howley for hypocrisy in ordaining non-graduates for the colonies.[31] Some meaningful examinations for the degree were set up in the short term but the system's fate was sealed. It was abolished by the 1850 University Commission.[32]

---

26 'Minutes of the Committee of the Privy Council to whom the Prince Regent has referred returns made by the Archbishops and Bishops of the Residence of the Clergy', 15 February 1814, LPL FP (HP) 32, ff. 144–47.

27 'Abstract of the number of Incumbents ... according to Diocesan returns ...', 3 July 1817, LPL FP (HP) 32, ff. 162–63.

28 London Episcopal Registers, MS 9531, 24 pt 2, Guildhall, London.

29 Alexander Argo to Howley, 9 January 1821, LPL, FP (HP) 6, ff. 139–40.

30 D.A. Winstanley, *Unreformed Cambridge* (Cambridge, 1935), 69.

31 [Samuel Perry], *A Letter to the Public Orator of Cambridge University on the Ordination of Non-graduates under the Ten Year Divinity Statute* (London, 1825), 8 and *passim*.

32 Winstanley, *Unreformed Cambridge*, 71.

Half of all Oxford and Cambridge graduates were ordained up to the 1840s, despite a doubling in the size of both universities since the turn of the century. The problems inherent in a large increase in personnel without a concomitant large increase in opportunities for employment were obvious.[33] If Howley gave licences to incumbents for non-residence, then the diocese would have a large number of curates. The continuing and increasing oversupply of clergy meant that many were never more than that, working for absent incumbents. The Curates Act of 1813, which had been promoted by Lord Harrowby with the co-operation of Archbishop Manners Sutton, attempted some regulation of the situation of badly paid junior clergy. The bishop could direct an incumbent to pay a curate a salary of up to £75 with an additional £15 if there were no parsonage house. If the living were worth more than £400 a year the salary could be increased to one-fifth of the whole value, but no curate could earn more than £250.[34] The dilemma for the bishop was that allowing a decent salary to a curate often caused the incumbent of a poorer parish genuine financial difficulties. Despite being sensitive to that issue, Howley insisted that each church had a right to 'full service' or 'double duty': that is a morning and evening service every Sunday. Frequency of double duty around the country had fluctuated in the previous century, declining in the Diocese of London. Non-residence was the most common reason why 'full service' was not performed and therefore Howley rarely allowed it and generally imposed the highest salary possible for the curate. The Act had a beneficial effect on assistants' salaries over twenty-five years: in the Church of England as a whole in 1813, 868 stipends did not match £40; by 1838 this had reduced to 161.[35]

Howley often complained that he had so few jobs in his own gift that he could rarely act to help a deserving candidate. Removing unsatisfactory or incompetent clergy could also absorb a disproportionate amount of time. The ailing Archdeacon of London agreed to resign only if his son was given 'suitable recompense' – which in his eyes should have been a prebend of St Paul's Cathedral.[36] The Bishop of London was patron of only 77 of the 640 benefices

33 Frances Knight, *The Nineteenth Century Church and English Society* (Cambridge, 1995), 107–08 (more generally 107–30).

34 Jacob, *Clerical Profession*, 69 and more generally 64ff.

35 John Walsh and Stephen Taylor, 'Introduction: The Church and Anglicanism in the "Long" Eighteenth Century', in *Church of England c.1689–c.1833*, ed. Walsh, Haydon and Taylor, 1–64 at 11; Barrie-Curien, 'Clergy in the Diocese of London', 97; Virgin, *Church in an Age of Negligence*, 232, 239 (more generally, 223–40).

36 James Bingham to Howley, LPL FP (HP) 6, ff. 261–68 *passim*; G.O. Cambridge to Howley, 23 December 1813, LPL FP (HP) 32, ff. 56–57; Howley to James Bingham, 7 May 1816, LPL FP (HP) 5, no. 61.

in the diocese recorded in the 1835 *Liber Ecclesiasticus* and many of these paid the incumbent a pittance. But he also had some of the wealthiest in his gift as well – twelve city of London livings and others like St James', Piccadilly and Kensington.[37] Howley tended to make personal acquaintances prebendaries of St Paul's. W.S. Goddard, former Head Master of Winchester and the preacher at his consecration, was his first choice in 1813. In 1819 he appointed his uncle Samuel Gauntlett. Despite the wealth of one or two, the average income of the prebends meant they were some of the poorest in the land. Those Howley appointed had generally achieved considerable eminence academically, and in other ways. The bishop also appointed the 'dignitaries' – precentor, chancellor and treasurer – all sinecure offices. Howley made his brother-in-law C.A. Belli (his wife's youngest brother) Precentor: 'in the third year after his ordination and on the eleventh day after the death of his predecessor; he died, still Precentor in January 1886 aged 94'. Belli seems to have attended the cathedral about once a decade and was once ejected from his stall by the vergers who had never seen him before.[38]

There was financial mayhem. The provision for many clergy in the City of London was unsatisfactory and becoming intolerable. After the Fire of London in 1666 and the consequent rebuilding of churches and amalgamation of benefices, rates of payment of tithes had been fixed so that they could not rise without special legislation. Bishop Randolph had received several deputations on the issue from the incumbents of these 'Fire Act' churches. The issue was further complicated by the existence of lay impropriators who had the right to receive the tithes and then were obliged to pay the clergy – and often did not.[39] The system for collecting tithes had all but collapsed. John Moore, a Minor Canon of St Paul's and Chairman of the Fire Act Committee, was the moving force behind a bill proposed to Parliament in 1817 to increase revenues, simply

37 *Liber Ecclesiasticus: An Authentic Statement of the Revenues of the Established Church compiled from the Report of the Commissioners appointed to inquire into the Revenues and Patronages of the Established Church in England and Wales* (London, 1835), Table III, 81.

38 W.M. Jacob, 'History 1714–1830', in *St Paul's: The Cathedral Church of London 604–2004*, ed. D. Keene, A. Burns, A. Saint (New Haven and London, 2004), 71–83 at 75 (Table 4); G.L. Prestige, *St Paul's in its Glory: A Candid History of the Cathedral, 1831–1911* (London, 1955), 9–10; Cox, *Recollections of Oxford*, 91.

39 *London Tithes: Statement on Behalf of Roger Kynaston, Esq., the Lay Impropriator of St Botolph without Aldgate* (1825), LPL FP (HP) 28, ff. 142–43; James Bingham to Howley, LPL FP (HP) 6, ff. 261–68 *passim*; G.O. Cambridge to Howley, 23 December 1813, LPL FP (HP) 32, ff. 56–57; Howley to James Bingham, 7 May 1816, LPL FP (HP) 5, no. 61.

to increase the amount which clergy would receive in lieu of tithes, but had no support from the Common Council of the City of London.[40]

The dispute was a godsend to those who loathed both tithes and the Church of England. An anonymous pamphlet (identified in Howley's papers as the work of D.V. Harvey, a 'Socinian Dissenter') claimed that the Rector of St Botolph's, Bishopsgate would receive the astronomical amount of c. £7,000 a year from tithes. The fact that the Rector's average annual income from 1812 to 1814 was actually £1,175 proved the system's gross inefficiency.[41] This was reconfirmed by Richard Mant (Rector from 1815 until his consecration as Bishop of Killaloe & Kilfenora) who calculated tithes based on a much reduced property value and took account of the expense of collection and lack of income from empty houses and from those who could not afford to pay in confirming this lower figure.[42]

Howley's immediate concerns were at the other extreme of clerical income. Again, one example can stand for many. Thomas Archer's job as curate of Pitsea and South Church was divided in June 1815 and he accepted the living of Foulness in part compensation, but almost immediately came to regret it. Its annual income was a paltry £86. Queen Anne's Bounty, established to help parishes and incumbents in financial difficulties, could not help because the living's value had been miscalculated and a proposed augmentation was refused. Howley gave Archer £5 of his own income every year for essential expenditure. Archer tried to sell his poetry to generate income. He was still corresponding with Howley in exactly the same vein eleven years later and at the age of 78 was 'quite unable' to contemplate retirement.[43] Nationally though, despite isolated incidents like these, clerical income did improve appreciably in the eighteenth and early nineteenth centuries, since income from land and tithe commutation (money paid in lieu of tithes) increased. 'By the early nineteenth century only one third of livings fell below the clerical poverty line ... estimated at £150, compared with half in 1736.'[44]

---

40 [John Moore], *The Case of London Clergy whose Livings are Regulated by the Act of 22 & 23 Ch II, Commonly Called the Fire Act; Amended by the Act of 44 Geo III* (London, 1817), LPL FP (HP) 28, ff. 109–10; John Moore, *Case Respecting the Maintenance of London Clergy Further Considered* (London, 1818), 12, 14 and *passim*.

41 [D.W. Harvey], *An Address to the Owners and Occupiers of Property within the City of London and its Liberties, Occasioned by Two Bills Now Pending in Parliament upon the Subject of Tythes, by a Member of the Court of Common Council* (1817); for Howley's MS. comments, see LPL FP (HP) 28, f. 145, 150v.

42 Richard Mant to Howley, 5 December 1815, LPL FP (HP) 29, f. 175.

43 Thomas Archer to Howley, 17 February 1816, LPL FP (HP) 6, ff. 117–19; Archer to Howley, 23 June 1827, LPL FP (HP) 6, ff. 137–38.

44 Walsh and Taylor, 'Introduction', 7.

Church Building

The provision of new Church accommodation was always an issue in London. Building new churches and creating new parishes was difficult, expensive and time-consuming because it required an Act of Parliament. It took six Acts between 1770 and 1818 simply to arrange the building of a new parish church for St Marylebone, though some thought that had been done in a repellently extravagant way.[45]

The Chancellor of the Exchequer's 1816 speech which proposed a grant of £1,000,000 for building additional churches showed that proportionate to population the diocese of London had only a quarter of the churches of the diocese of Oxford. The dioceses of London, Winchester, Chester (including Liverpool and Manchester) and York (including Sheffield) were the worst provided. If existing parishes were divided, then what would happen to the income from pew rents, paid by those who could afford to hire their own pew? This was a cause of serious concern. Churches which now received a reasonable amount might well lose much of their income. Similar fears about the receipt of fees and Easter offerings were echoed throughout the country. The Archdeacon of Essex suggested things that Howley seemed not to have considered, including the simplest: that a church was doubled in size if it held two morning and two evening services.[46] Howley took soundings amongst the incumbents of wealthy parishes and leading laity which resulted in his formal submission to the commissioners for building new churches to the effect that there was little or no hope of voluntary donations and even less of church rate increases assisting in their work. Large and difficult parishes had far more than their share of those who were in no position to contribute. His example was St Matthew's, Bethnal Green where the number of houses exceeded 7,000 and only forty-two were assessed at a rent of more than £50 a year, and upwards of 5,000 at under £10. Huge arrears of parochial taxes had built up in the parish and there was absolutely no prospect of their recovery.

In 1815, Richard Yates, Chaplain of the Royal Hospital, Chelsea, had estimated that of the 1,162,300 inhabitants of London (excluding the City of London), 946,000 people were 'excluded from the advantages of parochial

---

[45] T.V. Parry, 'The Incorporated Church Building Society, 1818–1851' (Univ. of Oxford unpubl. M.Litt., 1984), 19; *A Letter to The Right Reverend the Lord Bishop of London, upon the Society for Promoting the Enlargement and Building of Churches and Chapel, by a Clergyman of the Church of England* (London, 1818), 11.

[46] Wollaston to Howley, 21 May 1818, LPL FP (HP) 10, f. 255.

worship'.[47] No parish could be officially divided until the death of the present incumbent; district churches could be created within a parish, but this often led to tension over fees. There were some nebulous proposals about compensation for the incumbent, possibly by donation of the Easter offerings (the collection traditionally retained by the vicar as part of his annual income).[48] Howley knew that imposing rates for building additional churches and chapels would never be carried in an open vestry even where the burden was lightest. The prospect of calling together all the householders of a parish and asking them to stump up yet more money for a new church was unthinkable. The Established Church would have been at the mercy of its implacable opponents, who already criticised it for its worldliness, wealth and self-indulgence. Howley wanted the commissioners just to press ahead with building new churches in parishes like Bethnal Green. He reinforced his request by showing that Shoreditch, Bethnal Green, Whitechapel and Stepney, which collectively contained a population of over 100,000, supplied less than 11,000 'sittings' in their churches. That there was only room for one in ten parishioners was a proportion which Howley and most of the Church's leaders found totally unsatisfactory and lay behind the 'unprecedented resources and efforts to strengthen the Church at the parish level' made in the early nineteenth century.[49]

Churchmanship played its part in these issues as well. Joshua Watson, the foremost High Church layman, brother of the incumbent of Hackney and a linchpin in the formation of the National Society, was at the heart of the Church Building Society and the Church Building Commission. He had been a co-signatory of a letter to Howley in 1818 protesting the ease of building a dissenting chapel and the difficulty of building an Anglican church. The concern that barely one in ten in Middlesex could be seated in church at any one time appeared again. The co-signatories thought that a number of free churches (which charged no pew rents and had no reserved seating) might constitute a national offering of thanks for the victories that ended the Napoleonic Wars.[50] Watson and John Bowdler, another generous lay supporter of the National Society and the Society for Promoting Christian Knowledge (SPCK), organised a memorial on the need for more churches to Lord Liverpool. They thought

47 Richard Yates, *The Church in Danger: A Statement of the Cause, and of the Probable Means of Averting that Danger Attempted; in a Letter to the Right Honourable the Earl of Liverpool* (London, 1815), 49–50.

48 Church Building Commission Papers s. 32, LPL FP (HP) 10, f. 276.

49 Jacob, *Clerical Profession*, 9 and *passim*; Howley's submission to the Commissioners, LPL FP (HP) 10, f. 266; cf. Walsh and Taylor, 'Introduction', 10.

50 Parry, 'Incorporated Church Building Society', 31–33.

that these churches would supplement the National Schools in bolstering High Church principles. Archbishop Manners Sutton thought that the schools would do more harm than good without extra churches. Howley's hesitation was rather that the Government might slacken in its efforts and reduce its contributions if the society were too successful.[51]

The newly created Church Building Society of 1818 (Incorporated Church Building Society from 1828) helped parishes of more than 4,000 where there was not accommodation for more than a quarter of the population, or in parishes above a certain size, possibly 20,000. Otherwise the society could assist parishes of more than 2,000 where there was not accommodation for one half or all the parishes where there were c. 20,000 or more for whom there was no accommodation. In fact it made little difference which criterion was applied. Thirty-two parishes nationwide fulfilled both conditions. Five of these had too little space for between 59 and 70,000 of their parishioners. In London the parish of St Marylebone (referred to above) required five new churches; St Pancras, two.[52]

Howley, his Chaplains and Favourites

Howley spent most of the day in the company of his chaplains. They were responsible for his daily appointments and for access to him. It was clearly of the highest importance that they be personally congenial to him and his wife and sympathetic to his doctrinal position. Cyril Jackson recommended two candidates for appointment in 1813: Charles Lloyd (later Bishop of Oxford) who had 'twenty times more sound materials in him' than any others at Christ Church and whose learning, both classical and mathematical, made him 'just the sort of man we want in the present years' and Hugh Chambres Jones (Domestic Chaplain to the Duke of Portland and a former Student of Christ Church) whose current appointment Jackson had also arranged.[53] Howley knew Jones from when he had been a private tutor for the Hamilton family and appointed him.

Jackson told Jones that, unlike some domestic chaplaincies, it would not become an 'unpleasant confinement'. When Jones was wanted for business and

---

51 Parry, 'Incorporated Church Building Society', 34–35; Alan Webster, *Joshua Watson: The Story of a Layman 1771–1855* (London, 1954), 61.

52 MS details of allocation of funds, LPL FP (HP) 8, f. 173.

53 Jackson to Howley, 18 August 1813, LPL MS 2186, f. 50; Jackson to H.C. Jones, 17 July [1810], Ch Ch Copy Correspondence of H.C. Jones, f. 86.

ceremony, the only difference would be that his bed would be at St James's Square and not in Dean's Yard.[54] Jackson thought it very important that there should be more than just one channel to the bishop – his secretary – particularly bearing in mind the appalling precedent of Randolph's service from Wright. A clergyman 'much preferred dealing with another cleric on professional matters' in any case.[55] Chaplains often described themselves as 'coming into the family' (with the resonance of the *familia* of a medieval bishop's domestic establishment), so close a relationship did they have with the bishop and his wife and children. Howley and his wife encouraged this with his chaplains. Other duties involved leading daily prayers and attending on the bishop at confirmations.

Benjamin Harrison, Hugh James Rose, W.H. Mill and F.B. Wells were all resident either at Fulham or Lambeth (when Archbishop) with Howley for a considerable period of the year. Sir Herbert Oakeley, Bt. was ordained in 1814 to serve as Howley's chaplain, having been a Student of Christ Church from 1807. He lived at Fulham for twelve years before his marriage. Others were Examining Chaplains whose primary role was to interview those seeking ordination. These included Jones, W.R. Churton, W.S. Goddard, Blomfield, W.R. Lyall (future Dean of Canterbury), John Lonsdale (future Bishop of Lichfield) and William Vaux. Harrison was originally appointed as an Examining Chaplain but spent more and more time at Howley's side.[56]

Howley worked particularly closely with Charles James Blomfield. He appointed him Rector of St Botolph's, Bishopsgate in 1820 when he was 34 and in 1822, Archdeacon of Colchester as well. When Blomfield became Bishop of Chester in 1824 he kept the parish as a *commendam* because the income of the Bishop of Chester was amongst the lowest of all dioceses. After Blomfield succeeded Howley as Bishop of London in August 1828 he wrote several letters to his wife that provide a glimpse of domestic life. Mrs Howley had shown Blomfield around Fulham Palace to discuss arrangements. In total, the housekeeping, including coal, liveried uniforms for servants, wages and linen washing cost no more than £1,800 a year. Carriages were about £900 a year, wages £800. The Howleys spent c. £1,000 on clothes and other necessities. Bills were paid quarterly. In 1827, 970 people had dined with them. Calls on Blomfield's generosity for subscriptions and the like should not amount to

54 Jackson to Jones, [12 September 1813], f. 99.

55 Jackson to Howley, 13 September [1813], f. 102.

56 *Some notes relating to the Life (1791–1845) of Sir Herbert Oakeley, 3rd Baronet*, edited by his daughter The Hon Mrs Francis Drummond (1892), 3; more generally, see Gibson, *Social History of the Domestic Chaplain*, 145–61.

more than £1,500.[57] London House in St James' Square was, however, barely 'convenient'. The office areas and kitchens were not as good as in the Blomfields' present London home. Very little entertaining was done here. Dinners were 'very much what ours are – not at all superior – and so for breakfast'. Vegetables, fruit and cream arrived from Fulham Palace every day. Howley told Blomfield that he would be able to live very well on £8,000 a year, which would allow him to take out some investment for his parents and despite other financial obligations he would have c. £13,000 a year so that £4,000–£5,000 could be used every year in paying off debts.[58]

Howley, Blomfield and Liverpool

Lord Liverpool consulted Howley and Blomfield frequently over church appointments. Charles Lloyd, when Regius Professor of Divinity at Oxford, knew the use of Howley and Blomfield's *imprimatur*. He wrote a number of times to his former pupil Robert Peel after the Bishop of Durham's death in 1826 asking him to recommend his name to them. Not only did he want to be a bishop, he was equally concerned not to be bested to the Oxford turn by the Provost of Oriel College. Peel told Lloyd to contact Van Mildert or Howley directly. Lloyd refused on the basis that Howley was 'the Privy Councillor of Lord L[iverpool] in these matters'. He did not wish to enter the House of Lords 'with a chain of gratitude' around his neck to Howley, since he felt it likely that he would have to differ from him in the future and that would be difficult to do if he had been the 'overt instrument' of his elevation. Lloyd was depressed both at himself and at the system, having thought that he would have no trouble becoming a bishop and would then have asked Peel's help in getting translated to a bigger and better see.[59] He was nevertheless made Bishop of Oxford.

Liverpool did not follow Howley and Blomfield's advice slavishly, several times appointing people other than those they had recommended or without consulting them at all. John Kaye, newly Bishop of Bristol, wrote to Howley in 1820 hoping that J.H. Monk, Regius Professor of Greek might become Master of Trinity College, Cambridge. Monk had asked Kaye to write to Liverpool on the matter and Kaye knew that it would carry much more weight if Howley sent

57 Blomfield to Dorothy Blomfield, 6 August 1828, LPL MS Film 20.

58 Blomfield to Dorothy Blomfield, 2 August 1828, LPL MS Film 20.

59 Peel to Lloyd, 22 February 1826, BL Add MS 40342, f. 322; Lloyd to Peel, n.d., BL Add MS 40342, f. 324; Lloyd to Peel, 28 February 1826, BL Add MS 40342, f. 328.

the recommendation with a covering letter of his own.[60] Blomfield also wrote a paean to Monk's erudition and abilities to Liverpool. However, Archbishop Manners Sutton and Joshua Watson had already suggested Christopher Wordsworth, who had founded the National Society with Watson in 1811 and was Chaplain to the House of Commons and a former Domestic Chaplain to the Archbishop. Liverpool appointed him. He translated George Pretyman Tomline from Lincoln to Winchester in 1820 without consulting Howley, Blomfield or Joshua Watson, whose advice he also valued highly.[61] He told Dean Hall of Christ Church that his patronage was never influenced by personal considerations. By April 1820 he had appointed seven bishops 'with no one of the Individuals so made had I any connexion near or remote – and with some of them I was not even personally acquainted'.[62] Liverpool welcomed the advice of those he trusted, and preferred to appoint those who would be congenial to his views, but in the end was guided by what he was convinced was best for the Church.

Controversies with the Unitarians and Jeremy Bentham

High Churchmen were particularly prone to a fevered concern about an impending popular rebellion which would overthrow the Church along with the State. Howley had a horror of the principles and violence of the French Revolution of 1789 like the vast majority of his fellow bishops and clergy.[63] Threats to religion and social order went hand in hand with rebellion against rightful divine and human authority. Deviation from the Church of England was suspect enough, let alone Trinitarian Christian faith. Goddard's sermon at Howley's consecration on the pitfalls of unorthodox belief in this world and the next was entirely typical of countless others, and exactly what Howley would himself have said.[64] He gave a standard defence of the High Church attachment to the doctrine of 'apostolical succession'. Since the process of making decisions

60 Kaye to Howley, 28 June 1820, BL Add MS 38285, f. 340.

61 Tomline to Liverpool, 27 March 1820, BL Add MS 38283, f. 366; Edward Churton (ed.), *Memoir of Joshua Watson* (London, 1861), i, 219–21.

62 Liverpool to Hall, 17 April 1820, BL Add MS 38574, f. 176.

63 See N.U. Murray, 'The Influence of the French Revolution on the Church of England and its Rivals, 1789–1802' (Univ. of Oxford unpubl. D.Phil. thesis, 1975), 45–78; Peter B. Nockles, *The Oxford Movement in Context: Anglican High Churchmanship, 1760–1857* (Cambridge, 1994), ch. 1.

64 W.S. Goddard to Howley, 15 August 1813, LPL MS 2184, ff. 116–17.

within the Church was not clear simply from Scripture, the 'agency of men' was of vital importance in developing the norms of the Church's daily activity and this was as Christ had wished it to be. It was a short step to defend the supremacy of the Anglican Church in the State by distinguishing between the needs of Church and civil government. Although the liberty of worshipping God according to conscience was freely conceded to all, the State reserved the right to restrict offices of trust and power to those 'who have given the surest and most unequivocal pledge of their principles and attachment by the conformity to the National Religion'.

The sermon provoked a counter publication by Thomas Sanden, a well-known Unitarian.[65] Howley gave the subject plenty of his own attention in his first Charge to the clergy of the diocese of London in 1814. The French Revolution was evidence of a 'desperate wickedness'. Having linked infidelity with political rebellion and moral collapse, he traced its origins back to the rise of Deism and Unitarianism. He felt for the conscientious Unitarian, who accepted the general truth of Christianity but rejected its 'peculiar dogmas'. Yet anyone who refused to see that Trinitarian doctrines should be derived from the Bible was, to some extent, guilty of infidelity. Unitarianism had 'little to captivate the affections', and disgusted the 'unsophisticated reason by its obvious contradiction to Scripture'. He claimed it appealed only to those who had not thought matters through well enough and (even worse) those who loved to question everything and had too little respect for divine authority.[66] Other High Churchmen like Thomas Burgess, Bishop of St David's and Charles Daubeny, Archdeacon of Sarum, who had both been involved in acrimonious disputes with Unitarians, thought that Howley had been far too generous. Burgess believed that anyone rejecting Christianity's peculiar dogmas could not hold the general truth of the faith. Muslims admitted as much of Christianity as Unitarians: how much of the 'general truth of Christianity' did Howley think Unitarians held?[67]

The dispute was regarded as far from arcane. Thomas Belsham, the Unitarian Minister of the Essex Street Chapel off the Strand who had had a dispute with Burgess previously, sent Howley five substantial letters which sold enough copies to go into a second edition the same year. He objected that Unitarians had done

[65] W.S. Goddard, *Sermon Preached at the Consecration of William Howley as Bishop of London* (London, 1814); [T. Sanden], *A Second Letter to the Rev Dr Goddard* [by a layman] (Chichester, 1815), *passim.*

[66] W. Howley, *Charge at his Primary Visitation ... of William, Bishop of London* (London, 1814), 14.

[67] Thomas Burgess to Howley, 5 December 1814, LPL MS 2184, ff. 176–77; Charles Daubeny to Howley, 11 January 1815, LPL MS 2184, ff. 189–90.

little to warrant attack, neither attacking the revenues of the Church nor the character of the clergy. Belsham suggested that if the Scriptures were substituted for the Thirty-Nine Articles and the Liturgy reformed, then a 'very considerable majority' of Unitarians would become members of the Establishment, at least in 'the upper and more cultivated classes of society'. Many Unitarian clergy had remained in the Church of England because it gave a wider sphere of influence. Belsham took offence at the explicit or implicit suggestion that Unitarians did not reverence the 'inspired writings' and were all of a piece with deists, atheists and 'licentious Free-Thinkers'.[68]

However acrimonious, the disagreement was a dull echo of the conflicts that had threatened huge damage to the Church of England in the early eighteenth century.[69] It was nevertheless still notorious enough for Jeremy Bentham to attack Howley at length in *Church of Englandism* three years later, in particular objecting to the National Society encouraging 'a humble docility' to the rulers of the Church of England and their subordinates. He took as his refrain a phrase from Howley's Charge that the true Christian exhibits 'a prostration of the understanding and will' to the authority of the Church and her teaching and described Howley as the 'Prostrator-general of wills'. This was slavery beside which that found in the West Indies would be freedom. Bentham said that since Howley's Charge spoke of all but 'Church-of-Englandists' as 'enemies' and other Christians as 'schismatics and men of guilt' its practical effect was to justify oppression as a form of punishment.[70] Joseph Lancaster, a Quaker, had adapted the Anglican priest Andrew Bell's monitorial system of education, expunging the Anglican content from the scheme. Under Lancaster's system the Bible became a 'battering-ram against the Established Church' and Bentham thought that when the hierarchy had realised this, unable to suppress the use of the Bible, they had turned to the use of the Catechism to distort its message.[71] Howley's Charge seems to have been the catalyst for Bentham making public objections

68 Thomas Belsham, *Letters Addressed to the Right Reverend the Bishop of London in Vindication of the Unitarians from the Allegation of his Lordship in the Charge delivered to the Clergy of the Diocese of London at his Lordship's Primary Visitation* (2nd edn, London, 1815), 2–4, 17–23, 30–33.

69 E.G. Rupp, *Religion in England 1688–1791* (Oxford, 1986), 243–47.

70 Jeremy Bentham, *Church of Englandism and its Catechism Examined: Preceded by Strictures on the Exclusionary System as Pursued in the National Society's Schools ...* (London, 1818), xliii and *passim*.

71 Bentham, *Church of Englandism*, 43, 55 and *passim*; R.A. Soloway, *Prelates and People. Ecclesiastical Social Thought in England 1783–1852* (London and Toronto, 1969), 370–79.

which he had been nursing for over forty years but which he only began to publish between 1817 and 1832.[72]

The Bible Society and the National Society

The National Society had been founded only in 1811 but by the time of Howley's Charge already had many of the most influential bishops and leading clergy amongst its benefactors. It unashamedly propagated the High Church Anglican version of the Christian faith. Many of those who were friends and collaborators of Howley, like Christopher Wordsworth and Joshua Watson, the great lay leader of High Churchmen, had been involved in founding it. Bentham's strident criticism underlined how central the dispute over education had become. Supporters and detractors both realised how effective the National Society schools could be in ensuring attendance at Anglican parish churches. Bentham described them as 'the Bench of Bishops' schools' and thought that Bell's system of catechetical teaching would make this part of clergymen's ministry 'smooth and easy' by having their parishioners initiated, virtually suborned, into Anglican churchgoing from infancy.[73]

Amongst evangelical Anglican clergy there was more enthusiasm for the non-denominational British and Foreign Bible Society. H.H. Norris, Curate of St John's, Hackney and a chaplain to the Earl of Shaftesbury (father of the famous evangelical), published *A Practical Exposition of the Tendency and Proceedings of the British and Foreign Bible Society* in 1813. He dedicated it to Howley, as Bishop Elect of London. He concentrated on its supposed encouragement of 'erroneous and strange doctrines'. Since Anglican priests undertook to use 'all faithful diligence to banish and drive away' these at ordination, Norris could scarcely credit any Anglican support for the society. Whenever another auxiliary branch was set up there was a flurry of such feelings. Norris wrote his book after an attempt to set one up in Hackney itself, where Joshua Watson's brother was the rector, and a leading High Churchman himself.[74] Howley welcomed the

---

[72] Robert Hole, *Pulpits, Politics and Public Order in England 1760–1832* (Cambridge, 1989), 200–04.

[73] Hole, *Pulpits, Politics and Public Order*, 91.

[74] H.H. Norris, *A Practical Exposition of the Tendency and Proceedings of the British and Foreign Bible Society* (2nd edn, London, 1814), viii.

dedication warmly. He made Norris a prebendary of St Paul's in 1825 (just as Herbert Marsh had done at Llandaff after his consecration in 1816).[75]

Within four years the antagonism between evangelical and High Churchman had become focused on the competition and mistrust between the National Society and the Bible Society. Although clergy of different schools of thought had subscribed to societies like the Society for the Propagation of the Gospel in Foreign Parts (SPG) and the SPCK as well as the Bible Society in years past, many High Churchmen very soon became single minded in supporting the one and denigrating the other. The Bible Society's work in England itself, in direct competition with the National Society, particularly infuriated them. Christopher Wordsworth said that it would have caused few ripples if it had been solely an overseas missionary society.[76] The Royal Lancastrian Society, which existed to develop Lancaster's non-denominational system of education, was similarly abused after 1811. Despite its royal patronage, many deserted it.[77] The new National Society somehow made the older societies seem like upstarts, whose very existence was offensive.

If opposition to the Bible Society had been restricted merely to a small clique of fanatical High Churchmen, Norris's writings and the other protests would have been in vain. But antagonism went deeper and wider. A major dispute had taken place at the University of Cambridge between 1810 and 1814 after an auxiliary branch of the society was set up there. Herbert Marsh, the Lady Margaret Professor of Divinity, was prominent in attacking it on the basis that it was not solely allied to the Church of England. Marsh was an idiosyncratic self-aggrandising character who had been involved in a bitter dispute at Cambridge in 1805 when he preached a series of fiercely anti-Calvinist sermons, yet neither had he been at all popular with High Churchmen because of his 'liberal' views about biblical criticism.[78] Christopher Wordsworth told Norris that the Bible Society was as unpopular with government ministers and the Royal Family as it was amongst the bishops.[79] The creation of a separate sister British and Foreign Schools Society in 1814 simply added fuel to the fire. J.D. Macbride, of Magdalen Hall and an officer of the auxiliary branch of the Bible Society in

---

75 Howley to Norris, 22 November 1813, Bodl Lib MS Eng Lett c 789, f. 56; Churton, *Memoir of Joshua Watson*, i, 142–43.

76 Christopher Wordsworth, *Reasons for Declining to Become a Subscriber to the British and Foreign Bible Society, Stated in a Letter to a Clergyman of the Diocese of London* (London, 1810), 9.

77 Hole, *Pulpits, Politics and Public Order*, 193.

78 Cyril Jackson to Howley, 6 December 1810, LPL MS 2186, ff. 26–31.

79 Christopher Wordsworth to Norris, 5 February 1813, Bodl Lib MS Eng Lett c 789, ff. 42–43.

Oxford, wrote to Howley to attack Norris. Howley replied that he disapproved of the expression of Scripture without gloss or comment and of the Society's association with Dissenters, because its objects could be 'attained by charitable competition with greater safety'.[80]

The Prayer Book and Homilies Society was in some ways an attempt to bridge the gap between High Church societies like the SPCK and the Bible Society. The evangelical Bishop Henry Ryder was a keen patron and men like William Wilberforce were subscribers. Ryder tried to keep a foot in both camps, praising all three societies in his Primary Charge at Gloucester. By 1818 the society had distributed nearly 50,000 prayer books and nearly 40,000 'Homily tracts', and copies of the Articles as well.[81] Howley never took an interest in it, not least because it was formed 'as a handmaid to the British and Foreign Bible Society'. Howley disapproved of setting up any new branches of the Bible Society. His often repeated argument was that since both the SPCK and the National Society provided bibles already, there was no need for the Bible Society, which actively interfered with their work.[82] A contribution he had made to the Bible Society ten years earlier (well before the foundation of the National Society) led to his name being mentioned as a supporter in an advertisement in the *Salisbury Journal* and the *Hampshire Chronicle* announcing a meeting in Winchester to form an auxiliary branch, which caused him to express great irritation which was roused to fury when he discovered that the society later described him as one of its vice-presidents.[83]

The work of the National Society was one of Howley's highest priorities. He always commended it in his Charges. Like other bishops he gave it a remarkable amount of his time. He regularly attended its weekly meetings at the joint offices of the SPCK and the SPG in Bartlett's Buildings on the Strand. It had the highest priority amongst the fund-raising which went on in the diocese. He spoke at its town branch meetings for donations and support towards the building of schools. He told the organiser of the Colchester National Schools Committee that he regretted that so much money had been collected for the society for the

80 J.D. Macbride to Howley, 22 December 1813, LPL HP (FP) 29, f. 79 [with a note of Howley's reply].

81 Henry Ryder, *Charge ... to the clergy of the diocese of Gloucester ... at the Primary Visitation* (Gloucester, 1816), 31–33; *A Sermon ... before the Prayer Book and Homilies Society ... also the Report of the Committee* (London, 1818). I owe this reference to Dr Mark Smith.

82 See, for example, Howley to G. Heathcote, 15 December 1813, LPL FP (HP) 20, f. 125; Howley to William Whinfield, 16 June 1817, LPL FP (HP) 5, no. 95.

83 Richard Hobyln, Rector of All Saints', Colchester to Howley, 5 December 1815, LPL FP (HP) 20, f. 258.

conversion of the Jews because that would reduce the money available for the far more important work of mass education.[84] He vetoed a cheap day school for the children of clergymen as liable to distract from the education of the poor. He was always fearful that the National Society, even with financing from the 'zealous and rich', would suffer a lack of funds, particularly when collections for the society were suspended in 1815 in favour of the sufferers of Waterloo.[85]

The High Church, Nobody's Friends and the Hackney Phalanx

Peter Nockles shows how the 'old High Churchmen' looked backed to the Fathers and to the Caroline Divines for their inspiration. They held elevated views of sacramental grace both in the Eucharist and at Baptism and were concerned for the Catholic Church whilst being, in the main, anti-Roman. He explores how the term might be used as an indicator of a general 'political, ecclesiological, liturgical, spiritual and sacramental' position without tying 'high churchmen' down to too rigid a set of beliefs.[86] Different adherents would emphasise different parts of this heritage. Such a broad definition means that some terminology needs careful reconsideration as well. Nockles attacks the later historiography of Tractarianism which gained currency with the widespread success of the Oxford Movement in the latter part of the nineteenth and the first half of the twentieth century. Although a looser definition of the term 'High Church' has the advantage of allowing for the fact that several protagonists of the 'party' did hold differing views, notably on the correct relationship of the Church with the State, it does of course have the disadvantage of making it difficult to ascribe particular strategies to the 'party' as a whole. Sometimes the terms 'Orthodox' and 'High Church' have been used as virtually interchangeable and at others 'Orthodox' has defined a particular type of High Churchman.[87] Nevertheless Edward Churton's *Memoir of Joshua Watson* and J.W. Burgon's *Lives of Twelve Good Men* presupposed that a 'party' could be identified. Burgon's chapter on Hugh James Rose identified men of 'old fashioned piety' who 'had retained their

84 Howley to Edward Crosse, Rector of Mount Bures, Essex, 27 June 1815, LPL FP (HP) 5, no. 21.

85 Howley to Thomas Gurney, 12 September 1815, LPL FP (HP) 5, no. 31.

86 Nockles, *Oxford Movement in Context*, ch. 1 and *passim*.

87 Peter Nockles, 'Church Parties in the pre-Tractarian Church of England 1750–1833: The 'Orthodox' – Some Problems of Definition and Identity', in *Church of England c.1689–c.1833*, ed. Walsh, Haydon and Taylor, 335, 338–41 and *passim*; Nockles, *Oxford Movement in Context*, 25–32 and *passim*.

hold on Catholic Truth amid every discouragement'. Amongst these he listed Howley.[88]

The group of High Churchmen that has attracted particular interest is the 'Hackney Phalanx'. This was a broad coalition of like-minded clergy and some laity whose name merely reflected the fact that many of its leading lights, like Norris and J.J. Watson mentioned above, were incumbents or curates in and around Hackney.[89] Howley became increasingly close to its members when Bishop of London. His connection with Liverpool and through him to Joshua Watson has already been discussed. Christopher Wordsworth was another point of contact.

The High Church dining club, Nobody's Friends, was founded in 1800 by William Stevens (Nobody himself), the Treasurer of Queen Anne's Bounty. Amongst the society's founding members were leading High Churchmen, ordained and lay. These included James Allan Park, K.C., later a Justice of the Court of Common Pleas, both Joshua and his brother J.J. Watson (who became Archdeacon of St Albans in 1816) and H.H. Norris. Almost all of Howley's chaplains during his time at Fulham and later at Lambeth were or later became members of Nobody's Friends. John Lonsdale (later his Domestic Chaplain at Lambeth) and William Rowe Lyall (later Dean of Canterbury) were both elected in 1818. Blomfield and Sir Herbert Oakeley, Bt. were likewise both elected in 1821; as was William Vaux, Chaplain at Fulham in 1824; Benjamin Harrison (former Chaplain and future Archdeacon of Maidstone) in 1840 and William Hale Hale, a Chaplain at Lambeth, in 1845. Several members subsequently became bishops, like Van Mildert, Blomfield, Charles Lloyd and John Lonsdale of Lichfield (later Lichfield and Coventry.)[90] Howley was never a member, probably because he did not know the society's other members before his consecration. His 1813 letter thanking Norris for his book on the Bible Society shows that they had not previously met.

Politically too Howley espoused views typical of High Churchmen. He became entangled in the public wrangling over Queen Caroline's divorce when he spoke briefly in the debate on the Bill of Pains and Penalties against Caroline. He could see no good reason to oppose the divorce, since many previous divorces had been passed through Parliament when the conduct of the husband was notoriously reprehensible. Since there was 'certain proof' of the Queen's adultery, he supported the bill 'in a moral, constitutional and religious point

---

88 J.W. Burgon, *Lives of Twelve Good Men* (London, 1888), i, 154–55.

89 Nockles, *Oxford Movement in Context*, 14–16.

90 *'The Club of Nobody's Friends.' Biographical List of the Members since its Foundation, 21 June 1800 to 30 September 1885* [printed for private circulation] (London, 1938).

of view'.[91] He was misreported and then pilloried in the press for having said that the King could do no wrong 'morally or physically'. This was a distortion of some apparently private remarks in which he had discussed the view that, constitutionally, the King could do no wrong 'morally or politically'. An anonymous pamphlet printed for William Hone, the leading anti-clerical writer, *The Right Divine of Kings to Govern Wrong!*, claimed that Howley had said that the King could commit no folly, much less crime. Hone conjured a picture of a cringing, promotion-seeking Howley recommending 'Passive obedience and Non-resistance'. Howley's view of the fountain head of political, ecclesiastical and royal authority certainly stemmed from 'a widely held patriarchal theory of the origin and nature of all political authority'.[92]

Not every plan endorsed by Hackney got Howley's approval. Bishop Hobart of New York, seeking funds for the General Theological Seminary, attempted to undermine the fund-raising being done by Nathaniel Wheaton from Hartford, Connecticut for the college planned there and of Bishop Chase of Ohio, who was taken up by the Evangelicals in his search to finance missionary education in his diocese. Neither Chase nor Wheaton was really a party man. Chase nevertheless ended up not only with Howley's support but that of both archbishops. Two of Chase's sponsors were members of Nobody's Friends – Lord Kenyon and G.W. Marriott.[93] H.H. Norris was livid that James Gaskin, Secretary of the SPCK 1783–1823, had persuaded Howley to back Chase. Despite an agreement between Chase and Hobart to reach a compromise, Norris would not let the matter rest. Chase returned with £5,000 in funding, whilst Hobart returned with approximately £1,000 and books for his seminary. Geoffrey Best saw this as a good example of Howley's ability to act independently of the High Church party.[94] One might rather say that in the blurred edges of the High Church movement, which remained right up to and through the Oxford Movement, Howley's independence never stopped him being regarded as a High Churchman.

91 *Hansard*, n.s. ii (1820), col. 1711.

92 [William Hone], *The Right Divine of Kings to Govern Wrong! Dedicated to the Holy Alliance (by the Author of the Political House that Jack Built)* (London, 1821), 6–7; Nockles, *Oxford Movement in Context*, ch. 1.

93 G.F.A. Best, 'Church Parties and Charities: The Experience of Three American Visitors to England, 1823–24', *EHR*, 78 (1963), 255–56, (more generally) 243–62.

94 Best, 'Church Parties', 258–61.

The Church Overseas

It had long been accepted that the Bishop of London had some sort of responsibility for the Anglican Church overseas, and it had been a source of confusion and frustration to all concerned for almost as long. Howley's concerns, like those of many of his predecessors, were that he had no explicit jurisdiction for the ministry and that anything he could do would be hopelessly inadequate to the task. His own definition of its compass was extremely narrow. He could grant certain documents, vouching for the character and qualifications of those appointed to overseas postings by the Government. He could use his influence on the Government, which itself was unclear about the limits of his authority, for the benefit of the churches and clergy in foreign settlements.[95] Howley upbraided Earl Bathurst, the Colonial Secretary, over an Act of the Bahamas legislature for erecting and repairing churches and for the maintenance of ministers which took for granted that the Bishop of London acted as diocesan bishop of the Bahamas. Howley did not claim that and thought it would be thoroughly bad to be given the authority. Governors were habitually given the authority of an ecclesiastical Ordinary. He nevertheless objected to the proposal to give a governor authority to suspend clergy guilty of vice or immorality because there was no appeal procedure. This he thought should be available through the Privy Council.

Edmund Gibson, Bishop of London 1723–48, had been determined to know the full extent of his powers before granting any commissions for the exercise of jurisdiction beyond the diocesan boundaries. He discovered that he himself needed a Commission under the Great Seal to award any more commissions. Gibson did obtain one, but it was for him personally. In a strict sense no jurisdiction had been exercised by a Bishop of London in the colonies after Gibson's death yet they had continued to ordain candidates for service in the colonies. Bishop Porteus had given advice to clergy which was almost indistinguishable from discipline, even though he was under no illusion about the true extent (or lack) of his formal powers. Howley thought that it would be the utmost stupidity to risk the authority which he did have and which might be put to some good use by pushing the matter too hard. He thought that colonial regulation could handle clergy discipline but his dearest wish was to see a vast increase in the number of bishoprics. That would be by far the best way to deal

---

95 Howley to John Armstrong, Chaplain of British Honduras, 31 January 1817, LPL FP (HP) 5, no. 87.

with the problem.[96] Hardly surprisingly many High Churchmen thought this a plan well worth pursuing. Joshua Watson concentrated on raising the profile of the SPCK and the SPG for this reason. He encouraged both Howley and Manners Sutton to back an SPG grant of £5,000 to Bishop Middleton of Calcutta in 1818. Middleton was so closely associated with the SPCK and the SPG when Vicar of St Pancras and Archdeacon of Huntingdon that after he was consecrated he became the societies' model of a High Church colonial bishop.[97] Howley quashed a proposal that no cleric without a degree from an English, Scottish or Irish university could hold a benefice in the Bahamas. He drew an absolute distinction between ordaining those to serve in the colonies and overseas and those to serve in England, reminding Bathurst that a Scottish degree was no qualification for any situation in the Church of England. His willingness to ordain literates was based on the simple fact that not enough graduates were willing to work in the West Indies.[98]

Howley recommended *An Essay towards an Instruction for the Indians* (1740) by Thomas Wilson, the much revered Bishop of Sodor and Man, for instructing 'natives' in Ceylon. His book had originally been aimed at 'Red Indians' when the Governor of Georgia had asked for a primer. Wilson's book (like several similar ones by various authors) took the form of an extended series of questions and answers which expounded Anglican doctrine and provided suggestions for practical devotion. Howley stressed the need for a permanent relationship with the SPCK through a district committee. This way books would come far cheaper. Howley's dream was to see Bell's system of education spread throughout the British Empire, because of its 'astonishing' effects in teaching reading, writing and arithmetic with speed, certainty and 'I might almost say, with perfection'.[99]

Howley stayed in regular contact with colonial bishops even after they were released from his nominal oversight. Middleton wrote frequently from Calcutta for his advice. Howley could only be of limited assistance since letters took over three months to travel to and fro and were occasionally lost at sea. Middleton replied in February 1818 to a letter that Howley had written in April the previous year. He requested Howley's help in influencing the East India Company's training college in Hertford to provide religious instruction to its trainees and to continue the support from the various High Church societies.[100]

96 Copy Howley to Earl Bathust, 11 April 1817, LPL FP (HP) 3, ff. 71–77.

97 Webster, *Joshua Watson*, 115ff.; Hans Cnattingius, *Bishops and Societies: A Study of Anglican Colonial and Missionary Expansion 1698–1850* (London, 1952), 72 and *passim*.

98 Howley to Earl Bathurst, 11 April 1817, LPL FP (HP) 5, no. 93.

99 Howley to F. Thistleton, Ceylon, 10 January 1815, LPL FP (HP) 5, no. 1.

100 T.F. Middleton to Howley, 16 February 1818, LPL FP (HP) 1, f. 29.

Howley had particular contact with the West Indies, and made considerable efforts to find suitable candidates to serve there. He received detailed reports about the state of religion and society in the various islands. There were often requests for their own bishops, and if not, archdeacons.[101] The first Bishop of Jamaica, Christopher Lipscomb, was appointed in 1825. Howley often received questions from him and they were very similar to those he had previously received from the incumbents on Jamaica. Between February 1825 and December 1826, Lipscomb wrote nine letters crammed full of observations and questions for him to answer. Just as the priests of the island churches had complained about the attitude of estate owners to the catechising and baptism of their slaves, so Lipscomb did the same.[102] In the final analysis Howley seems to have resigned himself to the curious position into which his overseas 'responsibilities' placed him. He did what good he could by advice and suggestion. Virtually powerless in theory, he had a vast area of influence over clergy who looked to him more, not less, as the years passed at London.

---

[101] Theophilus Donne to Howley, 15 April 1820, LPL FP (HP) 2, f. 249.

[102] See, for example, Christopher Lipscomb to Howley, 18 February 1825, LPL FP (HP) 2, f. 389; Lipscomb to Howley, 2 December 1826, LPL FP (HP) 2, f. 493.

Chapter 3
Early Years at Canterbury

Appointment

Charles Manners Sutton had been Archbishop of Canterbury since 1805. As a grandson of the Duke of Rutland and brother of the Lord Chancellor of Ireland, and with a son who became Speaker of the House of Commons and later Viscount Canterbury, Sutton came from a social background that was palpably different from Howley's. Howley was generally thought to be his obvious successor. He had been Liverpool's clear favourite for the job, having been regularly relied upon by the Prime Minister for advice on appointments and other Church matters, but Wellington's appointment as Prime Minister in 1828 did not dampen speculation.[1] Howley's family background was as little impediment to appointment to Canterbury as it had been to London. Manners Sutton was an old High Churchman, closer personally to the leaders of the Phalanx than Howley, and had presided over the inaugural meeting of the National Society in 1811. They moved in the same ecclesiastical circles and used similar patronage networks. Many of Howley's close associates had been Manners Sutton's chaplains: they included Charles Lloyd, Lonsdale (who continued as Howley's chaplain), Christopher Wordsworth and Richard Mant.[2]

Wellington told the King that the two names to consider were Howley and Van Mildert. He would have preferred Van Mildert but Van Mildert had only recently become Bishop of Durham. Wellington's hesitations about Howley centred round his forthright opposition to Catholic Emancipation. George IV, adamantly opposed to it, naturally thought this a splendid qualification. Since Wellington's cabinet was in theory neutral on the question, Howley could hardly be openly objected to on the grounds of his opposition. Wellington suggested that if Howley went to Canterbury then Blomfield should go to London; if Van Mildert did, then Kaye of Lincoln could go to Durham. He inclined to appointing Howley but without great enthusiasm. The King had long been

1 Ffoliot Cornewall to Howley, 30 July 1828, LPL MS 2185, f. 39.

2 Dewey, *Passing of Barchester*, 140.

expecting and hoping that Howley would replace Manners Sutton.[3] Howley was elected Archbishop by the chapter of Canterbury on 8 August 1828. Amongst many letters of congratulations one from Sir James Allan Park, judge and leading High Church layman, stands for many:

> You are now to became the spiritual head of the first Protestant church, not only of Europe, but (looking to the East and West) of the world to advance the glory of God, the welfare of the Church against all Popery, heresy and schism.[4]

Pride in the term Protestant, confidence that the Church of England was a branch of the church catholic just like Rome or Greece and antagonism towards the 'errors of Popery' were entirely typical of the High Churchmen. Christopher Hodgson, Howley's secretary, said that Howley himself seemed almost more pleased by Blomfield's translation to London than by his own to Canterbury.[5] Howley was enthroned as Archbishop of Canterbury and Primate of All England and Metropolitan by proxy as was the common practice. His two immediate predecessors had been enthroned in the same way. A prebendary, William Welfitt, stood as proxy. He was 'inducted, installed and enthroned' by another prebend standing proxy for the Archdeacon of Canterbury. Welfitt was seated in the medieval throne, the chair and the Dean's stall and gave the blessing at the end as Howley would have done.[6] Sydney Smith lampooned Howley about the ceremony when the Archbishop was chairman of the Ecclesiastical Commission in the 1830s, in charge of re-organising cathedral finances and privileges. Howley might have forgotten his oath 'never to violate that foundation of piety' because 'detained in town by business or pleasure' he had sent down a messenger 'in the Canterbury Fly' to swear it. Enthronement in person would have attracted enormous fees in the first year of a bishopric which was always very expensive for the new incumbent.[7] Nonetheless the see was the source of great wealth. The

---

3 Owen Chadwick, *The Victorian Church: Part One: 1829–1859* (3rd edn, London, 1971), 13; Copy Wellington to King George IV, 21 July 1828, Southampton University Archives WP1/945/12; C.R. Sumner to Howley, 26 July 1828, LPL MS 2185, f. 9.

4 J.A. Park to Howley, 26 July 1828, LPL MS 2185, f. 15.

5 Blomfield to Mrs Blomfield, n.d., LPL MS Film 20.

6 'Form to be used at the Inthronization of the Most Reverend Father in God, William Howley, D.D., Lord Archbishop of Canterbury'. Thursday August 28th 1828, LPL MS 2195, f. 5.

7 Sydney Smith, 'First Letter to Archdeacon Singleton' and 'Second Letter to Archdeacon Singleton', in *The Works of The Revd Sydney Smith: Complete in One Volume* (new edn, 1850), 606, 627; R.M. Beverley, *Letter to His Grace the Archbishop of York, on the Present Corrupt State of the Church of England* (5th edn, Beverley, 1831), 5.

archbishop's estates were almost as lucrative as those of the Bishop of Durham. Hodgson estimated that Howley's income for 1828 would be £28,434. 6s. 9d. This included an average £3,300 from timber sales; an income of £11,785. 5s. 8d. from rents and an average of £12,000 a year in fines.[8]

Lambeth Palace

Lambeth had been the archbishop's official residence since the thirteenth century.[9] The buildings Howley inherited were in a very poor condition and he initiated a programme of extensive redevelopment, almost rebuilding, in his first year in office. He discussed possible architects within two months of taking office and was determined to employ one who favoured the gothic style. Edward Blore (1797–1879) had worked at Windsor Castle, Hampton Court and Buckingham Palace and was also architect of Westminster Abbey.[10] Blore had interceded with the Earl and Countess Spencer for the job and they recommended him to Howley with every confidence that he could give the palace the style it deserved and badly needed rather than making 'a sad mess of blunders in design, adaptation, addition and chronology'.[11] The initial survey showed that walls, chimneys, parapets and mortar were all in a ruinous condition. The interior 'with few exceptions is in as deplorable a state of neglect as the exterior'. Floors, staircases, windows and doors were all decayed. Lollards'

8 Estimate of the year Revenues in 1828 shewing the improvement since 1805

	1805	**1828**
Rents	5649.19.10	11428.7.6
Trust Funds	–	223.2.2
Fines	7653.10.6	12000.0.0
Manors	805.2.4	1187.19.11
Timber and Wood	2000.0.0	2300.0.0
Tenths	682.12.0	682.12.0
IMPROVEMENTS SINCE 1805	11030.16.11	
TOTALS	27822.1.7	27822.1.7

(Papers of Archbishop Manners Sutton, LPL MS 1916, ff. 31–68.)

9 C.R. Dodwell, *Lambeth Palace* (London, 1958), 11; Dorothy Mills, *Lambeth Palace* (London, 1951), 5.

10 B.F.L. Clarke, *Church Builders of the Nineteenth Century: A Study of the Gothic Revival in England* (London, 1938), 251.

11 Lavinia, Countess Spencer to Howley, 3 October 1828, LPL MS 1726, ff. 1–2.

Tower, the Tudor towers of the Great Gatehouse and the Great Hall were all in need of restoration. Blore was particularly critical of the neglect of the Hall and proposed sweeping away a 'jumble of buildings' which lay between it and the Gatehouse.[12]

Whether or not Howley had anticipated the scale of the proposals, he supported them immediately. Blore's own watercolours show the striking difference in scale of the two buildings.[13] Hodgson's 1838 financial statement shows how urgent the need for action had been and how little money had been available to start it. Alterations were also required at Addington Palace in Croydon which had been purchased during Manners Sutton's early years at Canterbury. The old palace at Croydon, which had served as the Archbishop's country residence since at least 1273, was deemed 'unhealthy' and had been sold in 1780.[14] The new palace was a mansion built in 1772, set in about 1,200 acres of land. Howley greatly improved the park and Blore added a chapel, library and several other rooms.[15] Manners Sutton's executors had paid only £3,957 in final settlement for the dilapidations at Lambeth Palace and £1,046. 1s. for the house at Addington before it was known that almost all the girders and joists in the floors there were affected by dry rot, and new floors were required through the whole house.

Howley's ordinary income could not cover the cost. An Act of Parliament enabled the raising of £60,000 from a forty-year mortgage on the estates of the see. The money was borrowed from the Governors of Queen Anne's Bounty. Howley also provided over £27,000 from his regular income.[16] At Lambeth, all the buildings extending east from the chapel, including the gallery, private dining rooms and the presence chamber, were demolished to clear a site for the courtyard. All expenditure had to be authorised by Howley, Archbishop Vernon Harcourt and Blomfield as commissioners prescribed in the Act of Parliament. As a result, each and every plan that Blore drew had to be countersigned by the three. The work meant that Howley's domestic and administrative life was in

12 Lambeth Palace Scrapbook, LPL MS 3563, ff. 25–26.

13 LPL MS 2949.

14 H.E. Malden (ed.), *Victoria County History of Surrey* (London, 1912), iv, 206.

15 A.W. Rowden, *The Primates of the Four Georges* (London, 1916), 389–90.

16 'Statement concerning the new erections and improvements at Lambeth Palace and Addington Park, Surrey ... drawn up in the month of March 1838, by His Grace's secretary', LPL MS 2197, ff. 2, 5.

upheaval for the first year or more as archbishop.[17] The final cost of rebuilding was more than £53,000 at Lambeth and more than £41,000 at Addington.[18]

Daily life at Lambeth was punctuated by state and other formal occasions. There was a quarterly evening dinner over which Howley would preside, available to all gentlemen who had been presented at court. Anyone in possession of court dress could attend simply by signing a book held in the palace's lodge. On these 'public days' servants were in full dress livery. The dinners attracted large numbers of bishops. On a typical public day in May 1829 the Bishops of London, Winchester, Durham, Bath & Wells, Gloucester and Lichfield & Coventry attended. Four public dinners in 1832 attracted 180 guests. In 1835, the four dinners attracted 253.[19] There still remained customs that had an echo of the medieval ceremonial which surrounded archbishops. None left the table before the Archbishop. Howley was 'preceded by servants bearing flambeaux when he walked across ... to what were called "Mrs. Howley's lodgings"'. It was said that no woman was ever allowed into the official apartments, not even to clean them. Mrs Howley was a keen admirer of the traditions of the palace and much regretted the passing of the public days, which Howley abolished in 1844.[20] After Howley's death in 1848 Benjamin Harrison constantly encouraged the

17 MS plans of Edward Blore for Lambeth Palace, LPL MSS 3104–3105; Howley to Burton, 3 July 1829, Ch Ch Microfilm Box 91.

18 Rebuilding costs at Lambeth and Addington:

Total expense at Lambeth	53,153.1.7
Total expense at Addington	41,611.19.6
General expenses	273.7.6
TOTAL	95,038.7.6

Monies received	
Dilapidation money for Lambeth	3,967.0.0
Dilapidation money for Addington	1,046.1.0
Mortgage	60,000.0.0
Chancery Fund	2,256.11.0
TOTAL	95,038.6.7

('Statement.' and 'Account of sums received and expended by Christopher Hodgson, nominee of William Howley, Edward Venables Vernon Harcourt and Charles James Blomfield under the Act of Parliament 10. Geo. IV ...', LPL MS 1561.)

19 Howley's notebook containing lists of names of guests invited to public dinners and luncheons at Lambeth and Addington, LPL MS 2918.

20 [G.W.E. Russell], *Collections and Recollections: By One who has Kept a Diary* (3rd edn, London, 1898), 84–85.

view that his 'self-forgetting simplicity' was at odds with the esteem in which he held the office of archbishop. This would then explain both the sumptuousness of the 'public days' at Lambeth and Howley's pleasure in being able to use his 1842 bout of cholera as a good excuse to stop them.[21] George Sikscomb served as gatekeeper at Lambeth for over forty years, first for Howley and lastly for Tait. Tait received far more post and welcomed far more daily visitors than Howley. It would have been very unusual for any except the higher clergy or senior lay officials even to write to Howley. Howley almost never used Lambeth for meetings or receiving deputations and there was no meeting in the Guard Room or Library until his successor John Bird Sumner's day.[22]

Repeal, Emancipation and Reform – the Challenge to the Church: Repeal of the Test and Corporation Acts

Howley had become Archbishop of Canterbury when many of the 'foundational myths' which bolstered Church and State – as two sides of the same coin – were under attack. Another, dependent on the first, was that the Houses of Parliament were a lay synod for the Church of England whose members were practising Anglicans, with the welfare of the Church as a prime concern. The years 1828–32 seemed to see several of the most cherished shibboleths of the High Churchmen destroyed. Their view of the 'interdependence of Church and State and not the dependence of the Church on the State' was damaged. Perhaps some High Churchmen had a more realistic appreciation of the many changes in the constitution from the seventeenth century onwards, but these four years undoubtedly dealt their morale a huge blow.[23]

The truth was that many non-Anglicans had been elected under various compromises and special permissions and that the affairs of the Church were only a small part of the interest of some of the nominally Anglican members. Nevertheless any proposal to change the nature or make-up of the House of Commons would excite the interest of the bishops and staunch churchmen. The Test Acts had prevented non-conformists from holding office in local

21 S.L. Ollard and G. Crosse, *Dictionary of Church History* (London, 1912), 289; Mrs Howley to F.B. Wells, 19 April 1844, West Sussex County Record Office, Add MS 7347, no. 6; Benjamin Harrison, *The Remembrance of a Departed Guide and Ruler in the Church of God: A Charge Delivered to the Clergy of the Archdeaconry of Maidstone* (London, 1848), 20–21.

22 Sikscomb's reminiscences, 16 May 1888, LPL Tait Ps, 104, ff. 108–13.

23 G.F.A. Best, 'The Protestant Constitution and its Supporters, 1800–1829', *TRHS*, 5th series, 8 (1958), 106; Nockles, *Oxford Movement in Context*, 63, 86–87.

government or being elected as MPs. Even though repealing the Acts changed virtually nothing because the legislation did little more than codify the annual Indemnity Acts which had allowed non-conformists access to elected bodies since the eighteenth century, it was undoubtedly a challenge to the myth at just the right time. The 'dissenting deputies' (as they were generally known) had been discouraged from pushing the issue before 1828 partly because the Protestant Society had been nervous of leaving the door open to Catholic Emancipation. Ironically, it was Wellington's appointment as Prime Minister which encouraged the Protestant Society and the Dissenting Deputies to make a combined attempt for Repeal since they assumed that his opposition to Catholic Emancipation would make a campaign for that pointless.[24]

In the first half of 1828 before he moved from London to Canterbury in July, Howley was unhappy at the prospect of repealing the Acts but it was Catholic Emancipation which most concerned him. Henry Phillpotts (who only became Bishop of Exeter two years later in 1830) proposed replacing the provisions of the Test and Corporation Acts with an oath condemning transubstantiation, which would admit dissenters and continue to exclude Roman Catholics from public office.[25] Peel, Home Secretary and Leader of the House of Commons, pressed Blomfield to give Phillpotts' proposals attention. Joshua Watson told Charles Lloyd that Blomfield was working on a compromise declaration. Lord John Russell's resolution in favour of repeal passed through the House of Commons in February 1828 by a margin of 273 to 193. Peel realised that retaining the sacramental test was impossible and rejected Blomfield's draft, probably influenced by Lloyd who reckoned that the leading bishops wanted matters sorted out once and for all, even if they would have preferred a different outcome.[26]

Lloyd advised Peel to oppose repeal, but if battling against an overwhelming current, then to allow himself to be carried along. Peel's inclination to allow repeal of the Acts grew stronger after a meeting at Lambeth Palace in March 1828 with Archbishops Manners Sutton and Vernon Harcourt, who were joined by Howley, Blomfield, Van Mildert and Copleston.[27] Peel believed that

---

24 G.I.T. Machin, 'Resistance to Repeal of the Test and Corporation Acts, 1828', *HJ*, 22 (1979), 116–19.

25 G.C.B. Davies, *Henry Phillpotts, Bishop of Exeter* (London, 1954), 64.

26 P.J. Welch, 'Bishop Blomfield' (Univ. of London unpubl. PhD thesis, 1952), 117–18; Van Mildert to Peel, 3 March 1828, in *Memoirs by the Rt Hon Sir Robert Peel, Bart*, ed. Lord Mahon and E. Cardwell (London, 1856), i, 72; Peel to Lloyd, 4 March 1828, BL Add MS 40343, f. 205.

27 Lloyd to Peel, 10 February 1828 in Peel's *Memoirs*, i, 65; W.J. Copleston, *Memoir of Edward Copleston, D.D., Bishop of Llandaff* (London, 1851), 123.

a declaration could be found which would satisfy both the House of Commons and the Church.[28] He recommended a Declaration be drafted for all who took corporate office in England and Wales never to 'injure or subvert' the Protestant Church.[29] The Third Reading passed the Commons without debate on 31 March. Peel reserved particular scorn for Van Mildert for hedging his bets on the question when he complained that a power which had been inserted by Peel to dispense certain people from taking the Oath had never been discussed. Van Mildert said that feelings would run high amongst the bishops unless all who were previously liable to the Test had to make the Declaration.[30] Peel refused to support any amendments that he might propose in the House of Lords.[31] The King wrote Wellington a furious letter, with much underlining, to insist as the Protestant 'head and protector of religion in this country' that the word Protestant must be in the Act or the Established Church would have virtually no security.[32] Wellington and Peel knew that the bishops could see the dangers inherent in the House of the Lords disagreeing with the Commons over an issue which had so much public support. Blomfield summed up this practical view neatly. Parliament had every right to repeal the Test and Corporation Acts even though it was quite acceptable for the civil rights of subjects to be circumscribed for the general good. The Acts had failed in their object before or after the annual Indemnity Bills. They had actually hurt the Church and this was the fundamental reason that he and his brother bishops supported the legislation.[33]

The Emancipation of the Catholics

Sir Robert Peel's anonymous biographer was in no doubt that repealing the Test and Corporation Acts had opened the floodgates and that nothing could stop further reform. The success of Catholic Associations could only make the

---

28 Peel to Lloyd, 15 March 1828, BL Add MS 40343, f. 212.

29 *Hansard*, n.s. xviii, cols 1185–89.

30 Peel to Lloyd, 22 March 1828, in Peel's *Memoirs*, i, 88; Lloyd to Peel, 23 March 1828, in Peel's *Memoirs*, i, 90.

31 Peel to Lloyd, 25 March 1828, in Peel's *Memoirs*, i, 94.

32 King George IV to Wellington, 25 April 1828 in *Despatches, Correspondence and Memoranda of Field Marshal Arthur, Duke of Wellington*, ed. 2nd Duke of Wellington (1871), iv, 406.

33 Wellington to the Duke of Montrose in Wellington's *Despatches*, iv, 411. G.E. Biber, *Bishop Blomfield and his Times: An Historical Sketch* (London, 1857), 50–52.

adherents of Catholic Emancipation hopeful.[34] Those opposed to Catholic Emancipation in the House of Commons were either in a minority (especially after 1820) or had a tiny majority, and Lord Liverpool had adopted a system of government neutrality on the Catholic question as early as 1812.[35] The King was immensely frustrated that it appeared impossible to form an administration which was exclusively 'Protestant' (i.e. opposed to Catholic claims). He had told Howley and Manners Sutton in April 1827 that he understood his Coronation Oath just as his father had and would never consent to the admission of Catholics to political power nor let any clergyman be promoted even to an 'inferior dignity' without the full assurance that he opposed it himself.[36]

At the end of the six-hour meeting, the King had instructed Manners Sutton to 'Tell it to all the bishops and all the world' and two weeks later wrote to Manners Sutton complaining that he had not given enough publicity to his views, which he wanted expressed in the House of Lords.[37] Howley repeated the King's views to the London clergy at their meeting in Sion College and when challenged by Lord Harewood later in the House of Lords to prove its authenticity had to beg not to be pressed to reveal his authority because of a long-standing ban on reporting royal opinion in Parliament.[38] Wellington and other ardent Tories did not have the luxury of the King's indignation and had to come to terms with the harsh political realities about Emancipation swiftly. Even Phillpotts realised the need 'to find a safe path for Wellington between the anti-Catholics and the voters of County Clare'.[39]

A year later, after Howley had become Archbishop and Blomfield had succeeded him at London, Wellington tried to persuade them that there was room for manoeuvre on the issue. He proposed that Catholics should be made eligible to serve in all but a handful of public offices and in return the franchise qualification (the level of property to be held before one was eligible to vote) in Ireland should be a £5 instead of a 40s. freehold. Individual Catholic priests would require a licence to officiate at mass. Howley, Blomfield and Van Mildert had two fruitless conferences with Wellington in November 1828 and again the

34 *Memoirs of the Right Honourable Sir Robert Peel, Bart. First Lord of the Treasury by the Author of 'The Life of the Duke of Wellington'* (London, 1842), ii, 39.

35 G.I.T. Machin, 'The Catholic Emancipation Crisis of 1825', *EHR*, 78 (1963), 458–59.

36 LPL MS 2189, ff. 4–13.

37 Trench to Wellington, 18 April 1827, in Wellington's *Despatches*, iii, 651; *The Diary and Correspondence of Charles Abbot, Lord Colchester*, ed. Lord Colchester (London, 1861), iii, 486, 496.

38 Colchester's *Diary*, iii, 508.

39 G.I.T. Machin, 'The Duke of Wellington and Catholic Emancipation', *JEH* (1963), 201–02.

following January when he tried to persuade them of the true state of affairs in Ireland and that the public interest, and the Church's interest too, demanded 'the adjustment' of the Catholic question. They turned him down flat.[40] When Peel finally did introduce a bill initiating Catholic Emancipation into the House of Commons, Howley gathered nine bishops to explore possible collective action against it. A couple favoured a petition to the King but no agreement was reached. Howley asked Lloyd, who had pointedly not been invited to the meeting, to give the Prime Minister details of what had been discussed. He told Greville that nine or ten Bishops would vote for Emancipation.[41] Blomfield summed up the feelings of the bench when he defended the clergy who had sent petitions to Parliament against it. He rejected the claim that the granting of the Catholic claims would improve Anglo-Irish relations. In his view the British Constitution, not the Anglican Church, was the obstacle to fulfilling the Irish claims. Nevertheless, the third reading of the bill passed through the House of Lords on 10 April 1829. Lloyd voted in favour, mainly out of loyalty to Peel. He was the only 'High Church' bishop to do so. Blomfield's vocal opposition to the bill was a cause of much irritation to Wellington, as was Lloyd's support of it to the King.[42]

Howley and the Reform Bills, 1830–1832

The failure of the first Reform Bill to disenfranchise some of the smallest boroughs, redistribute representation more fairly in terms of population and increase the electorate's size saw a Dissolution of Parliament and then a decisive victory for Lord Grey in the General Election of 1831. Whigs were returned in nearly all the constituencies with genuine electorates and the House of Commons agreed to the second reading of the reintroduced bill in July by a substantial vote. Grey had tried to frighten the bishops into reform by making dark hints about them setting their own house in order to avoid 'the tempest' to come. His announcement that no substantial change would be allowed to the bill in committee infuriated them and as a result Bishop Copleston refused to support the whole measure although he had become convinced it was necessary.[43] Howley was the only bishop who spoke against the bill and did so blandly: about

40 Welch, 'Bishop Blomfield', 147; Wellington's *Despatches*, iv, 276–78.

41 Edward, Lord Ellenborough, *A Political Diary* (London, 1881), i, 396; W.J. Baker, *Beyond Port and Prejudice: Charles Lloyd of Oxford, 1784–1829* (Orono, Maine, 1981), 189.

42 Welch, 'Bishop Blomfield', 149–50.

43 Mathieson, *English Church Reform*, 48–49.

the defects and anomalies in the Constitution and exterminating abuses. He was 'committed to a measure of gradual, temperate and safe reform'. He called for an agreement that would 'satisfy everyone' – impressing few of his contemporaries and fewer still of those who have written the history of this matter.[44]

Howley contributed barely two columns of *Hansard* on the last of five days' debate. Yet if the bishops thought that they would be saved from criticism by their silence they were woefully mistaken. The bill was defeated in the Lords by forty-one votes, twenty-one of which were episcopal. It was instantly obvious that had the bishops voted in favour then the bill would have passed its second reading and parliamentary reform would have crossed its most difficult hurdle. Many Tory peers, wary of criticism, had refrained from voting and this only exacerbated the fury that the coincidence of the voting brought down on the bishops' heads. Anger sometimes turned to violence. Howley asked the Home Secretary Melbourne to protect Lambeth. He even suggested having an armed force 'under the direction of the new police or military' inside the palace whilst he himself retreated to Addington. Melbourne said that Horse Guards was near enough if trouble broke out.[45] On the Wednesday following the negative vote nearly 70,000 people took part in a procession which carried a petition to the King objecting to what had happened. There were also many calls for the bishops to be excluded from the House of Lords and for disestablishment. Of course the 'constitutional revolution' of 1828–32 deeply dismayed the High Churchmen who saw their belief in the theoretical and practical union of the Church and State being fatally undermined. They bolstered their spirits by praising Howley's boldness, courage and wisdom in speaking up.[46]

Grey wanted to enlist King William IV into encouraging the bishops not to oppose the bill's re-introduction into the House of Lords and he tried very hard to persuade Howley and Carr of Worcester to reverse their opposition to it. Blomfield (who had not attended any of the second reading debates because of the recent death of his father) thought that Howley's tactics had been unwise and told Grey that he would vote for the second reading of the new bill, and was hopeful that several other bishops would do likewise. Howley admitted that rejecting the bill had caused much more anger than he had ever envisaged. The King duly told Howley and other bishops that voting to allow the bill into committee would only be an acknowledgement of the general principle of

44 *Hansard*, 3rd series, viii, 1831, cols 302–3; see, for example, John Cannon, *Parliamentary Reform 1640–1832* (Cambridge, 1973), 225.

45 Howley to Melbourne, 4 November 1831, Bodl Lib [Royal Archives microfilm], Melbourne Ps, Box 76, f. 1.

46 John Keble to C.A. Ogilvie, 2 November 1831, Bodl Lib MS Eng Lett d 124, ff. 23–24.

reform. The King 'did not doubt that he realised how important matters were nor the possible grave consequences for the House of Lords' if the bill were again rejected. The message was clear if Howley wanted to hear it.[47] Blomfield, acutely aware of Howley's frustration, framed his own support for the bill along these pragmatic lines.[48]

Grey was bothered that Howley had the impression that the King was opposed to increasing the representation of metropolitan boroughs. Howley told Aberdeen that he feared for his personal safety even in making the journey to Parliament. He certainly thought that the new bill would pass and was very tempted to turn his back on the whole process. He said that he had not contacted his brother bishops since the rejection of the bill 'from a dislike of politics'. He knew that Harcourt and Blomfield would vote in favour and 'one Bishop very determined in opposition' had already told him that he could see no further use in resistance and that others would follow suit. Nevertheless he did meet Lord Wharncliffe, Peel's Lord President of the Council, who briefed him on a meeting for those who opposed the bill.[49] Grey was furious to be rebuked by the King (who still wondered if the bill could be amended) for suggesting that he had changed his mind about the metropolitan districts. Unable to criticise the monarch directly, he told Sir Herbert Taylor, the King's Private Secretary, that the fact that Howley knew the King's private feelings could make matters difficult at the committee stage, not because Howley would make overt and improper use of the knowledge, but because the King's views would inevitably become known. Grey was so infuriated that he accused Howley both of 'weakness and indecision' and of intriguing successfully with his political opponents in the space of the same letter.[50]

The King tried again to persuade the Prime Minister that all his troubles would be over if he removed the provision about the metropolitan districts from the legislation. The King believed that even Howley would support a bill which omitted those provisions.[51] Grey had persuaded an extremely reluctant monarch that he would have to agree to create as many peers as was necessary to see the

47 Taylor to Grey, 27 November 1831, in *The Reform Act 1832: The Correspondence of the late Earl Grey with His Majesty King William IV and with Sir Herbert Taylor*, ed. Henry, Earl Grey (London, 1867), i, 447–48.

48 Grey to Taylor, 25 November 1831, in Grey's *Correspondence*, i, 443–45; *The Times*, 24 October 1831; Biber, *Bishop Blomfield and his Times*, 111.

49 Howley to Aberdeen, 22 November 1831, BL Add MS 43195, f. 73.

50 Taylor to Grey, 18 December 1831, in Grey's *Correspondence*, ii, 40–41; Grey to Taylor, 19 December 1831, in Grey's *Correspondence*, ii, 43–44; Grey to the King, 19 December 1831, in Grey's *Correspondence*, ii, 48.

51 The King to Grey, 22 December 1831, in Grey's *Correspondence*, ii, 50–51.

bill safely through the Lords. In the event, they were not required and the vote passed, but this did nothing to diminish Grey's contempt for Howley – 'such a poor, miserable creature ... that he would be frightened and vote any way his fear directed him'.[52]

The moderate conservatives who had decided that things must be changed for the sake of civil peace now had the enthusiastic backing of the King. Howley did seem to have been put into a state of indecision and confusion. Michael Brock's history of the Great Reform Act interprets his meeting with Wharncliffe as one of two men who knew that a deal needed to be done, however much they disliked it. This presumably accounts for the ferocity of Grey's impatience with his indecision. Lord Harrowby became more and more desperate for him to decide one way or the other.[53] At the third reading, a revivified Blomfield took centre stage. He supported the bill as something imperfect but less objectionable than before, which he wished to see slightly, but not essentially, altered. Phillpotts made a wild speech. Howley said nothing and voted against the bill along with fourteen of his episcopal colleagues. Twelve voted in favour, including Harcourt and Blomfield. As Howley had predicted, several of them had been opposed (like Carr) before.[54] A vain attempt to save some of the condemned boroughs meant that episcopal support melted away from the Government. The bill finally passed through the House of Lords on 4 June. Of the twenty-two who remained to vote against it, none was a bishop.[55]

Feelings ran high against the bishops after their actions over the Reform Bill. Around the country stories of bishops under threat were common. The Bishop of Bristol's palace had been set alight, Van Mildert thought it too dangerous to show his face in County Durham, Phillpotts was advised to postpone his confirmations and Copleston bought a brown coat in case he needed to escape from tricky situations.[56] Howley himself had faced a mob near Addington and had been 'assailed and grossly insulted'. He postponed his Primary Visitation from June 1831 because the pressure of the Reform Bill meant that he had to be

---

52 C.C. Greville, *A Journal of the Reigns of King George IV and King William IV* (3rd edn, London, 1875), ii, 249–50.

53 Michael Brock, *The Great Reform Act* (London, 1973), 245 and 247; Greville, *Journal*, ii, 262.

54 Taylor to Grey, 26 December 1831, in Grey's *Correspondence*, ii, 63–64.

55 *Hansard*, 3rd series, xi, cols 864–65; xii, cols 454–60; xiii, cols 373–74.

56 Chadwick, *Victorian Church: Part One*, 26–29.

in London all summer. Although he had planned to carry out the Visitation in September 1831 he did not feel safe to do so until August 1832.[57]

Howley seems to have retreated into the reassurance of the conventional. He made no mention of the Reform Bill in his Charge and restricted himself to expressing his humility in succeeding his illustrious predecessor and lauding the work of the societies which they had both done so much to support: the National Society, the Incorporated Church Building Society, the SPCK, the SPG and the Incorporated Clergy Orphan Society. He discussed pluralities and expressed the unremarkable view that the regulations were too lax and would have to be tightened.[58] Howley felt that the Visitation had been reasonably successful. Since the Reform Bill had passed the House of Lords in June the struggle was over. Nevertheless his carriage was pelted, the footmen had been attacked and one slashed an attacker across the face with a horse-whip after the carriage missed the turn into the deanery and had then to turn and face the mob. Howley even received an address from the Mayor and Corporation disavowing the behaviour.[59] The story that Howley's chaplain had a dead cat flung at him appears apocryphal.

---

57 Biber, *Bishop Blomfield and his Times*, 115; Howley to A.P. Perceval, 4 June 1831, PH, Pusey MS.

58 William Howley, *Charge at his Primary Visitation to the Clergy of the Diocese of Canterbury* (London, 1832), 5–13, 42–43.

59 Address presented to Howley by inhabitants of Canterbury, 10 August 1832, LPL MS 3355, f. 2; Howley to Mrs Howley, 7 August 1832, LPL MS 2188, f. 4; Harrison, *Charge to the Clergy of the Archdeaconry of Maidstone*, 28.

Chapter 4

The Reform of the Church

The Desire for Reform

The 1830s saw the bishops attempt to engage with the fact that great swathes of the industrial towns and vast tracts of London were all but outside the sphere of the Church's influence. Howley became the most influential apologist for the transformation of the Church's finances and organisation. As Archbishop of Canterbury he chaired the many meetings of the various commissions which were set up to examine the Church's problems in the 1830s. Yet as chairman he rarely participated actively in debate. It is therefore difficult to assess his particular contribution simply from the minutes of meetings. Claiming that Howley was more favourable towards and active in Church Reform than has often been realised does not imply that the energy and importance of others, especially Bishop Blomfield, was any less vital.[1]

Arthur Burns points out that 'the vocabulary of reform was deployed both by those seeking to reduce the power of the institution and those seeking to render it more effective and efficient'. Some of those most critical of the Church were wary of the push towards reform precisely because it might strengthen or legitimate the role of bishops or the institution in a way they found unpalatable.[2] Many of the Church's friends also questioned whether it was right or possible for it to continue with its traditional endowments. A vast number of pamphlets were published, both critical and supportive, and they proposed particular solutions to generally identified problems. Two of the best known showed the great difference of opinion that existed. First, Edward Berens, Prebendary of Salisbury, proposed to replace the system of income through fines with a fixed income for a bishop. He set it at a minimum of £4,000. He thought betting against the lives of one's tenants repugnant for a bishop. Like the vast majority of clerical reformers, Berens had a strong sense of the need for decorum within the framework of the old system. He disliked the system of *commendams* but was prepared to use them to best advantage. He proposed that stalls in St Paul's

1 See, for example, Knight, *Nineteenth Century Church and English Society*, 154.

2 Burns, 'English "Church Reform" Revisited', 149 (148–50 more generally).

Cathedral, Westminster Abbey and Durham be permanently annexed to various sees. Every archdeacon should be in residence and the pay for the job (on average less than £150 a year) should be dramatically increased by plum preferment.[3] The emphasis was all on preservation of the Church's historic role and endowments by judicious self-regulation.

In different vein, R.M. Beverley was well known as a pungent critic of the Church whose 1831 attack went through five editions in the year it was published. He dismissed the system of training ordinands as a dangerous sham and identified the Church's foremost evil as non-residence, which he would only have allowed on complex grounds if any surplus went into a special fund. Church property should be centrally administered by the Chancellor of the Diocese. No lease should be renewed before its proper time, rents should be regularised and curates should have salaries fixed by law.[4] The motivation here was very different. The Church must be accountable.

Howley and Early Reforms

Howley steered the first measures of Church Reform through Parliament. Lord Grey paid him a fulsome public tribute when Lord King, a pungent critic of the Church, asked for details of the number of resident and non-resident clergy in England and Wales on 14 February 1831. Grey said that he was convinced of the sincere desire amongst Church leaders to remedy the abuses in the establishment. Howley's own views were 'very moderate and liberal'. Later, in the 1832 debates on Howley's proposed bills, Grey told Parliament that Howley had told him 'shortly after he entered office' that he wished 'the general state of the property of the Church' to be comprehensively reviewed.[5] Howley introduced three small bills in June 1831: the first to provide facilities for the composition of tithes, the second to prevent the holding of pluralities and the third to extend an Act for perpetuating augmentations to small vicarages and curacies. Grey supported the measures, highlighting the difficulties which collection of tithes posed.[6]

Howley realised that payment of tithes in kind had often been damaging to agriculture because capital was never invested to improve the land. Composition, where tenants paid a sum of money to the receiver of the tithes instead of the

---

3 [Edward Berens], *Church Reform: By a Churchman* (London, 1828), 10–11, 101–03, 117.

4 Beverley, *Letter ... on the Present Corrupt State of the Church of England*, 27–28, 37.

5 *Hansard*, 3rd series, ii, col. 483; *Mirror of Parliament*, 27 March 1832, col. 1461b; *Mirror of Parliament*, 2 April 1832, col. 1562a: quoted in Best, 'Church Parties and Charities', 277.

6 *Hansard*, 3rd series, iv, cols 293–94.

fruits of the land, had been relatively successful compared to the difficulties in monitoring and collecting tithes in kind.[7] It was nevertheless a mixed success. The incumbent had to wait for the previous payment of the poor rates by the tithe payer and he also had to wait until the landlord was paid. Sometimes the incumbent received nothing because all that the tithe payer had was taken by the landlord or by creditors. Howley's bill gave the incumbent a 'power of distress' to recover what he was owed on a par with the landlord. The bill allowed commutations (where the incumbent received a once for all sum of money or piece of land to replace tithe or composition income) both of whole parishes and of particular compositions though permanent commutation was impossible.[8]

Howley's other two bills made transferring property to livings in the gift of cathedral chapters and colleges easier. Several bishops and chapters took advantage of the legislation to re-distribute funds. Bishop Van Mildert and the Dean and Chapter of Durham redistributed over £800 a year to parishes throughout the diocese. None of the Dean and Chapter's livings was left under £150 a year and several were much more generously paid. Parishes over a thousand paid at least £300.[9] Much to his irritation, Howley's Pluralities Bill was attacked by Lord Suffield who made play of the fact that even after it passed it would still be legal for the same man to be Bishop of Durham, Dean of Winchester and the holder of any number of church dignities.[10] Howley rejected criticism of the bill's timidity. He thought that the stipulation that two livings held in plurality could not be more than 30 miles apart would reduce the number of pluralities by nearly two-thirds.

The legislation exempted archdeacons from the rules about non-residence and pluralities to which the lower clergy would be subject. It was true also that the Archbishop of Canterbury's discretion to allow pluralities within the limit if the incumbent held a living worth less than £400 a year and if he were a Master of Arts or had a special recommendation from his bishop about his 'character and attainments' seemed like a typical loophole for a high flying cleric and compromised the bill's effectiveness.[11]

Suffield's demands for an upper limit on episcopal incomes and the enforcement of redistribution from wealthier to poorer bishops did not commend

7 Virgin, *Church in an Age of Negligence*, 36–40.

8 *Hansard*, 3rd series, iv, 18 July 1831, cols 1363–67.

9 *British Critic* (Jan.–Apr. 1838), 535–36; Chadwick, *Victorian Church: Part One*, 39; Welch, 'Bishop Blomfield', 230; *British Magazine*, iii (1833), 190.

10 *Hansard*, 3rd series, xi, 16 March 1832, cols 315–18.

11 Knight, *Nineteenth Century Church and English Society*, 167–68.

itself to Howley.[12] Grey was happy with the bill. Blomfield and Van Mildert opposed it because, even despite the exemptions mentioned above, it would put the 'higher orders' off ordination. Van Mildert opposed the financial cap on the value of the preferment held in plurality. He had a thoroughly idiosyncratic view of the whole subject – holding one benefice or see plus a prebend was not pluralism. On that basis he calculated that only two members of the Durham Chapter (which was renowned for being stuffed full of the over-beneficed and over-remunerated) were pluralists.[13] The *Christian Observer* perceptively claimed that the bill would irritate those who regarded the Church as a matter of property and family emolument without going far enough to satisfy those who really wished for the Church's spiritual efficiency and wanted to see a resident incumbent in every parish. Unfortunately for Howley an obscure alteration he had made in the bill came to light and was caricatured as trying to preserve the private patronage of a particular peer.[14] The reforming press had a field day with the bill's supposed inadequacies.

Geoffrey Best identifies Edward Burton and Lord Henley as the two most substantial of the welter of pamphleteers who published their views on how the Church should be reformed in an 'infinite variety of permutations and combinations'. Burton, Regius Professor of Divinity at Oxford since 1829, admired Howley's legislation. He believed that the great majority of those who held two benefices had received the second from a lay patron. He based this claim on surveys he had carried out in two unidentified dioceses.[15] If pluralism were a problem for the Church, then it followed that nineteen times out of twenty this was the fault of a lay patron, not necessarily because they were less careful than clerical ones, but simply because there were so many more of them.[16]

Like other pamphleteers friendly to the Church, Burton quoted a calculation ascribed to Blomfield that if the Church of England's entire property (including that belonging to deans and chapters) were equally divided there would only be funds to pay each working clergyman an annual stipend of £350 and that such a result could never justify the upheaval it would involve. Burton's remedy was to make the payment of tenths more rigorous than it had been. First fruits and

---

12 *Hansard*, 3rd series, xi, 23 March 1832, col. 789.

13 E.A. Varley, *The Last of the Prince Bishops: William Van Mildert and the High Church Movement of the Early Nineteenth Century* (Cambridge, 1992), 188ff.

14 *Christian Observer*, xxxii (March 1832), 195; *Christian Observer*, xxxii (May 1832), 365.

15 Edward Burton, *Thoughts upon the Demand for Church Reform* (2nd edn, Oxford, 1831), 20.

16 Edward Burton, *Sequel to Remarks upon Church Reform, with Observations upon the Plan Proposed by Lord Henley* (London, 1832), 43.

tenths were a royal tax on dignities and benefices, first fruits being a sizeable sum paid on first getting the preferment and tenths being a much smaller annual payment. The Crown had returned these taxes to the Church when Queen Anne's Bounty had been established.[17] Burton hoped that this would mean that the income of the bounty would increase rapidly and that all smaller benefices could quickly be augmented.[18]

Lord Henley's *Plan of Church Reform* (1832) aroused ire amongst leading churchmen. It was radical and he was influential; a peer, a Master in Chancery and Robert Peel's brother-in-law. He drew a parallel with recent parliamentary reforms. If a small measure had been conceded graciously straightaway, honour would have been satisfied. It was the squabbling that had been so dangerous for the bishops and therefore for the Church. Henley calculated that c. £300,000 a year was shared between about 600 cathedral 'dignitaries' – that is, well over a sixth of the estimated income of all the parochial clergy of England and Wales. There was still a solid body of opinion which thought it essential to encourage those from the upper echelons and – as Blomfield's opposition to Howley's legislation on pluralities had shown – this opinion was not solely confined to backwoodsmen or ultra-conservatives. Even Henley thought there should be some sinecures for the talented, who would then be free to write or do some particular work until appointment to a bishopric.[19] He proposed banning translations, regulating incomes, creating two new sees and that all episcopal and chapter estates go into the hands of a corporation for exclusive management and control and consequent redistribution of much finance. He reckoned that £150,000 could then be used to augment country livings, and endow and build new churches.[20]

Burton's *Sequel* claimed that after paying the commissioners who would administer Henley's system and bearing the cost of repairs and paying for the visitations of bishops and archdeacons and clergy pensions, the surplus left to be distributed to the wider Church would be negligible. If the figure of £300,000 was in any way an overestimate then Henley's reforms would actually have produced a deficit of £1,318 for augmenting all the parishes of the Church of England whilst abolishing the structure of cathedral and diocesan life.[21] The Church authorities looked to Burton above anyone else to provide lucid justification of their point of view. But there remained a stubborn distaste for accommodation

17 Virgin, *Church in an Age of Negligence*, 64.

18 Burton, *Thoughts*, 24–26.

19 Robert, Lord Henley, *Plan of Church Reform* (London, 1832), 26–31 and *passim*.

20 Henley, *Plan of Church Reform*, 36–39.

21 Burton, *Sequel to Remarks upon Church Reform*, 14–15.

and change amongst many High Churchmen. Benjamin Harrison complained that Burton was naive about Parliament, too generous in his assessment of Henley (which had surprised even Henley himself) and regretted that he had admitted that the 'dissenters' had a legitimate grievance over Church Rate.[22] In mid-December 1832 Howley and sixteen other bishops met at Lambeth to discuss Church Reform. Barely a month later Howley had to absorb the death of his elder and only surviving son at the age of 22.[23]

Arthur Perceval, the late Prime Minister's nephew, a Royal chaplain and old High Churchman in Howley's circle, put into print a general rebuttal of Henley's and other 'radical' plans which is a typical example of the revulsion which many conservative clergymen felt at his proposals. His sentiments are yet more evidence of the gap which was opening up between High Churchmen like Blomfield who took a 'practical' line on Church preservation and those who found little or nothing positive in reform proposals. Howley was generally recognised to have moved away from 'Perceval' and towards 'Blomfield' – a process that accelerated throughout the 1830s. As has been shown above, this description itself does not do complete justice to Howley's own commitment to some reforms which Blomfield found hard to accept. In 1836 Perceval complained to Newman that Howley was now pursuing with gusto the same proposals to amalgamate Welsh sees which he had criticised four years earlier. Perceval could not accept that Howley had changed his mind and put his new view down to 'sheer weakness and weariness'.[24]

The Ecclesiastical Duties and Revenues Commission and the Ecclesiastical Commission

Howley's previous expressed belief in the House of Lords that the Church had nothing to fear from inquiry, which he thought would be highly beneficial, had elicited from Grey the statement that Howley had told him soon after becoming Archbishop that he favoured a review of the 'general state of the property of the

[22] Harrison to Gladstone, 14 February 1833, BL Add MS 44204, f. 22; Henley to Burton, n.d. [September 1832], Ch Ch Microfilm Ps, Box 92 [Shrewsbury School MSS.], f. 92.

[23] Varley, *Last of the Prince Bishops*, 182–83 quotes Van Mildert to Archdeacon Thorp, 8, 31 January 1833, Thorp Correspondence, Durham University Archives, vol. 1, ff. 93, 101; Perceval to Newman, 18 March 1836, *LD*, v, 259; P.N. Shuttleworth, Warden of New College to Howley, 3 January 1833, LPL MS 2185, f. 110.

[24] Perceval to Newman, 18 March 1836, *LD*, v, 259; P.N. Shuttleworth, Warden of New College to Howley, 3 January 1833, LPL MS 2185, f. 110.

Church'. Geoffrey Best suggests that Howley's wish to ascertain the exact state of the Church's finances was a safety measure, little more than 'a mere means of giving the lie to radical and anti-clerical libels'. Yet he also recognises it as an indispensable first step towards the really extensive Church reforms which many 'friends of the Establishment' wanted.[25]

Joshua Watson was determined that any committee of enquiry into the Church's revenues and properties should be made up only of bishops and clergy, and Howley concurred. Despite the fact that these objections were overruled none of the members of the inquiry which Grey announced on 23 June 1832 were at all radical or antagonistic. It included Howley, Harcourt, Blomfield, Van Mildert, John Kaye, Christopher Bethell (Bishop of Bangor) and Sir Robert Inglis, the MP for Oxford University. Grey certainly believed that the Church should be reformed by this breed of men, not by radicals. Blomfield himself thought that Howley's views and his own were almost identical. He was convinced that a mixed commission of clergy and laity was necessary to consider changes both to Church discipline and to ecclesiastical property. Commutation of tithes would have to be settled immediately and coming to a final decision about pluralities and cathedral establishments could only be solved by a commission. The commission would have to act 'gingerly' since Parliament would be jealous of any body trying to legislate. Blomfield and Howley wanted to squeeze the advantages of convocation out of the commission without restoring that troublesome body.[26] Peel thought that money which came from impropriated tithes should in many cases be relinquished and used for its original purpose – supporting clergy in the same parish as the money was given. Howley also considered it second only in seriousness to the problem of crowded town parishes.[27]

Peel finalised plans to set up the Ecclesiastical Commission at the very beginning of 1835, in full agreement with Howley that reforms should come not from the Government but from a semi-independent commission.[28] He repelled criticism of his choice of bishops (Howley, Harcourt, Blomfield, Kaye and Monk) to sit on the commission and thought it well balanced: a commission either of ten laymen and the two archbishops or all the English bishops would

25 Best, 'Church Parties and Charities', 277–78.

26 Blomfield to Howley, 11 December 1832, LPL Fulham Ps (Blomfield Ps) 5, ff. 25–27.

27 Howley to Peel, 30 January 1835, BL Add MS 40412, ff. 207–08.

28 G.F.A. Best, *Temporal Pillars: Queen Anne's Bounty, the Ecclesiastical Commissioners, and the Church of England* (Cambridge, 1964), 297. For a detailed account of the foundation of the Ecclesiastical Commissioners, see ch. VII of *Temporal Pillars*.

have been rightly criticised.[29] There was no doubt that Howley and his fellow bishops felt confidence in Peel personally and much happier generally with a conservative administration.

Howley signally distrusted Lord John Russell then Home Secretary. He was wary of his motives in almost everything even to the extent of being uneasy about accepting Russell's questions about commutation of tithes over a period of two years and particularly chary of providing Russell with answers to written questions.[30] Howley complained he had received papers at too short a notice and that he had no 'consciousness that he had rejected the propositions of the Government' since previous conversations had never been explicitly Government policy. He was yet more frustrated by an assertion that he had passed the proposals on 'to the heads of the Church' and then rejected them himself.[31]

Suggestions for solving the problems of the tithe system appeared in protean variations. Each of the parliamentary sessions from 1833 to 1836 saw a major Tithe Commutation Act introduced by the government of the day.[32] When Peel became Prime Minister in November 1834 Howley and Blomfield worked with more ease with him and his Home Secretary Henry Goulburn in forming policy on the commission and they were worried when the Government fell after only four months. Nevertheless Howley negotiated happily enough the retention of the law officers on the commission with Melbourne who renewed the commission without hesitation when he came to power in April 1835.[33] Melbourne consulted him over Lord Chancellor Lyndhurst, Peel and Goulburn's joint decision that their places on the commission were only as government ministers and that they must withdraw. Howley insisted on vetting a list of the proposed replacements and Melbourne was happy enough to oblige.[34] The bishops tried to force Melbourne to promise to implement the report already given by the commission about uniting bishoprics, to transfer all the privileges of the bishoprics which were to be united to two new sees, to resist any motions hostile to the Church in Parliament and to refuse to appoint

29 Peel to Christopher Benson, Master of the Temple, 19 March 1835, BL Add MS 40417, f. 266.

30 Howley to Russell, 8 January 1834, LPL MS 1812, f. 1.

31 Howley to Russell, 31 December 1834, LPL MS 1812, f. 2; *Mirror of Parliament*, 3 July 1833.

32 See Eric J. Evans, *The Contentious Tithe* (London, 1976).

33 Best, *Temporal Pillars*, 300.

34 Best, *Temporal Pillars*, 297; Melbourne to Howley, 25 April 1835, Bodl Lib [Microfilm of Royal Archives], Melbourne Ps, Box 76, no. 2; Howley to Melbourne, 30 April 1835, Bodl Lib, Melbourne Ps, Box 76, no. 5; Melbourne to Howley, 30 April 1835, Bodl Lib, Melbourne Ps, Box 76, no. 6.

committees on matters connected with Church establishment.[35] Melbourne said that no government could engage unconditionally to implement the report but he did in fact give most of what Howley demanded. He also agreed that the on-going enquiries of the commission were good reason to resist motions on Church matters in Parliament and dealt deftly with further concerns about the upkeep of Church property.[36]

After Russell finally introduced the Tithe Commutation Bill of 1836, within seven years all claims had been weighed, all payments adjusted and tithe had ceased to be a political problem. It was remarkable that a subject that had caused years of dissension should have been settled so quickly.[37] An administrative structure to support the working of the bill was established along the lines of the Poor Law Commission. The proposal of Althorp (who in 1834 had proposed a reform of the Church rate system which had not gone far enough to satisfy dissenters who saw too much power left in the hands of the Established Church) to average the value of the tithes of the previous seven years was adopted and the sum to purchase wheat, barley and oats was converted into a money payment known as the tithe rent charge. Although Russell was determined that the legislation would contain compulsory clauses he accepted two amendments which allowed the bishop to see every agreement relating to clerical tithes before its confirmation by the commissioners and for lands not exceeding 20 acres to be given in part exchange for certain tithes if both sides agreed.[38]

The Problem of the Cathedrals

By the second half of the 1830s Howley had set himself firmly in favour of reform of every part of the Church. His position at the centre of all the reforming bodies had given him clearer evidence than anyone of the desperate need of the Church to do so, before events overtook it. Howley believed that a blueprint should be provided for cathedrals. His first priorities were to decide what funds were required for the fabric and to maintain cathedrals properly,

35 Howley to Melbourne, 5 May 1835, Bodl Lib, Melbourne Ps, Box 76, no. 9.

36 Melbourne to Howley, 6 May 1835, Bodl Lib, Melbourne Ps, Box 76, no. 10; Melbourne to Howley, 18 May 1835, Bodl Lib, Melbourne Ps, Box 76, no. 15a; Howley to Melbourne, 19 May 1835, Bodl Lib, Melbourne Ps, Box 76, no. 16; Melbourne to Howley, 23 May 1835, Bodl Lib, Melbourne Ps, Box 76, no. 17a; Copy Memorandum Russell to Melbourne, n.d., PRO 30/22, vol. 1E, f. 68.

37 See Evans, *Contentious Tithe*, 15.

38 Chadwick, *Victorian Church: Part One*, 88–89; Evans, *Contentious Tithe*, 125–27.

how many residentiary and minor canons would be required, what type of personnel were needed in the choir and how many stalls might be annexed to benefices or archdeaconries with 'slender endowments'. Only then did the question arise about what proportion of the revenues might go into a general fund on the principle of Queen Anne's Bounty and what proportion of the sinecure rectories and other revenues of the cathedral and collegiate churches should be used to improve administration by reimbursing rural deans, making better provision for archdeacons and improving livings that were overcrowded and poorly recompensed.[39] Howley stood firm against great protest, published and unpublished, from the cathedrals at the treatment meted out to them or which they feared would be meted out. This protest was often from personal friends. Perceval is again a good case in point.

Howley reassured Perceval that the fund that would be created from reform of cathedral income would receive £130,000 a year and therefore every eight years would see £1,000,000 devoted both to the augmentation of poor benefices and to the endowment of churches when new ones were built. There was therefore no reason why a thousand benefices should not each have an allotment of £1,000 within eight years with augmentation proceeding in the same ratio; so that in sixty-four years more than £6,000,000 could have been devoted to the Church's immediate needs. Perceval need only think what would have been achieved by 1837 if this system had been put in place when Queen Anne's Bounty had been restored.[40] Others were less easily mollified. William Bowles, a friend of Howley, was Canon of Salisbury. He objected violently to the removal of patronage traditionally vested in the chapter in his pamphlet *The Patronage of the English Bishops* (1836). Like Perceval, he could never reconcile himself to the fact that it was Howley doing this. He dedicated an address to Blomfield which compared his relationship with Howley as that of the 'wisdom of the serpent' with 'the harmlessness of the dove'.[41] There was awkwardness in Canterbury itself as high profile campaigners against change on the Chapter had to maintain courtesy and loyalty towards the Archbishop.[42] Bishop Kaye had to suffer the embarrassment of Lincoln's Chapter memorialising the commission against its proposals in the Dean and Chapter Bill in 1840.[43]

---

39 Howley to Peel, 16 February 1835, BL Add MS 40414, f. 267.

40 Howley to Perceval, 31 January 1837, PH, Pusey MS.

41 W.L. Bowles, *The Patronage of the English Bishops* (Bristol, 1836), 2–3, 9.

42 Peter B. Nockles. 'Aspects of Cathedral Life, 1828–48', in *A History of Canterbury Cathedral*, ed. P. Collinson, N. Ramsay and M. Sparks (London, 1995), 256–96 at 259.

43 Christopher Wordsworth, *The Ecclesiastical Commission and the Universities* (London, 1837), 20–22, 49; Knight, *Nineteenth Century Church and English Society*, 156.

Christopher Wordsworth used the most popular emotive argument against change at cathedrals when he listed eminent divines who had been Heads of Houses and held cathedral preferment at one and the same time – amongst them Lancelot Andrewes and John Cosin. Sydney Smith was as angry as many a Tory canon. He thought St Paul's was being singled out for especially harsh treatment. By November 1836 Smith was marginally more content but continued to resent the unfairness of the fact that bishops could keep all their patronage for life. He told Russell that Blomfield would hand out former St Paul's patronage to his own sons and sons-in-law when Smith himself died and his patronage passed to the bishop.[44] Russell passed the letter to Howley who rather diplomatically decided that it was inappropriate to show it to the commission or even to Blomfield since it was private correspondence.[45] The commissioners knew that they were hitting the cathedrals hard but the cathedrals were one of the very few sources of income over which they had even a measure of control. The pressure to augment parishes with the money they eventually liberated from the system was strong enough to preclude them recommending that every archdeacon should have a canonry.[46] Smith told a famous anecdote about Howley: fifty-three years earlier Howley had knocked him over with a chessboard for checkmating him at Winchester and now he was taking away his patronage – the only two acts of violence in his whole life.[47] Thomas Musgrave, the Whig Bishop of Hereford, told Melbourne that there was disquiet at the Church Rate Abolition Bill even amongst his supporters, adding presciently that if the 'alienation' of Church property at St Paul's Cathedral had taken place forty years earlier, the lessee purchasers would have had all the advantage of improved value, and the Church none.[48]

The Commissioners at Work

All did not run completely smoothly with Melbourne. The commissioners themselves had held back from suggesting wholesale change in the legal tenure of episcopal and cathedral property even for what they considered the most urgent of reasons – the augmentation of livings and a better supply of religious instruction. They were therefore appalled at a government proposal to abolish

44 Smith to Russell, 28 November 1836, PRO 30/22, vol. 2D, f. 80.

45 Howley to Russell, 2 December 1836, PRO 30/22, vol. 2D, f. 98.

46 R.A. Burns, *The Diocesan Revival in the Church of England c.1800–1870* (Oxford, 1999), 63.

47 Smith, 'First Letter to Archdeacon Singleton', 606, 621.

48 Musgrave to Melbourne, 2 April 1837, Bodl Lib, Melbourne Ps, Box 78, f. 10.

church rates by transferring management of episcopal and chapter estates to a board of commissioners.[49] The episcopal commissioners withdrew from the activities of the commission in protest, which both irritated and bewildered Melbourne. Howley believed that the Government had betrayed its undertaking to block the introduction of ecclesiastical legislation into Parliament, which had been the basis on which he had accepted membership of the commission. But Howley made sure that the spat did not derail the generally careful and fruitful relationship developing between the commission and the Government.[50] When the *Morning Chronicle* reported that Russell had accused the bishops of treachery, he was quick to rebut the report and Howley quick to thank him for doing so. Russell was willing to accommodate some of the commissioners' objections to the proposed Pluralities and Residence Bill but frustrated at their insistence that there should be no alteration at all in the way in which Church patronage was distributed, unless it had been suggested by the commission. Howley refused to offer an opinion without consulting Blomfield and Kaye.[51]

Howley received not a few protests from other bishops about the commission's work. Van Mildert had grave doubts about the revenues proposed for bishoprics. He could not see any option but using *commendams* for small sees. Apart from the five senior bishoprics, he thought that only Ely and Worcester could survive a drop in income. Reducing both these sees to an annual income of £5,500 each would produce a surplus of £6,500. Van Mildert thought that the archbishops should not lose income and if Durham were reduced to £10,000 'it must undergo some retrenchments which will affect its character'. That surely was the point, but Van Mildert hated it. For him transferring money from richer to poorer sees smacked of spoliation and was more objectionable than the use of *commendams*. Howley no longer saw things that way. Van Mildert would rather have had anything than a common fund which gave an individual bishop no discretion.[52] Bishop Allen of Ely felt that he was being made to suffer for the sins of his predecessor, Sparke, by having to pay over a far larger sum than he could possibly afford. In complete frustration, he suggested receiving a fixed salary of £5,500 and handing over his entire estates to its management in awkward correspondence with the Secretary. Allen complained on several occasions to Melbourne about his

[49] Commissioners to Melbourne, 10 March 1837, Bodl Lib, Melbourne Ps, Box 76, f. 46.

[50] Copy Melbourne to Howley, 20 March 1837, Bodl Lib, Melbourne Ps, Box 76, f. 50; Howley to Melbourne, 9 January 1838, Bodl Lib, Melbourne Ps, Box 76, f. 62.

[51] Howley to Russell, 16 March 1837, LPL MS 1812, f. 11; Russell to Howley, 2 April 1837, LPL MS 1812, f. 15; Howley to Russell, 5 April 1837, LPL MS 1812, f. 17; Howley to Russell, 27 September 1837, LPL MS 1812, f. 23.

[52] Van Mildert to Howley, 2 April 1835, BL Add MS 40419, f. 143.

treatment.[53] Phillpotts suggested many wide-ranging changes to the constitutions of chapters. Both he and Bishop Grey of Hereford (Lord Grey's brother) attacked the commission at various times in the House of Lords.[54]

Melbourne did his duty by Howley as Prime Minister. He did not try to place bishops with views more congenial to him on the Ecclesiastical Commission despite his friendly relations with Edward Maltby, whom he had translated from Chichester to Durham in 1836 to succeed Van Mildert, much to the High Church party's disgust. Since the commission only had the resource of cathedral endowments to play with, it was bound to be unpopular with backwoodsmen. Articulate Tories like Newman and Keble disliked the very existence of the commission and they were bemused by Howley's behaviour.[55] But Howley became committed heart and mind to its work and he and the other commissioners very rarely missed its meetings; of the first 103 meetings Blomfield missed only ten, Howley only eight.[56] Harcourt's quip that until Blomfield arrived at commission meetings the members would mend their pens and talk about the weather captured his energy and obscured the quieter and productive work of others, especially Howley. Owen Chadwick interpreted this comment as a subtle way of passing any criticism of the commission onto Blomfield's shoulders alone.[57]

Although more recent historians of Church Reform might be hesitant about Best's praise of 'modern' ways and the implicit criticism of inadequate 'old' ways (sometimes anything but), his tribute to Howley bears repeating.[58] He saw a man with a character that needed the support of strong friends like Blomfield and Peel, but with a will and mind of his own. It is also worth remembering that Howley was 70 in 1836 and Blomfield twenty years younger. The death of Van Mildert and the decline into illness of Rose in 1836 freed him from the strong influence of two of the most conservative of his intimate confidants.

---

53 *The Correspondence between the Ecclesiastical Commissioners and the Bishop of Ely* (London, 1837). See, for example, Joseph Allen to Melbourne, 14 January 1837, Bodl Lib, Melbourne Ps, Box 77, f. 116.

54 *Correspondence between the Lord Bishop of Exeter and Members of the Commission of Ecclesiastical Enquiry* (London, 1840).

55 Newman to R.H. Froude, 18 January 1835, in *Letters and Correspondence of John Henry Newman*, ed. A. Mozley (London, 1891), ii, 86.

56 Best, *Temporal Pillars*, 308.

57 Chadwick, *Victorian Church: Part One*, 133.

58 See, for example, Arthur Burns, 'A Hanoverian Legacy? Diocesan Reform in the Church of England 1800–c. 1833', in *Church of England c.1689–c.1833*, ed. Walsh, Haydon and Taylor, 281–82.

> The Howley of the later thirties is quite a different figure from the Howley of earlier times ... He gives the impression of a good man too easily influenced by strong personalities to be called firm or strong himself. After 1835 Howley veritably changes his spots. He may still have seemed 'the meek Archbishop' in private, but one would not gather that he was anything of the kind from *Hansard*'s reports of his speeches in the House of Lords ... whenever Howley was there, he had to lead for the prelates, and he always did it well ...
>
> Howley ... was not [j]ust a puppet pulled by Blomfield's strings. He believed in what he was doing. The truth must be, that ... the Ecclesiastical Commissioners' measures ... could not be much improved on by anyone who really tried to see church and nation as a whole ... in the modern way with the aid of maps, committees, circular inquiries, and tabulated statistics. This Howley did, however painfully, at the Ecclesiastical Commissioners' board. The result was infinitely creditable to him.[59]

The Church Discipline Bill, 1839–1840

At the same time as he sat on the Ecclesiastical Commission, Howley had to deal with the early days of the Oxford Movement and during the later travails of that controversy he had a huge amount of other business. He introduced the Church Discipline Bill into the House of Lords in May 1839. This regulated all offences in ecclesiastical law, doctrinal, liturgical and those to do with sexual immorality, drunkenness and crime. Perhaps he would have had objections to encroaching on the bishops' traditional rights in these matters if he had not had to change his views at the Ecclesiastical Commission. The Court of Arches, usually an appeal court from diocesan legal process, would hear all cases, subject to an appeal to the Judicial Committee of the Privy Council. Phillpotts protested vociferously about this potential infringement of his authority. He was supported too by Monk, despite his being a long-standing member of the Ecclesiastical Commission.[60] There were 300 other ecclesiastical courts in existence and jurisdictions were inevitably confused and many cases were grotesquely expensive. The bill cleared a path through some of this thicket by removing the power to try criminal cases from all the ecclesiastical courts, except those of the archbishops.[61] Howley's

59 Best, *Temporal Pillars*, 345, 346–47.

60 *Hansard*, 16 May 1839, 3rd series, xlvii, cols 1029, 1038.

61 *Hansard*, 16 May 1839, 3rd series, xlvii, cols 1307–08.

main concern was to find speedier ways to punish those clergy who had disgraced the Church and he was irritated by bishops disagreeing with him since he had consulted all his colleagues who had been in London when the plan was being developed. They had given unanimous approval to the scheme.[62]

Some of the proposals were developments of recommendations in the Special Report of the Ecclesiastical Courts Commission of 1832. Their complexity and the more pressing concerns of the Ecclesiastical Duties and Revenues Commission and of the Ecclesiastical Commission proper had left them unaltered for seven years. There was one major change. The report had asserted that the power to sentence or suspend clergy was one of a bishop's inalienable rights. Phillpotts objected to juries, just as Howley had done in 1836, even though Howely had now changed his mind.[63] Blomfield, though he had contributed to the 1832 report, supported Howley's change of mind specifically on the basis that the bill would increase the bishops' truly spiritual discipline. The bill was referred to a Select Committee which so mangled the proposal that the Lord Chancellor repudiated the legislation, which nonetheless passed the Lords in July 1839 by 21 votes to 12.[64] The bill came unstuck between those who thought that it left too much to the personal authority of the bishops and those who thought it 'derogated from the spiritual power inherent in their office'.[65] After two attempts nothing had been achieved. The final version of the legislation, which passed in 1840, owed much to Phillpotts.[66] When a clergyman was accused of any offence or had given 'occasion for scandal', a bishop could make up a five-man commission of inquiry, which had to include either the vicar-general of the diocese or one or more archdeacons. If they considered the evidence compelling, the bishop could then try the case summarily if there was a confession or with three assessors assisting if not.[67]

62 *Hansard*, 16 May 1839, 3rd series, xlvii, cols 1312–13; Burns, *Diocesan Revival in the Church of England*, 168 and more generally 162–91.

63 Mathieson, *English Church Reform*, 154ff.

64 *Hansard*, 25 July 1839, 3rd series, xlix, col. 772.

65 Howley to Perceval, 3 August 1839, PH, Pusey MS; Howley to Perceval, 5 September 1839, PH, Pusey MS.

66 Burns, *Diocesan Revival in the Church of England*, 169–70.

67 Mathieson, *English Church Reform*, 164.

Chapter 5
The Oxford Movement

The Canterbury Party

> What an afflicting consideration it is that no measures are taken by the Bench of Bishops collectively for arresting the progress of [Popery and Puseyism]. What, indeed, is to be expected, when the Primate has a Puseyite for a Chaplain, and the calumniator of Foxe for his Librarian?[1]

> I should wish as little as possible to be said in the way of praise or expression of confidence. I certainly do not feel the least of *that* towards the ABp ... unless he has been belied in all the newspapers, the whole of his proceedings in Parliament about these Church Bills is only to be accounted for on the notion of his being thoroughly Erastian.[2]

The first of these quotes was made by a typical Low Churchman frustrated that Howley had not disciplined what he considered the Rome-ward slide of the Tractarians, particularly by the early 1840s. The Tractarians were the High Churchmen in Oxford who, beginning in 1833, published a series of Tracts for the Times to protest about the encroaching of the State on the Church and whose famous leaders, John Henry Newman, John Keble and Edward Bouverie Pusey, became immensely influential in encouraging the clergy in particular to 're-discover' the catholic roots of the Church of England. The second is a quote of John Keble from an earlier period which shows how quickly some of the leading Tractarians, and those they influenced most closely, became critical of those in the High Church tradition like Howley, who held many of the same theological convictions as them but who had become increasingly disconcerted at the criticisms of that tradition which in Howley's opinion led some Tractarians dangerously close to Rome.[3]

---

1 J.H. Browne to C.P. Golightly, 18 March 1842, LPL, MS 1804, f. 106.

2 Keble to Pusey, 4 October 1836, PH, Pusey MS.

3 There are many histories of the Oxford Movement. The classic account is R.W. Church, *The Oxford Movement: Twelve Years 1833–1845* (London, 1891). Amongst more recent

Just as in London, Howley's advisers, chaplains and confidants were 'old High Churchmen'. W.N. Molesworth, son of one of Howley's chaplains, described them as the 'Canterbury party'.[4] The 'Puseyite' chaplain complained of was Benjamin Harrison who, although a close friend and former assistant lecturer to Pusey, became a symbol of the widening divisions between High Churchman and Tractarians very soon after becoming Howley's chaplain in 1838. When the flamboyant R.H. Froude characterised the evangelicals as Xs, the 'apostolicals' (the Tractarians) as Ys and the old High Churchmen as Zs, he chose Hugh James Rose and Harrison as absolutely typical Zs.[5] Rose, who served for a year as Professor of Divinity at the new University of Durham before illness forced his resignation, was the most important member of the group. He combined theological learning with political conservatism and his influence was particularly felt as editor of the *British Magazine*.[6] Howley made him his chaplain in 1834 and although he became Principal of King's College London in 1836 he very soon became ill again, which eventually resulted in his death in 1838 at the age of 43. All of Howley's most senior appointments came from this party; as often as not from his close circle as well. Not every bishop was as systematic in promoting one particular 'party'. As in many clerical patronage networks, these types of relationships were often cemented through marriages: for example, Howley's former chaplain Herbert Oakeley was given rich preferment. Nearly twenty years after Oakeley's death the continuing personal links between the families saw his third son marry Mrs Howley's niece.[7]

The Beginning of the Oxford Movement

The Government proposed the abolition of two archbishoprics and eight bishoprics of the Church of Ireland in February 1833. The sees were over-remunerated and under-populated by adherents of the Establishment. A wild furore broke out, and John Keble's sermon on National Apostasy on 14 July 1833 famously lambasted the idea. Before the bill reached the House of Lords

publications, see Michael Chandler, *An Introduction to the Oxford Movement* (London, 2005) and George Herring, *What was the Oxford Movement?* (London, 2002).

4 W.N. Molesworth, *History of the Church of England from 1660* (London, 1882), 313–17.

5 Nockles, *Oxford Movement in Context*, 20.

6 G.L. Molesworth, *Life of John Edward Nassau Molesworth, D.D., An Eminent Divine of the Nineteenth Century* (London, 1915), 34–38.

7 Henry Evelyn Oakeley married Caroline Howley Turner Belli, the daughter of W.H. Belli, Mrs Howley's younger brother, in 1862.

Howley had introduced a petition against it from the Archdeacon and clergy of Limerick, and Wellington had introduced one from the clergy of Clogher and Cloyne.[8] In debate on 17 July, Lord Grey pointed out that the diocese of Lincoln alone contained almost as many benefices as the whole of the Church of Ireland: in Lincoln there were 1,273; in Ireland, 1,456, and when sinecures were omitted, 1,306. The bishops did not speak entirely with one voice: Blomfield (party to another petition against the bill presented by Howley on 17 July) said that there were parts of it which did not offend him and despite the difficulties the legislation posed, he would support it; Van Mildert attacked it uncompromisingly.[9]

Howley regretted having to disagree with the Government: 'a position hardly befitting an Archbishop of Canterbury'. He had never thought that he would have to do so when he was appointed Primate. He thought the bill not only inadvisable but also impractical. Just as in England, he believed that the Church would incur a great deal of debt before enjoying the promised benefits of building glebe houses and augmenting small livings. He knew too that there would be an outcry if one man received two episcopal revenues.[10] The bishops split 15 to 11. Howley was joined by Van Mildert and Phillpotts; Blomfield, Whately of Dublin and both C.R. and J.B. Sumner, the evangelical brother bishops of Winchester and Chester, voted in favour. Whately told Newman that Howley had been consulted long before him and had given a general consent to the proposals, differing from the ministers only about whether the revenues of six or ten sees should be alienated.[11]

In July 1833 Rose had invited William Palmer (of Worcester College, Oxford) and Arthur Perceval to join him and Hurrell Froude in a conference at his rectory in Hadleigh barely two weeks after Keble's Assize Sermon.[12] In the years that followed the Zs would act time and again on Howley's behalf. Just how far and fast they fell away from sympathy with the views of Froude gives some indication of the differences of view and style that characterised the Oxford Movement even between 1833 and Newman's secession to Rome in 1845. Palmer and Perceval collaborated on creating an Association of the Friends of the Church. The Address to the Primate of 1834 pledged help in preserving the 'apostolical doctrine' of the Church, the doctrine of the Prayer Book and 'the

8 *Hansard*, 3rd series, 1833, xix, cols 550–51.

9 *Hansard*, 3rd series, 1833, xix, cols 718, 741, 765–66, 924–34.

10 *Hansard*, 3rd series, 1833, xix, col. 347.

11 *Hansard*, 3rd series, 1833, xix, col. 617; Whately to Newman, 3 November 1834, *LD*, iv, 356.

12 Chadwick, *Victorian Church: Part One*, 70–71.

orthodox and primitive faith'. It collected 7,000 clergy signatures but Keble and Newman were not keen on it and even Joshua Watson and Edward Burton (who refused to sign it) were uneasy.[13] Watson's qualms about the 'Oxford school' did not stop him being chary of Howley on occasion. As early as 1834 he was grumbling about him allowing far too much lay interference in the Ecclesiastical Revenues Commission. He was cautious on hearing of

> a general Address to the Primate, expressive of (the clergy's) concurrence in all that he has effected, and their confidence in his zeal and discretion, and devotion to the Church in all that he contemplated. Such a declaration, if attainable in the present state of the clergy would doubtless strengthen the hands of the Archbishop, and comfort him amazingly; but I fear in losing the advantage I was most anxious he should make of the Ecclesiastical Commission, he let the best, if not the only, opportunity for doing this go by.[14]

The machinations which accompanied the idea of, agreement on and execution of the Address are revealing. Newman and Keble slid from one person to another. Newman was disingenuous. Just as he was announcing his lack of confidence in an association to his school and college friend J.W. Bowden, he was courting Benjamin Harrison (dubious about the idea himself) for support in setting it up. Well-known Phalanx members like Watson and Norris disagreed with each other, and Rose was claimed as both a supporter and critic of the association and a supporter and critic of the Tracts. Harrison knew how diffident Keble and Newman really were and that Newman had now thrown all his energies into stopping organisations appearing around the country. Harrison felt that the association could exacerbate party spirit and splits and that they would end up acting like 'contending churchmen', with all the public drawbacks that entailed.[15]

Many of the fault lines were blatantly obvious from the beginning. Keble complained about the bishops' 'coyness' to Newman in August 1833, less than a month after the Assize Sermon. Those who had met at Hadleigh were already disagreeing over tactics. They used Rose as an intermediary with the bishops to get private and unattributable guidance for the Tractarian leaders. Keble and Newman's attitude to Rose was also hardening – they would support his *British Magazine* 'until he actually rats'. Keble was yearning for direction on his conduct

---

13 A.P. Perceval, *A Collection of Papers connected with the Theological Movement of 1833* (London, 1842), 17, 19; S. Butler to Burton, 30 October 1833, f. 190; Palmer to Burton, 25 November 1833, f. 205, Ch Ch Microfilm Ps, Box 92 (both letters with Burton's MS notes).

14 Watson to Norris, 24 October 1833, in Churton, *Memoir of Joshua Watson*, i, 26–28.

15 Harrison to Gladstone, 15 November 1833, BL Add MS 44204, f. 37.

over the bill to suppress the Irish bishoprics. He favoured an Address to the Archbishop but was wary because of ill luck with the 'many' he had attempted to organise in the past. Newman's delight that Howley was on the Tractarians' side soon gave way to similar and grandiloquent ambivalence:

> I wish the Archbishop had somewhat of the boldness of the old Catholic Prelates; no one can doubt he is a man of the highest principle, and would willingly die a Martyr; but if he had but the little finger of Athanasius, he would do us all the good in the world.[16]

Earlier discussions about whether the Address should include an expression of confidence in bishops other than Howley had been the source of considerable unease and potential embarrassment. Harrison thought it best for clergy to be able to support the Archbishop and through him the whole bench without seeming to attack their own less committed bishops.[17] The Address was presented in February 1834. It contained approximately 6,500 names, excluding Addresses which came through the Bishops of Exeter and Llandaff. Howley himself was touched by the event, 'almost affected', and said that the Church would come out of this present trial with an increase of honour and usefulness. The concomitant Lay Address to the Primate was in the hands of Joshua Watson. It was popular enough to bring in the names of 230,000 heads of families by the time of its presentation in May. But Howley's mood was considerably darker now. He was much less convinced of the good that such trials might bring.[18]

Flushed by the success of the initial Tracts, the Tractarians saw the death of the Chancellor of the University Lord Grenville in January 1834 as an opportunity to assert themselves more widely within Oxford. Peel and Wellington had been fancied as possible candidates for the vacancy. Peel felt insult added to injury when Wellington stood for election without reference to him, having made it quite clear that he was dubious about the whole idea. It was then alleged that Wellington had been wrongly told that Lord Talbot, the former Lord Lieutenant of Ireland (who as a member of Christ Church would have been a very strong

16 Newman to H.A. Woodgate, 7 August 1833, *LD*, iv, 27; Newman to Bowden, 31 August 1833, *LD*, iv, 33.

17 William Palmer, *A Narrative of Events Connected with the Publication of the Tracts for the Times, with Reflections on Existing Tendencies to Romanism, and on the Present Duties and Prospects of Members of the Church* (2nd edn, Oxford, 1843), 11; Harrison to Newman, 25 December 1833, *LD*, iv, 148–49.

18 Newman to Bowden, 9 February 1834, *LD*, iv, 189; Newman to T.D. Acland, 23 June 1834, *LD*, iv, 287.

candidate), did not wish to stand. Nevertheless, a coalition of liberal Tories and Whigs massed an unassailable majority for Wellington and sunk Peel.[19]

Bowden had suggested Howley as a candidate to Newman in November 1833. He hoped that the position would 'athanasiize' him.[20] Newman thought that Routh and the other Heads were supporting Wellington because they believed he was the only man who could conciliate the semi-liberal MAs. He also convinced himself that Charles Ogilvie (a Fellow of Balliol and one of Howley's chaplains from 1834) had destroyed any chance of Howley's election by 'ratting' from Howley to Wellington. The truth was that the Tractarians had been incapable of commanding a single Common Room for Howley. Keble strongly preferred Wellington to Peel but professed his mourning the loss of Howley to Ogilvie.[21] W.R. Ward dismisses the Tractarian campaign as a romantic folly powerless to increase the political resources of the university which never stood a scintilla of a chance of success.[22] None of Howley's letters on this matter survive but it is inconceivable that Ogilvie would have supported a different candidate had Howley wanted to stand. The job would have been a misery, hounded by the problems in Oxford as it was.

The Regius Professor of Divinity

The deaths in 1836 of both Edward Burton and Hugh James Rose were not only personal blows to Howley and their fellow High Churchmen. They were perhaps the two most substantial characters with the best chance of maintaining unity amongst High Churchmen in the ten years ahead, and as such their deaths had a real effect on the speed of the decline in relationships between the High Churchmen and the Tractarians. Henry Parry Liddon, Pusey's biographer and one of the most important leaders of the second generation of Tractarians, thought 1836 was the most important year in the history of the Oxford Movement for another reason – Renn Dickson Hampden's appointment as Regius Professor of Divinity to replace Burton. Hampden was the High Churchmen's liberal bogeyman. He had already gained some notoriety with his

19 Norman Gash, 'Oxford Politics in the Chancellor's Election of 1834', in *Pillars of Government and Other Essays on State and Society c1770--c1880* (London, 1986), 93–97; 'Papers relating to proceedings of the University', Bodl Lib GA Oxon c 50, ff. 112–13.

20 Bowden to Newman, 25 November 1833, *LD*, iv, 111.

21 Newman to Henry Wilberforce, 17 January 1834, *LD*, iv, 178; Keble to Ogilvie, 18 January 1834, Bodl Lib MS Eng Lett d 124, ff. 68–69.

22 W.R. Ward, *Victorian Oxford* (London, 1965), 84.

1834 pamphlet *Observations on Religious Dissent* which was based on his 1832 Bampton Lectures. Liddon's summary of Hampden's views (and therefore the views which many High Churchmen believed him to hold – whatever objections Hampden made to the caricature) was that moral and theological truths were things distinct from religion and that no 'inferences' ought to be drawn from Scripture; that the language of the Creeds themselves was thus a mistake, even though they expressed only what was taught by Holy Scripture. Everyone knew that Hampden had called for the abolition of the subscription to the Articles by newly arriving undergraduates.

Pusey and Newman supported a vigorous campaign against Hampden. Even his champion Archbishop Whately wondered whether Hampden's 'love of originality' was dangerous.[23] Rose thought the lectures so mischievous and un-Christian that it was a calamity that they should pass with nothing more than an anonymous review since the public would inevitably gain the impression that Hampden's publications had the authority of the entire university.[24] Howley had submitted a list of names to Melbourne for consideration to replace Burton: Pusey was his first choice, Newman and Keble his fourth and fifth. Melbourne passed the list to Whately and Copleston, Bishop of Llandaff and former Provost of Oriel, who rejected them all and suggested Hampden instead.[25] Howley soon heard that Hampden had been offered the Regius Chair and told Melbourne of his disappointment. Liddon thought that Howley had agreed to the appointment and then regretted it when he was 'fully conversant' with Hampden's writings but he was opposed to him from the start.[26] A petition against Hampden signed by more than half the resident MAs in the university was forwarded to Howley for presentation to the King. It asked that the Archbishop have a veto over the appointment and predicted dire consequences if Hampden were to educate those intending to enter the sacred ministry.[27]

Hampden told Melbourne that those who had organised the petition had also been putting together digests of his writings in an attempt to prove his theology unsound. Hampden absolutely refuted that claim. Both archbishops saw Melbourne in a final attempt to dissuade him from the appointment, urging

23 H.P. Liddon, *Life of Edward Bouverie Pusey* (3rd edn, London, 1891), i, 299–303; [Copy] Whately to Hampden, [1835], LPL MS 2164, f. 28.

24 Rose to Newman, [1 January 1836], PH Pusey MS.

25 Newman to Henry Wilberforce, 21 January 1836, *LD*, v, 209; Liddon, *Life of Pusey*, i, 370.

26 Howley to Melbourne, 9 February 1836, Bodl Lib, Melbourne Ps, Box 79, f. 3.

27 Newman to Rose, 8 February 1836, *LD*, v, 229.

him that Hampden would be fatally compromised if appointed.[28] Hampden's supporters made much of the fact that his appointment to the chair of Moral Philosophy in 1834 had been uncontroversial and ridiculed several Heads of House who had elected him then and now were amongst those petitioning against his appointment as Regius Professor.[29] It was only when the *Observations* went into a second edition that the Tractarians decided that it would be worse not to protest. But Hampden's detractors remained seriously compromised by their previous silence and his supporters, like Thomas Arnold, said so at every opportunity.[30] Newman took cold comfort from the support for the Tractarians' 'Theological Society' that the appointment would garner.[31]

The King asked Melbourne to let him withhold his sanction from the appointment until he could consult Howley.[32] Melbourne chastised him for impugning Hampden on no evidence and infringing on the rights of private judgement and free enquiry which were the 'foundations of the Protestant faith'. Melbourne could also rely on the fact that he had considered Howley's suggestions but that Whately and Copleston, both 'distinguished ornaments' of the university, had suggested Hampden.[33] A rumour had earlier gone round Oxford that Melbourne had in fact finally allowed Howley a veto so it was all the more of a shock when Hampden's name was announced.[34] The Tractarians began to agitate for the bishops to withdraw their insistence on ordinands having certificates of attendance from the lectures of the Regius Professor.[35]

Hampden began a correspondence with Howley which was later published. He protested vigorously that he always sought to uphold the doctrines and established formularies of the Church of England and that his Bampton Lectures were nothing more than a history of the technical terms of theology and also

---

28 Hampden to Melbourne, 10 February 1836, Bodl Lib, Melbourne Ps, Box 79, f. 5; Viscount Howick to Melbourne, [11 February 1836], Bodl Lib, Melbourne Ps, Box 79, f. 11; Howley to Melbourne, 13 February 1836, Bodl Lib, Melbourne Ps, Box 79, ff. 12–13.

29 W. Falconer to N.D. Macdonald, 13 February 1836, Bodl Lib, Melbourne Ps, Box 79, f. 14.

30 Edward Churton, *A Letter to an Edinburgh Reviewer, on the Case of the Oxford Malignants and Dr Hampden* (London, 1836); cf. Arnold's article in *Edinburgh Review*, April 1836; Nockles, '"Lost Causes ... and Impossible Loyalties": The Oxford Movement and the University', in *The History of the University of Oxford*, vol. VI: *Nineteenth Century Oxford, Part I*, ed. M.G. Brock and M.C. Curthoys (Oxford, 1997), 223–24.

31 Newman to Bowden, 17 February 1836, *LD*, v, 237.

32 William IV to Melbourne, 14 February 1836, Bodl Lib, Melbourne Ps, Box 79, f. 16.

33 Melbourne to William IV, 15 February 1836, Bodl Lib, Melbourne Ps, Box 79, f. 17.

34 Pusey to Melbourne, 22 February 1836, Bodl Lib, Melbourne Ps, Box 79, f. 28.

35 Nockles, '"Lost Causes"', 227.

that his *Observations on Religious Dissent* had been deliberately misinterpreted to imply that he attacked the doctrines of the Trinity and the Incarnation. He admitted a lack of clarity in some writings.[36] Howley refused to discuss the substance of the matter with Hampden, claiming it was a matter for the university and that whatever Hampden's intentions his writings undoubtedly did seem to criticise the 'vital truths of Christianity'.[37]

Howley agreed to Newman's suggestion of a more general petition to the King to take the advice of the Heads of the Church in making ecclesiastical appointments. Newman told Keble of petitions brewing in archdeaconries in Bath, Devon and Somerset and advised him to drop a hint amongst the 'zzz' that Howley was in favour.[38] Newman's memory twenty-five years later was that Howley was somewhat alarmed by the chain of events to which he appeared to have given sanction and that Melbourne was furious. Several petitions against Hampden were raised around the country.[39] There were persistent rumours that Melbourne would offer Hampden a bishopric, to the extent that Thomas Arnold told Whately that he would like to succeed him as Regius Professor.[40] Hampden felt persecuted by Howley who had told the House of Lords that certain of his 'modes of conveying theological opinions left much to be desired'. He accused him in return of cravenness towards the Tractarians and published their correspondence as part of a self-proclaimed determination to vanquish his opponents.[41]

The most important literary result of the Hampden controversy was the creation of the 'Library of the Fathers'. Froude had suggested to Newman as early as September 1833 that Howley have the works of Ignatius and Clement of Rome printed and recommend the clergy to preach on them.[42] Newman and Pusey sketched out a general scheme for the publication of selected writings of

36 [Copy] Hampden to Howley, 27 February 1836, Bodl Lib, Melbourne Ps, Box 79, f. 32.

37 [Copy] Howley to Hampden, 1 March 1836, Bodl Lib, Melbourne Ps, Box 79, f. 33.

38 Newman to H.F. Lyte, 26 February 1836, *LD*, v, 242–43; Keble to Newman, 25 January 1836, KCL, Keble MS; Keble to Newman, 5 March 1836, *LD*, v, 254; Newman to Keble, 6 March 1836, *LD*, v, 253.

39 Editors' note, *LD*, v, 255; Newman to Rose, 14 March 1836, *LD*, v, 257.

40 Arnold to Whately, 16 May 1836, LPL, MS 2164, f. 30.

41 *A Letter to His Grace the Archbishop of Canterbury Explanatory of the Proceedings at Oxford, on the Appointment of the Present Regius Professor of Divinity, by a Member of the University of Oxford* (3rd edn, London, 1836, ii–iv, 4–7; *Correspondence between The Rev Dr Hampden, Regius Professor of Divinity in the University of Oxford, and the Most Rev Dr Howley, Lord Archbishop of Canterbury* (London, 1838), Letter III, Hampden to Howley, 23 January 1838, 5–27 and Letters IV–VII, 28–38.

42 Froude to Newman, 8 September 1833, *LD*, iv, 47.

the 'Catholic Fathers'. By the time the project was coming to fruition Howley had begun to make his intentions plain about the direction of Church Reform and Newman heard that Keble would object to dedicating the work to him as a result. Newman thought that Howley might well refuse the offer but that he should be asked. It would be right to allow him to do something right after doing things with regard to Church Reform that they disliked.[43] Keble, always more extreme, did not want Howley to think that the Church was satisfied with him. He was rumoured to be planning to avoid meeting him on a visit to Sir William Heathcote's home in Hursley.[44] Pusey was disturbed by these reports. He believed that Howley had made a good stand in the Hampden business. Rose said that he had done all that could be done and Pusey was inclined to believe him.[45] Keble preferred to be churlish. He disagreed with Pusey's judgement that there was 'general approbation' of pending Church Reform and that he knew no clerics, whether High or Low Church, parochial or cathedral, who approved of it. He went on: 'we are told that he has remonstrated privately about H[ampden], but what public steps has he taken? What has he done that has the least tendency to warn the Church against the results of such teaching?' This was the same letter in which he described Howley as 'thoroughly Erastian' (n. 2 above) although it is important to remember that this is personal correspondence between old friends and Keble would have felt free to express himself more pungently than ever he would have publicly. By contrast, two days earlier he had told Pusey that he liked the idea of paying tribute to Howley's 'episcopal kindness' even though Newman thought it sounded strange. Pusey said that the original suggestion was Benjamin Harrison's and although those who did not value episcopacy would think it strange, it was the strongest word of which he could think.[46]

Pusey wrote to Howley asking him to accept the dedication and left the fine details of the wording aside. Newman was thrilled that Howley accepted immediately – 'I had no notion that he would put himself at the head of a "party".'[47] By August 1838, Howley was listed as a patron of the Library of 'ancient bishops, fathers, doctors, martyrs, confessors of Christ's most Holy Catholic Church'. Seven other bishops had subscribed, though Pusey wanted more.

43 Newman to Keble, [22 September 1836], *LD*, v, 359.

44 Newman to Pusey, 23 September 1836, PH, Pusey MS.

45 Pusey to Newman, 23 September 1836, PH, Pusey MS; Pusey to Newman, 25 September 1836, PH, Pusey MS.

46 Keble to Pusey, 2 October 1838, PH, Pusey MS; Keble to Pusey, 6/8 October 1838, PH, Pusey MS; Pusey to Newman, 19th Sunday after Trinity, 1838, PH, Pusey MS.

47 Newman to Pusey, 13 October [1836], *LD*, v, 368.

Pusey's translation of Augustine's *Confessions* had the careful introduction that Howley had advised when he did meet Keble in Hursley, making particular play of the fact that the Fathers could not and did not encroach on the supreme authority of Scripture. The Tractarians considered the publication of the 'Library of the Fathers' one of the most important things that they ever achieved, far more so than the companion 'Library of Anglo-Catholic Theology' of Caroline and other Anglican Divines which first appeared in 1841.[48]

Harrison, Howley, Bishop Bagot and the 1838 Charge

The most extensive account of Howley's particular views about the Tractarians and their relations with the old High Churchmen is recorded in a letter that Harrison wrote to Pusey after Howley invited him to be his chaplain. Howley told Harrison that the position would give him considerable insight and influence in what was going on regarding the Church and its operations 'which were daily becoming more and more important and extensive'. He expressed his high regard for 'the Oxford Divines' and fully understood that he would be generally regarded as giving them his 'unqualified sanction' by appointing Harrison. Howley paid fulsome tribute to Pusey, Keble and Newman by name. He feared that some opinions had already been carried too far, as had certain practices such as the wearing of crosses, which 'would be apt to be regarded by uninstructed persons as an approach to Popery'. It was no surprise that he thought that the worst thing that they had done was to publish Froude's *Remains* (1838) after his untimely death. Howley had been only one of countless churchmen horrified by them. Froude's brilliance for the cutting phrase made his extreme statements about the Church of England all the more able to shock. The loyal High Churchman Edward Churton told Pusey that he would rather have lost his right hand than see whole sentences and pages published.[49] Newman and Keble knew what effect publication would have. Nothing caused greater offence than the disparaging comments about the English Reformers, or Froude's loathing for the Reformation, which he described as a limb badly set which needed breaking again to come right.[50] Howley's biggest regret about the book was the influence it gave 'to parties of whose designs and motives he highly disapproved'. Howley

48 Keble to Pusey, 16 October 1836, PH, Pusey MS; Nockles, *Oxford Movement in Context*, 128.

49 Piers Brendon, *Hurrell Froude and the Oxford Movement* (London, 1974), 180.

50 Brendon, *Hurrell Froude*, 187; [R.H. Froude], *Remains of the late Reverend Richard Hurrell Froude, M.A.* (Oxford, 1838), Part One, i, 389.

did not ask Harrison for 'a confession of faith' but made it clear where he differed from the Oxford men so that he would not be understood, by making the appointment, 'to be expressing an unqualified approbation of their whole system'.[51]

Pusey was delighted that Howley had asked Harrison to be his chaplain and urged him to accept immediately although aware of the division of loyalties which Harrison might face. Keble was equally pleased, because he thought that Harrison was less likely to be 'corrupted' than almost any one whom Howley might have chosen. He said that Rose would have been delighted if he had lived.[52] Liddon's biography of Pusey shows how difficult matters did in fact become:

> The traditional caution of Lambeth was too much for him. His tone became gradually more official and less sympathetic; he was, as years went on, less the friend of the Movement than its critic. Pusey felt the change deeply ... although they remained on terms of affectionate friendship ... [he] always referred in later years to the move to Lambeth as an 'unfortunate experiment'.[53]

Liddon clearly felt that Harrison had put pressure on the episcopate. 'In those days there were no recalcitrant Bishops. A word from Lambeth was taken as a command – and no doubt was often a relief from responsibility, and did not necessarily imply weakness on the yielding Bishop's part.'[54] A MS addition to the transcription at Pusey House, Oxford (perhaps by W.J. Copeland, Fellow of Trinity College who collected materials for a history of the movement) quotes Joshua Watson: 'you must make allowance for Lambeth "atmosphere"'.[55] Bishop Bagot of Oxford found himself torn, 'almost pressed to death' between 'Lambeth' and 'Oriel'. Bagot's 1838 Charge, which made some mild and unremarkable cautious remarks about the dangers of reintroducing practices that had ended up elsewhere in superstition and might create schism and avoiding expressions that might be 'dangerous to certain minds', gave Newman cause to make a huge

---

[51] Harrison to Pusey, 11 August 1838, PH, Pusey MS.

[52] Pusey to Harrison, [13 August 1838], PH, Pusey MS; Pusey to Newman, 9 August 1841, PH, Pusey MS; Newman to Pusey, 13 August 1841, PH, Pusey MS; Keble to Newman, 23 August 1838, KCL, Keble MS.

[53] Liddon, *Life of Pusey*, ii, 45–46.

[54] Copy Letter Bishop Robert Eden, Primus of Scottish Episcopal Church to W.J. Copeland, 12 January 1879, PH, Pusey MS.

[55] *Oxford Movement in Context*, 1.

fuss, so much so that Bagot put an extra footnote in the second edition making it explicit that he never intended a general censure on the Tracts.[56]

The Martyrs' Memorial

As has been seen already an attachment to the Reformation was a hallmark not only of the Low and Latitudinarian Churchmen but was held with equal conviction by the High Churchmen who surrounded Howley. Charles Pourtales Golightly, a former curate of Newman, was already renowned for his distrust of the Tractarians. As early as April 1837 he had called for the erection of memorials to the Protestant martyrs in the various places in Britain where they had suffered under Mary, and Froude's *Remains* were just the extra spur he needed to give fresh impetus to the twenty-year-old idea of commemorating the martyrs in this way.[57] He planned to erect a memorial to Cranmer, Ridley and Latimer and build a church dedicated to their memory. By the time the memorial was finally prepared, nine Heads of Houses had subscribed, as had nine bishops. Howley, Harcourt and Blomfield subscribed £50 each in January 1839 specifically towards a church. Benjamin Harrison, Archdeacon Watson, Norris and Gladstone all subscribed in the same year.[58] Harrison thought that if he did not join he would be tarred with the Froudeian brush whose contempt for the Reformers he considered outrageous.[59] Bagot told Pusey several times that it would be invaluable for the Tractarians if they subscribed to the memorial but Pusey would only subscribe if it were made public that he had been instructed to do so. If Pusey could not subscribe in the normal way to the memorial, Bagot urged him at least to make a declaration of his attachment to the Reformed Church to stop all the accusations of his hostility to the Reformation. Howley had previously told Bagot that the editors of *Remains* should take the

---

56 Richard Bagot, *A Charge Delivered to the Clergy of the Diocese of Oxford ... at his Third Visitation, July and August 1838* (2nd edn, Oxford, 1838), 19–21, see 21n. for Bagot's extra comment. For fuller discussion see Liddon, *Life of Pusey*, ii, 52–64 and Richard Mead, 'Richard Bagot, Bishop of Oxford, and the Oxford Movement, 1833–1845' (Univ. of Oxford unpubl. B.Litt., 1966), 44–60.

57 Peter Toon, *Evangelical Theology 1833–1856: A Response to Tractarianism* (London, 1979), 39; E.M. Goulburn, *Reminiscences of Charles Pourtales Golightly* (Oxford and London, [1886]); Nockles, '"Lost Causes"', 236; Nockles, *Oxford Movement in Context*, 284–86.

58 'Martyrs' Memorial Subscription List', Wadham College Library, Oxford, A.11.4.

59 'Martyrs' Memorial Subscription List', Wadham College Library, Oxford, A.11.4; Harrison to Pusey, 30 October 1838, PH, Pusey MS; Harrison to Pusey, 6 November 1838, PH, Pusey MS.

opportunity of saying this or most of the benefit of their talents that the Church enjoyed would be lost.[60] Keble refused – Cranmer was an unwilling sufferer and professed doctrine 'which the ancient Church would have called heretical'. He also had no intention of publicly disavowing Froude's view of the Reformers.[61] Pusey suggested an allusive Latin inscription for the memorial which made vague references to the persecution and fire which had purged the Church in Mary's day.

Pusey had tried to get Bagot to agree a form of words, in concert with Howley, which could be recommended for the sake of union to all parties.[62] Howley was keen on Pusey's plan of building a church in the parish of St Ebbe's for the destitute population. Pusey drafted his own set of words for a tablet inside the church praising the manifold blessings of the Reformation, especially the giving of the cup to the laity, a pure liturgy and the introduction of the vernacular. The main object of all this effort was to mollify Bagot and Howley and others who wanted the Tractarians to make amends in the eyes of their critics, but the committee in charge of the memorial rejected Pusey's proposals wholesale.[63] When Bagot told Pusey that any alternative plan would look like rivalry, Pusey washed his hands of the matter. It was typical of the convolutions of the matter that two months later Pusey told Keble that he had never wanted to disown the Reformers: 'whatever faults there were, we should never have been Apostolical without them'.[64]

Tract 90

The publication of Tract 90 in 1841 was regarded either as the nadir or zenith of the Oxford Movement according to the views of its readers. Newman regarded his own examination of the Thirty-Nine Articles as a valiant attempt to prove to his extreme supporters that the Church of England was a valid home for a 'Catholic'. His interpretation of the Articles as the 'stammering lips of ambiguous formularies' which allowed interpretations opposed to their express and obvious

60 Mead, 'Richard Bagot, Bishop of Oxford', 62ff; Bagot to Pusey, 18 January 1839, PH, Pusey MS.

61 Keble to Pusey, 18 January 1839, PH, Pusey MS.

62 Pusey to Keble, 13 January 1839, PH, Pusey MS.

63 Pusey to Newman, 23 October 1838, PH, Pusey MS; Pusey to Keble, 24 January 1839, PH, Pusey MS; 'Monument to Cranmer, Ridley and Latimer', PH, Bricknell MS.

64 Keble to Pusey, St Paul's Day 1839, PH, Pusey MS; Pusey to Keble, 29 January 1839, PH, Pusey MS.

meaning raised to a new height the pitch of the concerns that had been dogging them about the duplicity and sophistry of the Tractarians. It was most painful for High Churchmen like Howley who had expended considerable efforts to affirm the views of the Tractarians as a valid, although perhaps excessive, perspective on Anglicanism. They were presented with a document that would be read widely, despite Newman's genuine hopes, as an attack on Anglicanism and all it stood for – a sneering, too clever by half, disingenuous misrepresentation. The younger Zs were even more unhappy than men of the older generation like Howley and Watson because of their previous personal loyalty to Newman, which they felt had been betrayed.[65] Bagot and Howley kept in very close touch and Bagot passed on Howley's advice, often unacknowledged and verbatim, in his letters to Pusey and Newman.[66]

Howley was adamant that any punitive action by the university would be disastrously counter-productive although he was very happy with the resolution of the Heads of Houses of March 1841 that the Tracts did not embody the teaching of the University of Oxford.[67] Bagot wanted Newman to calm the situation by declaring certain of the 'most obnoxious' opinions to be opposed to the *spirit* if not the *letter* of the Articles, but Howley was opposed to Newman publishing anything further at all since an 'unsatisfactory' explanation could do irreparable damage.[68] Newman reacted much the same way as he had over Bagot's Charge in 1838. Pusey thought that Newman's 'open questions' about the latitude in teaching permissible to the Church's ministers, if supported by the leaders of the Church, would save many who would otherwise go to Rome. Newman decided to remove the reference to 'stammering lips' (its most controversial phrase) from the second edition. His *Letter to Dr Jelf* was also careful to acknowledge that the Articles condemned the authoritative teaching of the Church of Rome whilst reiterating Charles Lloyd's distinction between 'official' and 'popular' Roman teaching: a device which he was to use to effect in later years.[69] Bagot made vast

65 Mead, 'Richard Bagot, Bishop of Oxford', 94–110; Peter Nockles, 'Oxford, Tract 90 and the Bishops', in *John Henry Newman: Reason, Rhetoric and Romanticism*, ed. D. Nicholls and F. Kerr (Bristol, 1991), 49 (more generally 28–87). For a general account of Tract 90, see Chadwick, *Victorian Church: Part One*, 181–89.

66 'Memorandum', March 1841, PH, Pusey MS.

67 Harrison to Gaisford, 15 March 1841, Bodl Lib, Oxford University Archives, NW 21.5, no. 54; Harrison to Gaisford, 17 March 1841, Bodl Lib, Oxford University Archives, NW 21.5, no. 56.

68 Bagot to Pusey, 17 March 1841, PH, Pusey MS.

69 Bagot to Newman, 17 March 1841, PH, Pusey MS; [J.H. Newman], *A Letter addressed to the Rev. R.W. Jelf, D.D., Canon of Christ Church, in Explanation of No 90, in the Series called The Tracts for the Times. By the Author* (Oxford, 1841), 7, 11.

numbers of copies of letters which he sent around for advice. Howley did what he could to avoid public controversy and was unimpressed by Newman's more emollient tone.[70] W.J. Copeland thought Bagot had been leaned on by Lambeth to tell Newman that *submission to authority* was different from *succumbing to controversial adversaries*.[71]

Many old High Churchmen thought that Newman had made a 'dangerous misapplication of a legitimate principle. The Church's formularies were being tried by a merely private judgement as to what was and was not antiquity.'[72] The Tract was criticised by High Churchmen more closely associated with the 'Oxford conspirators' than Howley. Edward Churton told Perceval that Joshua Watson condemned it: 'all good Churchmen of my acquaintance do'. Most High Church criticism focused on the Tract's disloyalty to Anglican formularies, 'which to some seemed suspiciously akin to the latitudinarian evasiveness that seemed to characterise the old Low Churchmanship'.[73] Nockles concludes that Newman's kindly words about Bagot in the *Apologia* masked a shifty account of a 'supposed' understanding between himself and the bishops. Newman certainly thought that if he were to withdraw Tract 90 from sale, he would avoid censure and avoid the impression that it had been withdrawn because it was doctrinally unsound. Pusey said the same in his *Historical Preface* to the work in 1866. Newman convinced himself that not only Bagot but 'they' (i.e. all the bishops) would not condemn him. In a note to Copeland of 1868 explaining that the sixth volume of the Tracts never had a dedication, he was explicit: 'Jelf came to me, on the beginning of the row ... from Archbishop Howley to say that, if my friends would consent not to move, nothing should be done on the other side.' There is no other reference to any such understanding amongst his voluminous correspondence, and Bagot was certainly surprised that the Tract remained on sale.[74]

Bagot passed Pusey the letter from Howley which had endorsed the arrangement for stopping the Tracts.[75] Howley agreed with Newman that Tract 90 should appear in the final volume of the collected Tracts, along with his *Letter to Jelf* with its postscript. He also thought it would be good to reprint

70 Howley to Bagot, 19 March 1841, PH, Pusey MS.

71 Draft Bagot to Newman, [21/22 March 1841], PH, Pusey MS; Howley to Bagot, 22 March 1841, PH, Pusey MS.

72 Nockles, *Oxford Movement in Context*, 139. For Tract 90's view of antiquity, see 136–42 and ch. 2 more generally.

73 Nockles, 'Oxford, Tract 90 and the Bishops', 50, 60.

74 Newman to Coleridge, 16 October 1864, *LD*, xxi, 262; Newman to Copeland, 1 July 1868, *LD*, xxiv, 96. J.H. Newman, *Apologia pro Vita Sua*, [ed. M. Svaglic] (Oxford, 1967), 128–29; Nockles, 'Oxford, Tract 90 and the Bishops', 56–58.

75 Howley to Bagot, 26 March 1841, PH, Pusey MS.

some of Newman's previous writings on 'Romanism', which would allay the fears of some.[76] Howley had a personal meeting with Pusey some months later to discuss the furore.[77]

The Jerusalem Bishopric and the Church Overseas

Some of the Tractarians attacked Howley bitterly for his role in the setting up of the Jerusalem Bishopric. The proposal to set up a bishop in Jerusalem who could minister to the Protestant congregations, both Anglican and Prussian, commended itself to many High Churchmen explicitly because it would extend episcopacy. Howley and Blomfield both knew Baron Bunsen, King Frederick William of Prussia's envoy, quite well. He had married Bishop Monk's cousin and was a friend of Lord Ashley (the future Earl of Shaftesbury), the most famous and feted evangelical of his time, whose fame stems mostly from the role he took in pursuing legislation to limit the hours of child labour.[78] The Evangelical press was gleeful at the prospect of the bishopric. Ashley and his followers talked in apocalyptic terms. Howley supported Bunsen's proposals in letters to Peel and Aberdeen. The ministers were taken with how keen Howley and Blomfield were on the scheme.[79] The proposal suited well; the money for the venture would be put up by Frederick William until there was enough raised to erect a wholly Prussian Bishopric at Bethlehem, when the Jerusalem Bishopric would become solely English. In addition, the Archbishop of Canterbury would be responsible for consecrating the candidate, who would be nominated alternately by the British and Prussian Governments. He would also have the right of veto over any Prussian candidate. Until the restoration of a Christian Jewish Church, the Archbishop would act as Metropolitan. Although the German congregations would use the German Protestant Liturgy, those consecrated would have to subscribe to both the Thirty-Nine Articles and the Augsburg Confession.[80]

---

76 Howley to Bagot, 27 March 1841, PH, Pusey MS; Palmer to Pusey, 1 April 1841, PH, Pusey MS.

77 Pusey to Newman, 1 October 1841, PH, Pusey MS.

78 P.J. Welch, 'Anglican Churchmen and the Establishment of the Jerusalem Bishopric', *JEH*, viii (1957), 193–204; R.W. Greaves, 'The Jerusalem Bishopric, 1841', *EHR*, lxiv (1949), 332–33.

79 Aberdeen to Peel, 16 September 1841, BL Add MS 40489, f. 47.

80 Bunsen to Melbourne, 6 August 1841, Bodl Lib, Melbourne Ps, Box 79, f. 96; Welch, 'Anglican Churchmen', 193–95.

Nockles notes that it was the old High Churchmen who had little difficulty in dispensing with the Tractarian objections to the scheme. High Churchmen had always been eirenical towards the continental Protestant churches, although there was an increasing unhappiness at churches which did not take every opportunity to recover the historic episcopate.[81] Pusey and Manning had both famously been initially in favour of the scheme, and Pusey wriggled later when he tried to explain that he had been under the impression that there was a pre-existing congregation when he spoke more positively about the idea.[82] Even Perceval, who opposed the scheme, followed this line. He rejected the contention of strident Tractarian William Palmer (of Magdalen College) that non-episcopal foreign churches were heretical per se and denied that Roman and Greek anathemas had any authority for Anglicans. Many High Churchmen thought that the scheme was an excellent method of extending episcopacy, and that it answered many of the objections about Protestant Churches that had been slow to re-introduce it. The official statement about the bishopric was commonly thought to have been written by Howley.[83] It described Rome as

> continually labouring to pervert the members of the Eastern Churches and to bring them under the Pope's dominion, sparing no arts nor intrigues, hesitating at no misrepresentations, sowing dissension and disorder amongst an ill-informed people, and asserting that jurisdiction over them which the ancient Churches of the East have always strenuously resisted ...
>
> ... the two great Protestant powers of Europe will have planted a Church in the midst of them, the Bishop of which is specially charged not to entrench upon the spiritual rights and liberties of those Churches; but to confine himself to the care of those over whom they cannot rightfully claim any jurisdiction.[84]

---

81 Nockles, *Oxford Movement in Context*, 156–62.

82 Rowan Strong, 'The Oxford Movement and the British Empire: Newman, Manning and the Jerusalem Bishopric', in *The Oxford Movement: Europe and the Wider World 1830–1930*, ed. Stewart J. Brown and Peter Nockles (Cambridge, 2012), 78–98 at 79; Pusey to Harrison, 17 February 1840, PH, Pusey MS; Pusey to Harrison, 17 February 1840, PH, Pusey MS; Pusey, *Letter to Jelf*, 40, 50ff., 84; 92 and 111ff. (on Jerusalem bishopric); Liddon, *Life of Pusey*, ii, 275: Pusey to Harrison, 22 January 1842, PH, Pusey MS.

83 A.P. Perceval, *A Vindication of Proceedings Relative to the Mission of Bishop Alexander to Jerusalem* (London, 1843); Greaves, 'Jerusalem Bishopric', 347; E.B. Pusey, *A Letter to His Grace the Archbishop of Canterbury, on Some Circumstances Connected with the Present Crisis in the English Church* (London, 1842), 104–05.

84 *Statement of Proceedings Relating to the Establishment of a Bishopric of the United Church of England and Ireland*, [published by authority] (London, 1841), 6.

Howley strongly disapproved of a Memorial from Oxford Diocesan clergy which Bagot forwarded to him in January 1842, complaining about the choice of Frederick William as the Prince of Wales's godfather. It would obviously seem a studied insult, not only to the King but also to Queen Victoria herself. He cited a few precedents. Howley gave Bagot (who was constitutionally most unsuited to it) the trickiest of challenges – to shut the agitators up, without seeming to stifle their protest.[85] James Hope (later Hope-Scott, a Scottish lawyer and Fellow of Merton College whose path to conversion to Rome in 1851 was marked by ever more determined Tractarian views) had met Sir Robert Inglis, MP for Oxford University, Benjamin Harrison, Bunsen and his associate Abeken in a final attempt to thwart the scheme. Hope wanted the candidates proposed for consecration to be subject to approval by majority vote of the Archbishop of Canterbury and his fellow bishops. He secured a meeting, in company with Inglis, with Howley and urged him to avoid any suggestion that the Church of England was Protestant, but Howley was happy that it was so. He was in this, as in everything else, a typical High Churchman.[86] The more advanced Tractarians thought all this naked Erastianism. Palmer's petition to Howley attacked the suggested bishopric first because it would interfere in the prior jurisdiction of the Oriental Churches and second on the question of subscription to the Confession of Augsburg and his concerns about the admission of Lutherans and Calvinists into the ministrations of an Anglican bishop. He and his fellows were deeply alarmed, feeling that their allegiance was due to the Church of England 'as a Catholic Church and not a Protestant persuasion'.[87] Newman solemnly disowned the Archbishop's actions and later identified the issue as the one which 'brought me onto the beginning of the end' of his Anglican days. Even Keble was in two minds about whether Newman's approach was wise.[88]

Howley thought that protests about the jurisdiction of the new bishop were based on a false premise. Even the Patriarch of Constantinople had no jurisdiction except over the members of his own Church. One had to consider communions not localities. If that were not the case there would be no justification for allowing a minister in Malta or anywhere else in Europe where there had been clergy under the jurisdiction of the Bishop of London for many

85 Howley to Bagot, 15 January 1842, PH, Pusey MS; cf. Howley to Perceval, 15 January 1842, PH, Pusey MS.

86 Robert Ornsby (ed.), *Memoir of James Robert Hope-Scott* (London, 1884), i, 286–89.

87 Palmer of Magdalen to Howley, [November 1841], PH, Pusey MS.

88 Copy Newman's protest against bishopric of Jerusalem to Bagot, 11 November 1841, PH, Pusey MS; Newman, *Apologia pro Vita Sua*, 136; Keble to Newman, 15 November 1841, KCL, Keble MS.

years. If the Bishop in Jerusalem (a carefully chosen title) invaded the rights of Greek Prelates or seized their churches like some Latins, then there *would* be cause for complaint.[89] Churton was not alone in finding the 32-year-old deacon's censure of the 76-year-old Primate insufferable. He told Pusey that Newman and Palmer of Magdalen's protests would just seem an attempt to weaken Howley and Blomfield's authority: what difference was there between the new bishop's appointment and Bishop Luscombe's to the West Indies? Churton obviously thought none.[90]

Howley did later admit in his meeting with Hope and Inglis that the scheme had been put into operation too hastily.[91] He outlined the final details of the bishopric in a letter to King Frederick William of June 1842. Ordinands from German congregations would subscribe to the Nicene, Apostles' and Athanasian creeds. Young Germans who came for confirmation would be instructed and the rite would be administered according to the Prayer Book. Gladstone correctly believed that Howley and Blomfield were utterly opposed to obliterating the broad distinction between a Church which had maintained Apostolic succession and one which had not, whatever its tenets were now. King Frederick William caused them both considerable embarrassment by encouraging the notion in Prussia that the English hierarchy felt that the two Churches were on an equal footing. Reading German accounts of the scheme suggesting not the assumption of German Protestants into the Anglican Church, the theme which had been played to placate High Churchmen in England, but a union based upon the existing principles of agreement of the Anglican Church with German Protestantism made Gladstone much more uneasy about the scheme.[92]

Michael Solomon Alexander was appointed bishop. A converted Prussian Jew who was Professor of Hebrew at King's College London, he seemed, and should have been, well suited. Howley's Letter Commendatory of Alexander to 'the Prelates and Bishops of the Ancient and Apostolic Churches in Syria and the Countries adjacent' was exceptionally carefully drafted. Alexander's mission went only so far: 'not to intermeddle in any way with the jurisdiction of the Prelates or other Ecclesiastical Dignitaries bearing rule in the Churches of the East; but to shew them due reverence and honour'.[93] Alexander was

89 Howley to Perceval, 27 October 1841, PH, Pusey MS.

90 Churton to Pusey, 9 December 1841, PH, Pusey MS; Churton to Perceval, 1 May 1843, PH, Pusey MS.

91 Ornsby, *Memoir of Hope-Scott*, i, 286–89.

92 Copy Howley to King Frederick William, 18 June 1842, BL, Add MS 44683, ff. 92–106; Welch, 'Anglican Churchmen', 199–200; Ornsby, *Memoir of Hope-Scott*, i, 295.

93 W.H. Hechler, *The Jerusalem Bishopric* (London, 1883), 39.

an unmitigated disaster. He attacked the Turkish Government as a 'usurped authority' in his first sermon in Jerusalem. Aberdeen, now Foreign Secretary, urged Howley to send a 'friendly admonition' of this habit post-haste. He obliged immediately.[94]

Although he had sometimes been cast as caught hopelessly between the rock of the need to please Queen Victoria and King Frederick William and the hard place of making the scheme palatable as possible to High Churchmen, which was only possible by trimming his principles and agreeing to something which he did not quite like, Howley never regretted his involvement in the scheme. He was stronger than ever in support of his actions when Perceval started agonising about his own involvement two years later.

> I should not have been justified before God and the Church if I had neglected any opening which might eventually lead to the healing of those divisions in the Christian Church, which have originated in the corruptions and usurpations of Rome, and have mutilated the fair proportions of the Catholic Church in many of the Churches which have renounced Romish error. I can imagine no greater blessing for Christendom, than the reunion of the different professions in one faith and one Church ... the Ch. of Rome would I believe be the last to renounce the errors by insisting on what she repels [*sic*] all others from her Communion.[95]

Rowan Strong shows how the launch of the Colonial Bishoprics Fund was given pace by the High Churchmen who believed that supported by the State or not, there was a close connection between the nature of the divine commission to spread the faith throughout the world and 'her obligation to extend the apostolic principle of episcopacy'.[96] This was at the root of the support from High Churchmen like W.F. Hook. In 1841 Howley chaired a meeting of the Colonial Bishoprics Fund, a favourite cause of Blomfield, and spoke of the great influence that a bishop's ministry would bring to bear on the morals and religion of a colonial population. So the Church should continue to inaugurate colonial dioceses with or without government support.[97]

---

94 Aberdeen to Howley, 3 March 1842, BL Add MS 43195, f. 91; Howley to Aberdeen, 4 March 1842, BL Add MS 43195, f. 93.

95 Howley to Perceval, 20 February 1844, PH, Pusey MS.

96 Strong, 'Oxford Movement and the British Empire', 95.

97 Rowan Strong, *Anglicanism and the British Empire c.1700–1850* (Oxford, 2007), 200–201.

Pusey's Letter and Howley's Anti-Tractarian Critics, 1842

William Rowe Lyall (one of Howley's London chaplains and Archdeacon of Maidstone since 1841) reported a long conversation with Howley about the state of the Oxford Movement to Bagot in January 1842. Howley displayed keen awareness of how difficult Bagot's position had been in Oxford. Howley thought that Pusey had accepted his advice that the Tractarians should choose total silence, neither publishing any further material nor answering any attacks made upon them. For whatever reason, the advice had not been followed. Howley now believed that they must make a formal statement of their true theological position and he was especially taken with William Goode's hugely detailed publication, in two volumes totalling 1,446 pages, *The Divine Rule of Faith and Practice*, which took on the Tractarians – on their own ground. Goode compared Pusey, Newman and Keble's views of 'patristical' tradition with the 'Romish' Church's view of the authority of the Fathers' writings against Scripture and made frequent use of the Caroline Divines to bolster his own case.[98]

Howley made it clear that his own view of Pusey and his friends would be diminished if they left such a book unchallenged. He wanted answers on Goode's factual claims, not more polemic. If Pusey and Newman believed that their position was based on the authority of the Ancient and Anglican Fathers, now they could prove it. Lyall wanted Bagot to persuade Pusey and Newman to produce such a work.[99] The Tractarians had found in Goode a theological adversary worthy of them. A future editor of the *Christian Observer* (1847–49), and no bigot, his knowledge of historical theology, ecclesiastical history and law marked him out as one of the most learned evangelicals of the day.[100]

Pusey's *A Letter to His Grace the Archbishop of Canterbury, on Some Circumstances Connected with the Present Crisis in the English Church* (1842) had its origins in his visit to Addington Palace to stay with Howley and later correspondence with Harrison about the episcopal Charges which had dealt with Tract 90.[101] Pusey claimed that all had the liberty to claim what was Catholic in the Church of England and reject the un-Catholic. So it was 'shallow and false' to ascribe the tendency towards 'Romanism' to the Tracts.

---

98 The book's second edition in 1853 saw it expanded to three volumes. By that time Goode thought that he had been thoroughly vindicated by Newman and others going to Rome.

99 Lyall to Bagot, 14 January 1842, PH, Pusey MS.

100 Toon, *Evangelical Theology*, 6.

101 Liddon, *Life of Pusey*, ii, 275; Pusey, *Letter to the Archbishop*, 9; Pusey to Hope, 27 September 1841, in Ornsby, *Memoir of Hope-Scott*, ii, 5; Harrison to Pusey, 15 January 1842, PH, Pusey MS.

He hid (as Tractarians were wont to do) behind his responsibility to his own bishop, and not to any other. But he was not coy about attacking other bishops' inadequate statements of Catholic truth.[102] Pusey expounded Tractarian qualms about the Church of England's behaviour: that it failed to build on the foundation laid, it undervalued good works, regular devotion, self-discipline, it 'but little' appreciated the doctrine of the Sacraments and had no thought at all of the Church as the mystical body of Christ. The Tractarians had not set themselves to 'oppose' but simply to 'supply what was lacking'. Here he included the explanation of his own early support for the Jerusalem Bishopric referred to above.[103] Liddon said that Howley had complimented him on the publication. In 1881, Pusey repeated what he had said in the Historical Preface to Tract 90, that none of the bishops had understood the Tractarians' aims but Howley.[104]

Newman was initially unenthusiastic about the prospect of Pusey writing the *Letter* at all, fearing that Harrison wanted Pusey to say the sorts of things that Harrison would say.[105] Their Oxford opponents thought it unbearably self-righteous and arrogant. It was certainly bluntly critical of several bishops by name which was not Pusey's normal practice.[106] Goode soon responded with *The Case As It Is*. This was a crisper, much briefer presentation of the arguments he had used in his major work. He accused the Tractarians of departing from the Anglican consensus of the primacy of Scripture and attacked them over Apostolical Succession, quoting Hooker and Bancroft against it. He used the same method systematically over Eucharistic sacrifice, transubstantiation, justification, sin after baptism, reserve in communicating religious knowledge, invocation of saints, purgatory and prayers for the dead, pardons, images and relics. Tractarian ambivalence towards the Glorious Revolution particularly galled him. The 'Tractators' were guilty of little less than Popery in Tract 90.[107] Goode next turned his fire on Bishop Bagot for being soft on the Tractarians, since they had claimed to obey him.[108]

It was Howley's calm reaction to Pusey's *Letter* which gave rise to the description of Harrison as a Puseyite which opened this chapter. Such a

102 Pusey, *Letter to the Archbishop*, 39-40.

103 Pusey, *Letter to the Archbishop*, 111ff.

104 Pusey to [?], 21 June 1881, PH, Pusey MS.

105 Liddon, *Life of Pusey*, ii, 277; Nockles, *Oxford Movement in Context*, 297 (n. 132).

106 Nockles, *Oxford Movement in Context*, 309–10.

107 William Goode, *The Case As It Is: Or a Reply to the Letter of Dr Pusey to His Grace the Archbishop of Canterbury* (London, 1842), 9–15, 44 (on Tract 90).

108 William Goode, *Some Difficulties in the late Charge of the Lord Bishop of Oxford, Respectfully Printed Out in a Letter to his Lordship* (London, 1842), 5, 8.

description, if meant to indicate that Howley and his chaplain were in thrall to Pusey or the Tractarians more generally, was very wide of the mark. There was no doubt that Harrison's personal friendship and Pusey's own more cautious personality meant on occasion that they seemed to have much in common and as has been shown extensively above, this can hardly be surprising. Howley, Harrison and the Zs were particularly critical of the tone of some Tractarian campaigning and highly sensitive to any sense of a change from their view of Rome or the Reformation. Certainly to describe Benjamin Harrison as a 'Puseyite' would have raised a wry smile from Pusey, Newman and Keble. The other person charged as the 'calumniator of Foxe' was S.R. Maitland, no great apologist for the Tractarians. In 1838 they had manoeuvred him out of his brief editorship of the *British Critic*, even though Edward Churton had backed his appointment to the hilt.[109] He had published an attack on Tract 89's view of 'primitive antiquity'. At times, especially as with the appointment of Hampden as Regius Professor, the Tractarians and the old High Churchmen stood completely united; at others, as with the publication of Froude's *Remains*, the fault line seemed stark. Yet in most controversies there was a variety of opinion and, as has been seen, this meant that the interplay between the two groups was somewhat subtle. In addition, there was no doubt that Newman, Keble and Pusey respected the office of the Archbishop and Howley himself personally, which had a beneficial influence.

[109] Nockles, *Oxford Movement in Context*, 278.

Chapter 6
The 1840s

The Education Bills of 1839 and 1843

Howley's distrust of Lord John Russell, then Home Secretary, was only increased by his announcement in 1839 that the annual education grant would rise from £20,000 to £30,000 and that he intended to set up an Educational Committee of the Privy Council with the right to inspect schools. Russell made it clear that he did not want any bishops on the committee, and that religious affiliation was in his opinion irrelevant to its membership. It was not that there would be no religious instruction in schools but that it would, as in previous interdenominational schemes, be 'limited to Biblical generalities rather than catechetical indoctrination'.[1] Always ready to think the worst of him, Howley objected with all the vehemence he could muster to the subversion of the Church of England's traditional role in providing and supervising education, and untapped feelings about the 'dangers' of allowing various dissenting denominations an equal hand in the process, which would relativise religious authority and encourage a tendency towards voluntaryism about Christianity itself, views which were little changed in style or content from those he had expressed more than twenty-five years earlier in his earliest years as Bishop of London.[2]

Blomfield spoke for Howley and the great majority of Anglican clergy when he attacked the tendency towards non-denominational religious instruction as

> in some cases uniform, even as the barren surface of the desert is uniform ... They talk indeed of neutrality in religion – neutrality in religion! To be neutral in religion (on the part of a religious teacher) is treason against the truth.[3]

1 R.A. Soloway, *Prelates and People: Ecclesiastical Social Thought, 1783–1852* (London and Toronto, 1969), 400.

2 *Hansard*, 3 May 1839, 3rd series, xlvii, col. 764.

3 *A Memoir of Charles James Blomfield, D.D., Bishop of London*, ed. A. Blomfield (2nd edn, London, 1864), 195–96.

Of course the bishops did not want non-Anglican schools abolished; it was the move to alter the funding of the Anglican educational societies that was unacceptable to them. Howley thought it impossible to teach two systems of religion in one school and the subject must either be excluded or taught as a single system of doctrine since it was wrong to teach people that there was any system as good as their own.[4] Russell's poor handling of the row conspired to force the temporary withdrawal of the idea. Russell acknowledged that fears that religious instruction would be ended in schools were powerful, although he attacked those who had complained that the change would have created 'religious indifferentism' since so many had no idea at all of the most basic concepts of Christianity. Lord Brougham was furious both that Russell had been routed by his critics and with Russell for his ineptitude.[5]

Russell's public reverse was an embarrassment but the intransigence of the Chancellor of the Exchequer, Thomas Spring Rice (from 1835 to 1839), was a much more substantial matter, and meant that the bishops' fears were grounded in a fair amount of evidence. Even his own Prime Minister Lord Melbourne found him narrow minded.[6] Despite a parliamentary grant of £10,000 being made towards education, neither the National Society nor the British and Foreign Schools Society had received any funding towards 'model schools' (schools for poor children), nor had the National Society received monies towards a proposed training institute to be built in Westminster. A greatly protracted and detailed correspondence covering the years 1835–39 was published by the National Society to protest at the delays.[7] Russell's plan was the subject of many petitions and protests to the Queen but he held firm and the Order was passed, following a two vote majority in favour of the £30,000 grant in the House of Commons. Howley continued to campaign against the bill, presenting several petitions in July 1839.[8]

Howley had statistics which showed that in 1837, the National Society was running 17,341 schools which educated 1,000,087 children. He wanted a school in every parish, under the guidance of bishops and cathedral chapters. Howley wanted clergy to think of running of a school as equally important to doing duty in church and so he was keen to drive a wedge between parliamentary grants and the Privy Council Committee. He lauded the parliamentary grants to

4 *Hansard*, 3 May 1839, 3rd series, xlvii, col. 764.

5 *Hansard*, 3rd series, xlvii, cols 1378, 1382.

6 'Thomas Spring Rice', *DNB*, xviii, 1921, 835–37.

7 *Correspondence of the National Society with the Lords of the Treasury and with the Committee of Council on Education*, ed. John Sinclair (London, 1839).

8 *Hansard*, 3rd series, xlvii, col. 1237.

the National Society and even to the non-denominational Lancastrian Society – which *was* different from what he would have said as a youthful bishop. He loathed the Privy Council Committee proposals, which would avoid Parliament altogether in the long run and leave schools and societies at the mercy of a board of ministers with large discretionary powers. He proposed a series of resolutions which would reaffirm the Church's central role in the religious education of the nation's children.[9] The Marquess of Lansdowne, Lord President of the Council, asked whether Howley really believed that the Church of England had a right to educate the millions who were not members of the Church. He was sarcastically happy at least that Howley was not completely opposed to non-Anglican schools receiving funding. Howley's motion, which praised the traditional view of the Church's role in the education of the whole nation, was passed by a majority of over a hundred, with a large episcopal turn-out and only Maltby, Stanley and Otter of Chichester dissenting.[10]

A parallel controversy flared up four years later over Peel's proposals to provide education for children working in factories. Peel and his colleagues were wary of dramatic changes, bearing in mind the outcry of 1839–40. As a Tory administration they were more in the bishops' confidence and wanted to increase state funding of education little by little. The Home Secretary, Sir James Graham, proposed compulsory scriptural education throughout the week, enforceable by statute. Unlike the situation in 1839 he proposed that as well as biblical exegesis three mornings a week would be given to the catechism and doctrine of the Church of England. A conscience clause was to be built in for the children of Dissenters. What really rankled was the clause stipulating that the headmaster of each school must be an Anglican.[11] The situation rapidly became one with which no one was satisfied. Churchmen opposed various provisions amongst Peel's proposals. Fear of Puseyite clergy increased the antagonism of the Dissenters. Howley told Peel of the National Society's decision to raise a fund towards establishing church schools in the manufacturing and mining districts which could be totally under the Church's control. They were to appeal for subscriptions, the Archbishops and the Bishop of London having pledged £500 each over five years. He asked that Peel should recommend the Queen to accept the patronage of the appeal. Peel, with far more reason than Melbourne, Russell or Spring Rice could ever have had, was genuinely bemused by the Society's proposals and felt let down by the Anglican hierarchy. He predicted

9 *Hansard*, 3rd series, xlvii, cols 1238–41, 1252–54.

10 *Hansard*, 3rd series, xlvii, cols 1256–66, 1332–33.

11 Welch, 'Bishop Blomfield', 490ff.

great misfortune for the Church if there were schism not only between Churchmen and Dissenters but amongst Churchmen themselves.[12] Criticised by Anglicans and Dissenters the Government had no option but to withdraw its plans. A series of negotiations which began in 1847 culminated in 1849 with an agreement to a limited form of inspection of schools and bore fruit in the creation of training colleges for teachers.[13]

The Oxford Regius Professorships, 1841

Charles Perry's pamphlet *Clerical Education, Considered with Especial Reference to the Universities* was one in a long line of calls for reform especially of his own university, Cambridge. He thought that theological colleges were always likely to reinforce like-minded ordinands in common prejudices. He thought that a Professor of Pastoral Theology in the Theology faculties would in effect provide formation and instruction on the clerical office without the particular influence of churchmanship. It is hardly necessary to add that this would have been entirely consonant with the prevailing orthodoxy of the two universities and therefore popular with the great majority of the bishops.

Specifically in Oxford, Edward Cardwell, Principal of St Alban Hall, had raised the issue of the teaching of divinity with the Hebdomadal Council, and the Dean of Christ Church, Thomas Gaisford, asked that its committee dealing with the matter show Howley its correspondence for his comments.[14] Howley himself had supported making candidates for orders follow a uniform system of study in theology at the universities since at least 1835.[15] The High Churchmen were impressed with what their influence had achieved at the new University of Durham, and especially Hugh James Rose's appointment as Professor of Ecclesiastical History there. As a result, Charles Thorp, Archdeacon of Durham and the Warden of the university, got the bishops to accept Durham graduates for ordination with remarkably little trouble. Bishop Bathurst of Norwich even

12 Howley to Peel, 5 July 1843, BL Add MS 40530, f. 409; Peel to Howley, 9 July 1843, BL Add MS 40530, f. 411.

13 'Education in the Manufacturing and Mining Districts', BL Add MS 40530, f. 411; Welch, 'Bishop Blomfield', 501–05.

14 'Memoranda respecting the Professorships of Pastoral Theology and Eccl. History and the Statute de Disciplina Theologica', 20–21, Bodl Lib, OUA, NW 21.5.

15 Charles Perry, *Clerical Education, Considered with Especial Reference to the Universities; in a Letter to the Right Reverend the Lord Bishop of Lichfield* (London, 1841), 14–18, 23; F.W.B. Bullock, *A History of Training for the Ministry of the Church of England in England and Wales from 1800 to 1874* (St Leonards-on-Sea, 1955), 56.

considered the degree better than Oxford or Cambridge.[16] Only one bishop, George Murray of Rochester, expressed unease but on the different grounds that he feared there were too many graduates chasing ordination already.[17] High Churchmen of all stamps wanted Oxford as well as Durham to have a professor of 'church polity'. The Tractarians were very keen that there should also be a chair in liturgy and related subjects. The Heads of Houses had vetoed that idea, but in the end the professorship of Pastoral Theology provided a reasonable amount of what the Tractarians wanted.[18]

Howley made reference to a plan of some years before 1840, which he had hoped would combat the combined lack of knowledge of many ordinands about what they were required to do as pastors, but Burton's death and the furore over Hampden had seen the end of it. Howley's ideas were modelled on the practice of the Navy 'in which no one can obtain a Lieutenant's Commission without passing an examination before a regular board and being reported fit'. Howley had wanted to see boards of examiners in the two universities without whose certificates of 'fitness' confirmed by a 'quasi degree' of the university, no one would qualify for ordination. Howley rejected the complaint that this would encroach on a bishop's rights since a bishop would still have power to examine, and would be relieved from the worry of rejecting incompetent candidates or 'admitting them from motives of kindness'. He wondered with gentle humour which rarely emerges in his correspondence whether the time was 'yet right' for such proposals since professors might dislike an examination that could reveal their efficiency as well as the progress of the students. His own concerns that private schools of theology in which 'peculiar systems' of doctrine were taught would become the order of the day had led him to hesitate even about the advisability of theological colleges in cathedral closes.[19]

Howley thought that even Lord John Russell would support a scheme if the university authorities were keen. The problem was the potential clash between the professors already in post and this was not just the problem of Hampden, but intrinsic in creating new roles with a new board of professors. Gaisford agreed that this was a significant issue. Meanwhile Gaisford cooled towards the idea of a Professor of Pastoral Theology and thought it much more sensible to learn the duties of a parish priest whilst a deacon in a parish. Both he and Howley were

---

16 University of Durham, Thorp Correspondence, vol. 5, ff. 139ff.; Bathurst to Thorp, 7 February 1834, f. 142.

17 Phillpotts to Thorp, [n.d.], f. 166a; Murray to Thorp, 19 February 1834, f. 168.

18 P.B. Nockles, 'An Academic Counter-Revolution: Newman and Tractarian Oxford's Idea of a University', *History of Universities*, x (1991), 164–65.

19 Howley to Gaisford, 9 October 1840, Bodl Lib, OUA, NW 21.5, ff. 12–15.

wary of creating a chair of 'Biblical Criticism' because of the patent dangers of yet more controversy.[20] Gaisford pushed harder for a chair in Ecclesiastical History, and was getting keener on a chair in some sort of biblical exegesis, possibly amalgamated with the Regius Professorship of Greek and given a canonry of Christ Church, thereby having equal status with Hebrew.[21] Nevertheless the final scheme was for Pastoral Theology and Ecclesiastical History.

Howley proposed taking the matter to the Duke of Wellington, as Chancellor of the University. He was still nervous of asking a Whig administration to create such positions because of the men they might choose to fill them. Gaisford wanted him to suggest the plan to the Government and to keep the Heads of Houses in the dark. The Vice-Chancellor and Wellington agreed to the scheme.[22] The Heads of Houses began to discuss what they wanted both from the new and the existing professorships. Howley did not wish to discuss the possibility of new chairs at Oxford with the rest of the bench, although he considered it a foregone conclusion that bishops would require certificates from the new professors if they were approved by the university. He was very keen that the chairs be set up, whether or not the new incumbents could have canonries at Christ Church immediately.[23] Howley put a scheme for the two professorships to Peel in late 1841. Peel's conditions for appointment were the same as those he used for bishoprics, persons 'free from suspicion of peculiar notions' who had not only the learning required in a professor but also the tact to deal with the breakdown in working relationships between the three existing professors.[24]

Peel thought that the bishops should be consulted before a plan affecting the whole of theological education was put into effect. Howley disagreed. He told Peel that they had agreed to the establishment of the professorships in principle and the various statutes suspending canonries and redistributing resources were waiting to take effect. Like Howley, the Heads of Houses on the committee wanted the chairs established whether or not there were canonries vacant.[25]

20 Gaisford to Howley, 17 October 1840, Bodl Lib, OUA, NW 21.5, ff. 16–19.

21 Howley to Gaisford, 29 October 1840, Bodl Lib, OUA, NW 21.5, ff. 20–21; Gaisford to Howley, n.d., Bodl Lib, OUA, NW 21.5, ff. 24–27.

22 Howley to Gaisford, 29 October 1840, Bodl Lib, OUA, NW 21.5, ff. 30–31; Copy Gaisford to Howley, 6 November 1840, Bodl Lib, OUA, NW 21.5, f. 22; Draft Gaisford to Howley, 21 November 1840, Bodl Lib, OUA, NW 21.5, ff. 34–35.

23 Howley to Gaisford, 12 February 1841, Bodl Lib, OUA, NW 21.5, ff. 44–45; Howley to Gaisford, 5 March 1841, Bodl Lib, OUA, NW 21.5, ff. 50–51.

24 Howley to Gaisford, 19 November 1841, Bodl Lib, OUA, NW 21.5, f. 58; Howley to Gaisford, 22 November 1841, Bodl Lib, OUA, NW 21.5, f. 60.

25 Copy Peel to Howley, 27 November 1841, Bodl Lib, Dep d 4, Wynter MS, f. 128; Copy Howley to Peel, 29 November 1841, Bodl Lib, Dep d 4, Wynter MS, f. 130.

Gaisford wanted Robert Hussey, already at Christ Church, for the chair of Ecclesiastical History and suggested Benjamin Harrison as a potential Professor of Pastoral Theology. Howley agreed that Harrison would be an excellent candidate but he thought it a bad idea for both professors to come from Christ Church. His preference was for C.A. Ogilvie, a former Fellow of Balliol and another of his chaplains. In any event Peel had a definite preference for a man with parochial experience (as Ogilvie had and Harrison did not). Hussey and Ogilvie were appointed.[26]

Phillpotts immediately announced that he would require attendance at the courses of both professors before ordaining curates. A voluntary examination in Theology was also begun at Edward Hawkins' suggestion but it was a damp squib. There were only seven successful candidates from 1844 to 1863.[27] Ecclesiastical History was as much Patristic Theology as anything and it is all too easy to see a connection with the content of Howley's own lectures as Regius Professor of Divinity. Since the provisions of the Cathedrals Act 1840 (Act 3 and 4 Vict. c. 113) only came into operation on the death of office holders, Ogilvie and Hussey were given £300 a year until they became canons of Christ Church. Hussey never did so before his death in 1856. The Regius Professor of Ecclesiastical History was to have the seventh stall on the death of the incumbent and Frederick Barnes (who had succeeded Howley in 1809 when Howley became Regius Professor) came within months of holding it for fifty years when he died in 1859 at the age of 88.[28]

Revamping the arrangements for the Oxford professors did not come without concerns. The 1842 statute which had created the new chairs also made the Regius Professor chairman of a five-member theology board. Many of Hampden's opponents quailed at the thought of him having absolute power over examination subjects and there was a notorious disagreement when Hampden deliberately tried to exclude the Tractarian R.G. Macmullen in 1844 from gaining a BD. Nonetheless this was far outweighed in Howley's mind by the positive value of having two new professors, both High Churchmen, who

---

26 Draft Gaisford to Howley, n.d., Bodl Lib, OUA, NW 21.5, ff. 62–63; Howley to Gaisford, 21 December 1841, Bodl Lib, OUA, NW 21.5, f. 64; Howley to Peel, 10 January 1842, BL Add MS 40499, f. 176; Howley to Gaisford, 6 January 1842, Bodl Lib, OUA, NW 21.5, f. 70; Wynter to Wellington, 16 December 1841, BL Add MS 40459, f. 113; Wellington to Peel, 22 December 1841, BL Add MS 40459, f. 118.

27 Henry Phillpotts, *Charge to the Clergy of the Diocese of Exeter* (1842), 3; Ince, *Past History*, 39.

28 J. Le Neve, *Fasti Ecclesiae Anglicanae* (1864), ii, 524ff.; *DNB*, ed. L. Stephen and S. Lee, 1921, x, 330–31 (Hussey) and *DNB*, xiv, 911–12 (Ogilvie).

enjoyed his complete confidence.[29] It took time for the new professors' function to be fully appreciated. Ogilvie complained that despite his lectures being well attended, a full four years after the Theological Statute was passed Scholars in Theology were not coming forward for examination. Howley was still looking forward to the day when 'academical testimonials of proficiency' would be required from candidates for orders – that is, some explicit training in pastoralia and theology. He thought that the good example of those trained at Durham and King's College London would probably be the key to getting this required of all ordinands.[30]

The North Wales Bishoprics, 1843–1846 and the New Dioceses Commission, 1847

An Order in Council of 12 December 1838 put into effect the Ecclesiastical Commission's own proposal that at the next vacancy in the diocese of St Asaph or Bangor, those sees would be united, keeping both cathedrals, and a new see would be created at Manchester funded by the surplus revenues. This proposal was a logical outcome of the commission's dual brief: to reorganise the Church's revenues so a better ministry could be given to the industrial North and not to increase the numbers of bishops. The proposals seemed relatively innocuous and opposition to the measure was muted at that time. Bishop Bethell knew that it should in theory be possible to administer both dioceses together since they contained only 255 parishes between them, whereas the diocese of Winchester alone had over 1,000. But there was unease, which had time to develop into full blown opposition whilst both bishops were still in position. Five years after the Order in Council St Asaph clergy sent Howley a Memorial saying that the circumstances of North Wales – the language, poverty, geographical problems and the prevalence of dissent – needed more not fewer dioceses.[31] Very soon after the rumblings of discontent about the measure began to be heard, Howley tried to get Peel to reverse the Government's policy of implementing the proposals of a commission which he himself had chaired. It was not a dignified position and

[29] Chadwick, *Victorian Church: Part One*, 205; *British Critic*, xxxii (1842), 161–65; *The New Examination for Divinity Degrees: Some Hints as to the Character of the Statute now Proposed by Convocation* (Oxford, 1844), 4–5; Nockles, *Oxford Movement in Context*, 242.

[30] Draft Ogilvie to Howley, 19 March 1846, Bodl Lib MS Eng Lett d 123 f. 11; Howley to Ogilvie, 6 April 1846, Bodl Lib MS Eng Lett d 123 ff. 12–13.

[31] R.L. Brown, *Lord Powis and the Extension of the Episcopate* (Cardiff, 1989), 14, 18, 4; Burns, *Diocesan Revival in the Church of England*, 196–97.

did not impress. Amalgamating dioceses had been one of the most unpopular proposals of the 1830s and Howley had never resolved his worries about it. He thought that every bishop wanted the proposals reversed. Even mild men like Bagot had ridiculed the idea in years past.[32] Howley had a face-saving scheme. If Peel announced that a diocese of Manchester was so urgent that the Church could not wait for the death of one or other of the bishops of St Asaph or Bangor to release funds, then he could endow Manchester from other sources and avoid the wrath of the clergy of North Wales. Howley wanted Peel to suggest the creation of two or three other bishoprics in the most populous dioceses when the Episcopal Fund was large enough. He believed that this would add to the credibility of changing the policy on the North Wales bishoprics.[33]

Peel knew how much the Ecclesiastical Commission and the Government would be compromised if he agreed. He feared the novelty of creating bishops outside the House of Lords even more since trying to increase the numbers of bishops in the House of Lords would have been political madness. Lord Powis, who led the opposition to the amalgamation, had already suggested that a new bishop could exist outside the Lords and Blomfield had rebuked him. There was a strong emotional attachment to the belief that bishops sat in the House of Lords by virtue of baronies and by 'immemorial prescription'. Howley knew that the consequences of rejecting the proposed bishoprics would be worse than accepting on these unsatisfactory grounds.[34] But the agitation which this proposal created prepared the ground for the inevitable abolition of the artificial constraint on episcopal numbers and the carving out of new dioceses in the latter part of the nineteenth century. Goulburn, like many politicians, wanted neither more bishops without seats in the House of Lords nor more bishops with the right to sit there.

Whatever his sympathies towards those who wanted to reverse amalgamation, Howley had to be loyal to the legislation which had passed through Parliament at the suggestion of a commission of which he was chairman. Howley could not welcome Powis' motion, however much he had tried to get his wishes implemented behind the scenes. Nevertheless by 1844 the only bishops voting to retain the policy of uniting sees were commissioners. Howley told Longley (the first Bishop of Ripon) that he fully supported the erection of a see at Manchester

32 Richard Bagot, *A Charge Delivered to the Clergy of the Diocese of Oxford ... at his Third Visitation, July and August 1838* (2nd edn, Oxford, 1838), 9–10.

33 Howley to Peel, 22 April 1843, BL Add MS 40527, f. 356.

34 'Historical note' [sent by Ogilvie to Howley, 23 February 1847], Bodl Lib MS Eng Lett d 123 ff. 14–15; Howley to Ogilvie, 2 March 1847, Bodl Lib MS Eng Lett d 123 ff. 16–17; P.S. Morrish, 'The Manchester Clause', *Church Quarterly*, i (1969), 324.

and two or three others, probably in Nottingham and Cornwall.[35] Agitation in North Wales continued. Howley tried to re-open the subject with Peel in 1845 by playing on the strength of Dissent and the poor condition of Anglican churches there. He told Peel that the Commissioners had not been aware of this when they recommended uniting the sees: they simply had statistics of the small numbers of benefices and low population. Kaye of Lincoln had already said publicly that he had only agreed to the union between St Asaph and Bangor because he despaired of obtaining an additional bishopric with a seat in the Lords. So he had changed his mind and would not oppose Lord Powis' motion.[36] Peel told Howley that he would not guarantee to support Powis' Bill if it came to the Commons. He was very wary of upsetting an arrangement which had been recommended by commissioners and had secured the support of both Whigs and Tories. If the plan were abolished and another bishopric was created with a seat in the House of Lords this would be an essential alteration to the scheme of Church Reform and would weaken the Ecclesiastical Commission's authority by encouraging more of the same on their other proposals. It would give the Church's opponents in Parliament a field day.[37]

All but four of the 173 clergy of St Asaph diocese signed another Memorial to Howley in 1846 opposing the union with Bangor. After Bishop Carey of St Asaph died, Lord John Russell (now Prime Minister) did not rush headlong into amalgamation and eventually conceded that he would establish Manchester with different funds.[38] Howley and Blomfield tried a last ditch attempt to persuade Russell to add new bishoprics with seats in the Lords to the present number.[39] Howley wanted time to discuss the situation with the whole bench partly because he still felt cagey about some criticisms of high handedness which had been levelled at him and Blomfield over the Jerusalem bishopric. But all Howley really could do was to brief the bishops on the Government's intentions.[40]

Sir George Grey, the new Home Secretary, felt it particularly necessary for the Bishop of Chester and someone connected with the Church in Wales to be members of the fledgling New Bishoprics Commission. Russell was considering retaining St Asaph and creating four sees, one at Manchester, one for

---

35 Brown, *Lord Powis*, 23–24; Howley to Longley, 15 June 1844, LPL, Longley Ps, i, ff. 254–55.

36 Howley to Peel, 28 April 1845, BL Add MS 40565, f. 238; Kaye to Peel, 28 April 1845, BL Add MS 40565, f. 259.

37 Peel to Howley, 30 April 1845, BL Add MS 40565, f. 264.

38 Russell to Howley, PRO, 30/22, 5C, f. 185.

39 Howley to Russell, 7 October 1846, PRO 30/22 5D, f. 94.

40 Howley to Russell, 8 December 1846, PRO 30/22, 5F, f. 94.

Nottinghamshire and part of Yorkshire, one which would make a better division of the dioceses of London and Norwich and one which would encompass Cornwall. Russell refused Howley's request that all the new bishops should have seats in the Lords. He would support a system of having a set number of bishops, sitting by rotation in order of seniority – the system which survives. Howley came to the rational conclusion that to have bishops without seats in the House of Lords was a lesser evil than to have no new bishoprics.[41]

When Howley's meeting of bishops did take place, it was much less exercised by the division or unification of St Asaph and Bangor than by Russell's new plans for reforming the Ecclesiastical Commission by introducing a paid Commissioner and the New Bishoprics Commission. Twenty-one bishops joined in expressing their disapproval of the measure. Russell's final nominations to the New Bishoprics Commission included C.R. Sumner of Winchester and Maltby of Durham as well as Howley, Harcourt, Blomfield and Kaye. The commission began to report, not only considering Russell's ideas for new sees but also drawing attention to the anomalies of previous schemes like the diocese of Rochester consisting mainly of the county of Essex, across the other side of the Medway. The bishops of Norwich and Lincoln were also unduly burdened. The commission proposed a see at Southwell, making use of the existing Collegiate Church; a see for South Yorkshire and a new see in the archdeaconry of Cornwall. The report never got beyond draft stage, as the Whigs became sceptical about increasing the episcopate beyond the bishopric of Manchester. A reference to the three further bishoprics was removed from the Bishopric of Manchester Bill.[42]

Howley's Letter of 1845

David Newsome described 1842 as the year when the Romeward movement of the Oxford Movement began in earnest. Newman's retirement to Littlemore coincided with the increasingly public profile of W.G. Ward and Frederick Oakeley. Their extreme pronouncements made Howley ever more suspicious of the Oxford men. This distrust was all pervasive and made politicians and Church leaders unduly cautious, avoiding anyone who might be tarred with the Tractarian brush. Howley had run out of patience with the trials and tribulations

41 George Grey to Russell, 9 December 1846, PRO 30/22, 5F, f. 109; Russell to Howley, 9 December 1846, PRO 30/22, 5F, f. 122; Russell to Howley, 10 December 1846, PRO 30/22, 5F, f. 130.

42 Draft Second Report of the New Bishoprics Commission, [June 1847], PRO 73/70.

in Oxford. Rather wearily he wished that the Tractarians would not do things which would inevitably bring them into difficulties. When Pusey's sermon on the Eucharist before the University of Oxford was delated on the grounds of its teaching unsound doctrine, Howley told Ogilvie that the last thing Pusey should do was publish it. Frederick Oakeley's attempt to distinguish between 'holding' and 'teaching' Roman doctrine as an Anglican priest was part of the curious deposit of apologies which kept the extreme Tractarians in the Church of England. Howley thought that Goode's *Tract XC Historically Refuted* and similar publications which scorned such reasoning were the inevitable result and could only redound to the discredit of men like Ward and Oakeley. Goode despaired of the Tractarians but equally disapproved of the silence of 'those to whom the Church has given the office of teaching' about their writings.[43]

Howley's *Letter Addressed to the Clergy and Laity of His Province* was in part a response to the furore caused by Blomfield and Phillpotts' heavy-handedness in dealing with the beginnings of ritualism. Blomfield had been exasperated by it. Advanced Tractarianism (as it was sometimes known) had been gathering strength in the diocese of London since at least 1839. Blomfield appreciated the importance which Tractarians were attaching to the Prayer Book rubrics and had always been keen on the necessity of conforming to them. His 1834 Charge had acknowledged that improvements were perfectly possible in the Liturgy but that there was no warrant for risking the peace of the Church. His 1842 Charge lambasted auricular confession, intercessions for the dead, prayers to the saints and the mixed chalice. He had approved of the Oxford Movement's strictness in observing the rubrics of the *Book of Common Prayer* and agreed that omissions were worse than unauthorised additions. He criticised those who denied that the Prayer Book taught baptismal regeneration and especially those who 'mutilated' the Office of Baptism as a result. So he did approve of apparent novelties, such as daily prayers and fasts and feasts' observance and the more frequent celebration of Holy Communion.[44]

W.H. Hale, Blomfield's Domestic Chaplain, told Norris that neither he nor Blomfield thought that the Archbishop need take action because total liturgical uniformity in every single parish was impossible to impose.[45] There

[43] Frederick Oakeley, *A Letter to the Lord Bishop of London, on a Subject Connected with the Recent Proceedings at Oxford* (London, 1845), 11; William Goode, *Tract XC Historically Refuted; or, a Reply to a Work by the Rev. F. Oakeley, Entitled 'The Subject of Tract XC Historically Examined'* (London, 1845).

[44] C.J. Blomfield, *Charge to the Clergy of the Diocese of London* (London, 1842), 23, 29–37, 49.

[45] W.H. Hale to H.H. Norris, 30 November 1842, Bodl Lib MS Eng Lett c 790, ff. 95–96.

was a concentration of powerful Evangelical clergy grouped around St Mary's, Islington whose intransigence induced Blomfield to make concessions to them. Seventeen of them told Blomfield that his directions on ceremonial would so disgust their congregations that conformity would be impossible. A weekly collection was particularly resented. Wearing a surplice had become a party badge to which they could not agree. Blomfield yielded to all their demands. The clergy announced to their parishes that services would continue unaltered. Blomfield was stunned by the turn of events and handled them poorly.[46] His insistence on strict adherence to the rubrics led to open rebellion against him in places and to obedience only where the changes were either liked or a matter of total indifference. Bishop Phillpotts issued a pastoral letter in November 1844 which also required the clergy to have a weekly collection and to preach in the surplice. The laity was in uproar. Phillpotts hung on until 23 December, when he withdrew the insistence.[47]

Howley's Letter appeared on 8 January 1845. The dissension caused by the rubrical controversy had caused him a great deal of concern in his declining years – he was now only one year short of his 80th birthday and in poor health. He had not expressed an authoritative opinion sooner partly because of the ambiguity of the rubrics, and partly from uncertainty about the powers given to the Archbishop of the Province in the preface to the *Book of Common Prayer* to pronounce on such matters. There was a long history of deviation from the rubrics. But since there was an increasing number of clergy who felt this irreconcilable with their ordination vows a diversity of practice had arisen, and had become associated with a particular theological persuasion. Howley would have preferred everyone to conform to the rubrics but knew this was impractical. He was obviously upset at the reaction to Blomfield's Charge. Benjamin Harrison's *Historical Inquiry into the True Interpretation of the Rubrics in the Book of Common Prayer* (1845) made very similar reading.

Howley thought it perfectly possible that the rubrics had not been designed to enforce rigid and universal conformity of practice and he wanted laity to understand more of why some clergy wanted to obey the rubrics, and clergy to understand that they could not make unilateral changes in the conduct of worship. He wanted an end to legal action on the disputed issues. He did not comment on specific disputes for fear of his judgments not being heeded.[48] Some

46 Malcolm Johnson, *Bustling Intermeddler? The Life and Work of Charles James Blomfield* (Leominster, 2001), 92–94; Welch, 'Bishop Blomfield', 433–38.

47 Burns, *Diocesan Revival in the Church of England*, 177.

48 William Howley, *A Letter addressed to the Clergy and Laity of his Province* (London, 1845), 6, 9, 11–12.

extreme Low Church opinion was critical but Howley had spoken sufficiently generally to avoid most controversy.[49] In Oxford the degradation of W.G. Ward and the censure of *The Ideal of a Christian Church* (1844) in which he had tried to justify an Anglican priest holding all Roman doctrine and the attempted censure of Tract 90 categorically underlined the end of an era. Gladstone and Pusey hoped that Howley would urge that the issue be left alone. Howley believed that the matter would not be 'controverted' again. In the event the resolution was vetoed by the university proctors.[50]

Bishop Hampden

Russell's appointment of Hampden as Bishop of Hereford in 1847 provided the finale to the theological controversies of Howley's twenty years at Canterbury. Howley's opinion of Hampden had changed little if at all since the controversy over his appointment as Regius Professor in 1836.[51] The depth of his distaste for Hampden found expression in the wearily clichéd story that he would rather go to the Tower of London than consecrate him. The same story was also told when Thomas Arnold was rumoured to have been made a bishop.[52] Hampden had been keen to become a bishop for several years. In 1847 Russell floated Hampden's name for Manchester 'as one qualified by his learning and virtue to adorn the Bench of Bishops'. Russell disingenuously told Howley that he would welcome his opinion about the possibility of making Hampden a bishop, because of the controversy which had surrounded him.[53] Although Howley rightly suspected that Russell's motives in getting him to give an opinion on Hampden were to have his admission that he had no reason to believe that he 'had taught any doctrine at variance with those of the Church' whilst Regius Professor in writing, he had to exonerate his publications of the same period. He refused to comment on

49 Peel to Howley, 12 January 1845, BL Add MS 40557 f. 338; Blomfield to Howley, 9 January 1845, LPL MS 2187 f. 7; Phillpotts to Howley, 8 January 1845, LPL MS 2187 f. 33.

50 See Pusey to Gladstone, 18 February 1845, PH, Pusey MS; Gladstone to Pusey, 22 February 1845, PH, Pusey MS.

51 See A.R. Ashwell, *Life of the Right Reverend Samuel Wilberforce* (London, 1880), i, 419–515.

52 For a refutation, see A.M.G. Stephenson, *The Victorian Archbishops of Canterbury* (Blewbury, 1991), 14.

53 Hampden to Melbourne, 13 July 1840, Bodl Lib, Melbourne Ps, Box 79, f. 61; Russell to Howley, 6 August 1847, Bodl Lib MS Eng Lett d 307, ff. 58–60.

Hampden's discretion or suitability for business, but played up how important these qualities would be in the first Bishop of Manchester.[54]

Russell showed what he really thought of Howley's advice after the death of the Archbishop of York later that year. Howley heartily recommended Kaye of Lincoln, a bishop for almost thirty years.[55] But Russell first offered the job to Maltby, his faithful supporter at Durham, who declined on the grounds of age (he was 77) and then to Thomas Musgrave, the Whig Bishop of Hereford, who accepted. Even Maltby thought Musgrave unimpressive.[56] Howley told Russell that Hampden's appointment would cause 'an unprecedented explosion of feeling'. Howley encountered vast opposition to the nomination.[57] Russell then took his moment to throw Howley's previous remarks back in his face. Howley had identified nothing objectionable in his writings and had not actively objected to the appointment to Hereford; all he had done was to say that a great outcry would ensue. Russell put most of the opposition down to the Tractarians, a tactic of which Hampden himself was of course fond. He received an immediate riposte from Howley that the opposition was far wider than that. If Hampden must be appointed, he thought he should make a public declaration of his belief in the doctrines of the Church.[58] Hampden was willing to do so, again telling Russell that the Tractarians were the prime movers against him. He was also wary of their friends:

> There may be some concerned who deny belonging to the party ... these borderers on a party, under the plea of impartiality are often those who work party-ends more effectually. It is some evidence of the character of the persons by whom the Archbishop is surrounded, that one of his Chaplains, Archdeacon Harrison, is an intimate associate of Dr Pusey, the Tractarian leader and well known to have adopted his views.[59]

Howley felt that for reasons of protocol it would be wrong for the Primate to sign the Remonstrance of the thirteen bishops against Hampden's nomination. Samuel Wilberforce of Oxford had cast himself in the role of crusader and was

---

54 Howley to Russell, 9 August 1847, PRO 30/22, 6E, f. 61.

55 Howley to Russell, 6 November 1847, PRO 30/22, 6G, f. 61.

56 Maltby to Russell, 9 November 1847, PRO 30/22, 6G, f. 71; Maltby to Russell, 22 November 1847, PRO 30/22, 6G, f. 215.

57 Howley to Russell, 26 November 1847, PRO 30/22, 6G, f. 259.

58 Russell to Howley, 27 November 1847, PRO 30/22, 6G, f. 261; Howley to Russell, 29 November 1847, PRO 30/22, 6G, f. 296.

59 Hampden to Russell, 1 December 1847, PRO 30/22, 6H, f. 42.

unimpressed at the reply, but his swashbuckling only got him into trouble. He signed the 'Letters of Request' which formally gave sanction to action against Hampden in the Court of the Arches and then had the humiliation of having to withdraw them, claiming that he had misunderstood their purpose and admitting that he could not find errors in Hampden's theology.[60] The bishops who signed the Remonstrance – amongst them Blomfield, Kaye, Wilberforce, Monk and Denison – all put paid to their promotion prospects by so doing. Wilberforce was frozen out of Queen Victoria and Prince Albert's intimate circle over the affair. Russell had his stock answer to every complaint about Hampden, and could also rely on the fact that the University of Oxford had required a certificate of attendance at Hampden's lectures for some years past.[61]

Phillpotts asked Russell if he had enquired explicitly of Howley whether he thought Hampden a fit person to be recommended for a bishopric: 'If you did not *ask* his opinion, few persons will be at all surprised that he abstained from giving it.' Howley's 'age and delicacy' and 'reluctance to obtrude without absolute necessity' meant that he would only offer such an opinion if directly asked for one.[62] Russell had clearly known this all too well. He had his own way and Howley reluctantly accepted it. He confirmed Hampden's election and had begun the arrangements for the consecration, but never had to perform the ceremony.

Death

Howley had become noticeably weaker during the Hereford bishopric controversy. He had indifferent health throughout his life and, in particular, was ill several times after he was 70. Far the most serious illness was the 'spasmodic cholera' which he suffered between August and October 1842, when 76. The doctors had given up all hope of recovery and Peel had decided to appoint Blomfield in his place.[63] Howley died on 11 February 1848, one day before his 82nd birthday. He was reputed to have left £120,000 in personal bequests. His funeral on 26 February saw a huge and lengthy procession from Lambeth to Addington, where he was buried in a vault in the parish church. The streets

---

60 Russell to Wilberforce, 18 December 1847, Bodl Lib MS Eng Lett d 307, f. 108; Ashwell, *Life of the Right Reverend Samuel Wilberforce*, i, 431, 453–54, 467ff.

61 Copy Russell to the remonstrating bishops, 8 December 1847, Bodl Lib MS Eng Lett d 307, pp. 100–02.

62 Phillpotts to Russell, 10 December 1847, PRO 30/22, 6H, f. 122.

63 Account by Mrs Howley, LPL MS 2203, ff. 63–65, n.d.; Ashwell, *Life of the Right Reverend Samuel Wilberforce*, ii, 185.

were lined from Lambeth to Kennington Gate, shops closed along the route, and when the cortège arrived in Croydon there was a huge crowd to see it. His long-serving chaplains Harrison and Mill took the service; Lyall and F.B. Wells (Howley's private secretary 1837–42) were amongst the pall-bearers. The remains of the Howleys' two children buried in London and the third buried in Fulham were removed and interred in the vault.[64] Howley was commemorated with a stone effigy by Richard Westmacott which Lyall and Harrison organised in a very prominent place in the choir of Canterbury Cathedral, between the tombs of the medieval archbishops Bourchier and Chichele. No memorial had been placed there since the Reformation. In 1853 Harrison paid for five windows dedicated to Howley's memory in the cathedral. Howley's library was left to Harrison to assist in the theological studies of the clergy in Canterbury. It formed the nucleus of the Howley-Harrison Library at the cathedral after 1887. It was the library he kept mainly at Addington, augmented by Harrison's own books and a library inherited from Harrison's uncle.[65]

Howley's death had come at a time when his own party were very much on the defensive. The Remonstrance against Hampden's consecration had ended their chances of promotion. Russell considered J.B. Sumner of Chester, Lonsdale of Lichfield and Pepys of Worcester. Whately's name was even mentioned, but quickly discarded. The Queen and Prince Albert were very keen on Sumner.[66] So the evangelical succeeded the High Churchman. Clive Dewey traces how quickly Howley's lieutenants lost their influence after his death. After Sumner went to Lambeth, Tait replaced Blomfield at London in 1856. Lyall's successor as Dean of Canterbury was the evangelical Henry Alford. Reforms to cathedrals meant that High Church patronage was a resource of diminishing importance.[67] The speed of this eclipse was quickened by the happenstance of Howley dying during a Whig administration. If Howley had died of the cholera in 1842 and Peel had appointed Blomfield, the High Churchmen's patronage networks might have survived more or less intact for another twenty years.

---

64 *Illustrated London News*, 26 February 1848, 121; *DNB*; LPL MS 2203, f 255.

65 Claude Jenkins, 'Archbishop Howley', *Canterbury Cathedral Chronicle*, 41 (October 1945), 10; K.G. Pilgrim, 'A Victorian Archdeacon: The Venerable Benjamin Harrison, M.A.' (unpubl. MA thesis, Univ. of Kent, 1994), 76.

66 Chadwick, *Victorian Church: Part One*, 247–48.

67 Dewey, *Passing of Barchester*, 102–03.

Conclusion

> [He was] one of the wisest prelates who ever graced the throne of Augustine. Because Dr Howley was no author, – was neither famous as a preacher, nor impressive when he spoke in public, – he has left a name with which churchmen of the present generation are but slenderly, if at all acquainted. But those who knew him best, bear eager testimony to a singularly lofty as well as lovely and attractive character ... His special claim to Church gratitude is founded on the fact that he presided wisely at the helm during a season of extraordinary trial to the Church, and under the Divine Blessing piloted the good ship safely through the storm, at a time 'when neither sun nor stars in many days appeared and no small tempest lay on her.'[1]

J.W. Burgon's tribute, couched in the florid style of the day, sums up the paradox of this study. One of the purposes of this book has been to show more clearly the reality of the leadership Howley and others gave to the Church at the end of the long eighteenth century. A series of questions might be asked: why was it that the Archbishop who chaired the Ecclesiastical Commission, and whose views became ever more fluid about the reality of the life of the Church in the changing nation in the middle of the 1830s, was left with a reputation for meekness, even weakness? Why did Blomfield's thoroughly deserved reputation as a Church leader who had himself made this transit obscure that of the Archbishop of Canterbury? Why is Howley's reputation, even if undeserved, so modest? The accounts that emerged of his part in Queen Victoria's coronation are one example – Howley trying to hand her the orb after she already had it: 'and he (as usual) was so confused and puzzled and knew nothing and went away'. His jamming of the Coronation ring on her fourth finger became a story which illustrated his incompetence rather than the incompetence of those who had wrongly made it to fit her fifth. Lord Melbourne tempered her youthful dislike of Howley and her affection and respect for him by the time he died was unforced.[2]

1 Burgon, *Lives of Twelve Good Men*, i, 189–90.

2 Elizabeth Longford, *Victoria R I* (London, 1964), 102; Chadwick, *Victorian Church: Part One*, 160–62, 247.

In an age where the expression of emotion was much more tightly constrained, it is impossible not to think that Howley provided a rare glimpse of his own thoughts and emotions when he told his newly arriving chaplain how difficult it was to know oneself and to draw the line between moderation and lukewarmness, and that a person might seem lukewarm even if he was very keen not so to do.[3] Part of it was a fabled inability to speak well in public. Samuel Wilberforce heard him addressing a girls' school: 'My dear young friends – My dear girls – My dear young catechumens – My dear Christian friends – My dear young female women'.[4] Nevertheless, he was not ineffective in Parliament, and that was where oratory counted. When Grey described him as a 'poor, miserable creature', Howley was doing an impressive hatchet job on his Reform legislation.[5] Behind the scenes he was more effective still. Naturally his views carried more weight with the Tory Lord Liverpool and Sir Robert Peel than the Whig Earl Grey and Lord John Russell, but as has been demonstrated at length, he was consulted over policy and patronage more than conventionally. Enough has already been said about why there are few records of his considerable contribution to the reform of the Church in the 1830s and something similar was true of his dealings with the Oxford Movement. It can only be seen with hindsight how closely Howley was involved in the immediate situation of dealing with the Tractarians in Oxford. The advice that Bagot followed slavishly, even to the point of the direct and unattributed transcription of it into correspondence with Pusey and others, was not visible. Tractarian judgements were partial, but they have retained their sting.

There was an abortive attempt to collect material for a biography soon after he died. Joshua Watson enquired whether enough of Howley's correspondence could be got together to do the job properly, since the truth about his character was best shown in it. The *Memoir* makes no further reference to it. There was a rumour that Mrs Howley destroyed papers relating to his time as Archbishop. Benjamin Harrison's widow is certainly understood to have burnt much of her husband's correspondence, 'to save herself the trouble of looking through and sorting out'.[6]

---

3 Harrison to Pusey, 11 August 1838, PH, Pusey MS.

4 *Memories of Old Friends: Being Extracts from the Journals and Letters of Caroline Fox from 1835 to 1871*, ed. Horace Pym (2nd edn, London, 1882), i, 214; Sparks, 'Howley and his Books', 34.

5 C.C.F. Greville, *The Greville Memoirs: A Journal of the Reigns of George IV and William IV* (London, 1874), ii, 250.

6 Churton, *Memoir of Joshua Watson*, ii, 262–63; Lambeth Palace Library Annual Report, 1968–69, 1. There is no written evidence that the papers were destroyed by Mrs Howley; *Letters of Mary Sibylla Holland*, ed. B. Holland (3rd edn, London, 1907), 180.

The biographical approach has provided a framework for examining some of the themes of late Georgian and early Victorian Church history. Reform in Church and State came from a group of men who had excelled in manipulation of the system they were called upon partially to dismantle. Howley could never have been in this position were it not for the years as Domestic Chaplain, Canon of Christ Church and as episcopal confidant of Lord Liverpool. The irony of such a man changing his views explains the fury of the cathedrals at someone they could only consider a turncoat. I have attempted to explain why the negative view of Howley was powerful and why it was reinforced by the reforming impulse which affected all parts of the Church of England in the following century. Howley's true influence and abilities as well as his weaknesses and failings are better appreciated by a subtler understanding of his context and his views than that.

Primary Sources

Section I Printed Works

1 Howley's Primary Charge as Bishop of London, 1814

Subject matter: residence; curates; double duty; French Revolution and irreligion; infidelity/deism/Unitarianism; education and the National Society

2 Howley's Charge of September 1840 as Archbishop of Canterbury

Subject matter: difference between 1814 and 1840, State interest in regulating many areas of life whereas in 1814 only in attending to some issues within Church; tithes; Clergy Discipline Act; Church Commissioners – bishops, parochial clergy, cathedrals; commendams and translations; decline in non-residence and pluralities; attacks on Establishment; lack of religious provision leading to immorality; education; colonies and conversion; National Society; 'evils of dissent'; worldwide Church East and West, the evils of Rome; early rubrical controversies

3 Letter Commendatory from The Most Rev. The Lord Archbishop of Canterbury, &c., 1841

Subject matter: To Eastern Patriarchs commending and explaining the Bishop's mission

4 A Letter addressed to the Clergy and Laity of his Province by William, Lord Archbishop of Canterbury, London, 1845

Subject matter: ritualism and rubrical controversy in full swing post-Blomfield 1842 Charge

Section II Parliamentary Speeches

1 *Augmentation of Small Livings, 1831*

First element of Church Reform introduced by Howley

2 *Pluralities Bill, 1832*

To restrict Pluralities. The beginning of the work of Ecclesiastical Commission in sight

3 *Reform Bill, 1831*

Speech during debate

4 *Education Bill, 1839*

Howley's most substantial outlining of his view of the link between religion and education. Also refers with approval to the Bell and Lancastrian schemes of education – moving away from the unyielding demand for Anglican education system as times change around him.

Section I
Printed Works

1 Howley's Primary Charge as Bishop of London, 1814

[p. 4] In the course of the last session we have felt the necessity of resorting to the extraordinary interposition of Parliament for the relief and protection of many respectable clergymen, who had incurred heavy and ruinous penalties by inattention to the provisions of the law, which regulates the very important concern of residence on ecclesiastical benefices. The statute, on which the proceedings against them were grounded, was originally designed to mitigate the intolerable rigour of a former law, which may just be termed **[p. 5]** unreasonable, since it neither regarded the practicability of the duties enjoined, nor apportioned its penalties to the degrees of guilt or the pecuniary circumstances of the offender. The new statute was then received as a favour, and in spite of its acknowledged imperfections might, in a great measure, have answered the purpose of protecting the clergy from vexatious attacks, had they acted with due circumspection and regard to their own security. Its enactments, it must be confessed, were sanctioned by penalties of excessive severity, because perhaps it was argued, that none but the criminal non-resident would incur the hazard of prosecution, when legal protection might be obtained, wherever it was due, at very moderate expense and trouble. The fallacy of this reasoning has been proved by the event. A very considerable number of the clergy through ignorance, forgetfulness, or inadvertency, have incautiously exposed themselves to informations, which, in many instances, if suffered to proceed, would have involved them in irretrievable ruin. The equitable interference of Parliament has afforded relief in this emergency, empowering the diocesan to discriminate between involuntary error, or venial omission, and substantial violation of the law. The result of the inquiries to which this arrangement has led, I am happy to state, has been peculiarly creditable to the clergy of this diocese. In the numerous cases referred to my decision, the fault has, almost without exception, been found to consist, not in wilful dereliction or criminal neglect of duty, but in the disregard of those precautions, which are necessary to legalize virtual residence, or to confirm the claim of justifiable absence to the indulgence allowed by law.

Among the **[p. 6]** objects of attack, it is bare justice to say, are many individuals irreprehensible in character, and exemplary in conduct, who have constantly resided in the bosom of their cures, and whose lives and affections have been uniformly devoted to the spiritual concerns of their parishioners. By men of this description, unaccustomed to reproach, the unmerited imputation of delinquency has been felt as a more intolerable grievance, than the pecuniary loss which would have followed the rigid execution of the law. But, whilst they stand acquitted of criminality, they have been deficient, it must be allowed, in that reasonable care of their own interest, which, in the complicated relations of civil life, becomes a duty to society, of stronger obligation perhaps on the Ministers of the Gospel, than on any other class of men. The salutary influence of the clergy, which gives efficacy to their exhortations, and weight to their instructions, is intimately connected with the general respectability of their persons. And the dignity of the sacred office will undoubtedly suffer in the estimation of the public, when men invested with this high character are placed in the humiliating situation of delinquents, and compelled to struggle with the disquietudes of mind, and the distress and embarrassment of circumstances which are the natural consequences of an expensive prosecution. To me, indeed, I frankly avow, the principle of maintaining order and regularity in the church, by the casual and indiscriminating agency of the common informer, appears to be founded on complete misconception and ignorance of the nature and ends of ecclesiastical government and discipline. The efficiency of ecclesiastical authority, of all authority I might say, **[p. 7]** which has for its object to regulate the conduct of individuals in a multiplicity of emergent cases, depends on the rational exercise of discretion, acting indeed by regular forms, and insisting on the observance of general rules, but maintaining a proportion between the offence and the punishment, and not leaving the determination of innocence and guilt to the technical interpretation of ambiguous statutes. To the system however established by the existing laws, whatever are its merits or defects, it is our bounden duty to conform: and that, not for wrath but for conscience sake, not merely by scrupulous attention to the letter, from regard to personal security, but in the liberal spirit of frank and loyal obedience to the injunctions of authority. By scrupulous attention to the admonition, and faithful performance of your professional duties without evasion or subterfuge, you will at once evince your gratitude for the protection of the Legislature, and prove to the satisfaction of the world, that you act under the impulse of nobler motives than sublunary hope or fear.

I now pass to the bill for the farther support and maintenance of Stipendiary Curates, which, in the first place, requires every incumbent not duly residing on his benefice to nominate, within a specified time, a proper Curate, to be licensed by the Bishop, or Ordinary of the place, having Episcopal jurisdiction. The regulation contained in this clause is not in substance new, but comes in aid of the ancient law which from motives of convenience had been relaxed, whilst a licence could not be obtained without personal attendance on the Bishop. The removal of this difficulty, by enabling the Ordi- **[p. 8]** nary to act by commission, has reasonably suggested the propriety of enforcing salutary regulation, which places every officiating minister under the superintendence, the control, and the protection of legitimate authority. But the primary object of the Bill is to secure a more adequate provision for the maintenance of stipendiary Curates; and if its enactments may, in certain respects, be considered as pressing too hard on benefices of inferior value, they afford little complaint to the wealthier incumbent. On the clause which allows a reduction of stipend, discretional within certain limits, where the Curate has the charge of more than a single parish, I embrace this opportunity of making known my determination to use every precaution against its possible effect in promoting the union of Curacies, a practice which should never be allowed without satisfactory evidence of its necessity. The primary duty of the Incumbent is personal residence on his cure, and the laws ecclesiastical and civil, which in various specified cases dispense with this obligation, insist on ample provision for the care and instruction of the parish. It would indeed be contrary to reason that the interest of the flock should be sacrificed to the convenience of the pastor. That which cannot be done by himself, the Minister is bound to perform by his deputy; and I leave it to the conscience of any thinking man to determine, whether full compensation is made for the absence of the Incumbent by the services of a divided Curate. To a conscientious Clergyman the cares and duties of a single parish will, in most instances, afford sufficient occupation of time and labour. And even when a scanty population creates an exception to this remark, the **[p. 9]** burden of an additional cure should not be lightly undertaken, without due consideration of the very material obstacles which a minister, not residing on the spot, will have to encounter in the adequate performance of his duty; an obvious, and in most cases an inevitable result, will be the retrenchment of duty on the Sabbath in places accustomed to the full service, and the continued omission of morning or evening prayer, when the necessity, which could alone justify the introduction of so reprehensible a practice, has ceased to exist. In directing my serious attention to the prevention of this abuse, I shall not however forget the regard which in reason is due to the convenience of poorer incumbents, more especially in contiguous parishes with few inhabitants. In some instances I am sensible that the most laudable anxiety on the part of the Clergy to second the wishes of their Diocesan in this important matter must necessarily fail of success; and that the want of a residence, or the unhealthiness of the climate, would leave many churches without a pastor, if the labours of a Curate were strictly confined to a single parish. An unfortunate combination of these causes has induced me, in a small number of cases, though with the utmost reluctance, to commit the care of three churches to the same hand. But in this unwilling concession to alleged necessity, I wish it to be distinctly understood, that I reserve the power of immediate revocation, if further enquiry should prove that I have acted without just reason.

The kind and, I may add, the equitable concern of the Legislature for the comfort and respectability of the Clergy has been **[p. 10]** further evinced in a temporary bill, by which the provisions and penalties of former acts on the subject of residence have been so far modified and altered, as to afford, at least for the present, sufficient protection against the vexatious acts of the informer. And the repeal of the acts *for burying in woollen*[1] has relieved us from the terror of statutes which had long slept, but, like the insect which stings after death, might have been awakened to mischievous activity by the call of malignity or avarice. The best demonstration of our gratitude for these favours is unequivocal fidelity in the discharge of those high duties, to which we are pledged by the most solemn engagements to God and to our country. Yet, in acting under the impulse of feelings the most exalted, your course must ever be shaped by the strictest attention to the letter of the law; nor can you with safety for an instant forget, that neither the discretion of the Diocesan, not the equity of the Judge, can dispense with the forms or mitigate the operation of a penal statute. On the importance of this caution I have insisted with greater earnestness, because this is a point on which the most conscientious Clergyman, engrossed by the duties of his charge, is not unlikely to fail; and I have found by experience, that the distress and vexation, occasioned by the later prosecutions, have not been universally efficacious in impressing the necessity for a more accurate acquaintance with laws, which in no single particular can be transgressed or neglected with impunity. I am equally disposed **[p. 11]** by inclination and duty to watch over the interests and promote the welfare of my Clergy: but in this, as in all other private concerns, the security of the individual is to be found in his personal circumspection and vigilance.

---

[1] The Burial in Woollen Acts 1666–80 required the dead, except plague victims and the destitute, to be buried in pure English wool shrouds. There was a potential £5 fee for noncompliance. The legislation was repealed in 1814.

From these considerations of domestic prudence our attention is now called to concerns of universal importance to the interests of the Christian world. The convulsions which threatened to subvert the hallowed and ancient fabrics of religion, of social order, and of civil and political liberty, are happily allayed. The storm has ceased to roar. In the sight of the nations assembled from the ends of the earth to be the ministers of God's justice, and the witnesses of his power, the pillar of usurped domination, erected on the ruin of thrones and the wreck of principles, has crumbled, at the bidding of the Almighty, into dust, and the tyranny, which made the world as a wilderness, and destroyed its cities [Isaiah 14.17], exists only in recollection, like the horrors of an oppressive dream. The restoration of peace has followed the triumph of truth and justice; and the moderation which has tempered the glories of victory with a milder radiance, may be hailed as an auspicious presage of settled and durable tranquillity. But prosperity has its dangers: the Spirit of evil is always busy: – though often confounded, he is never dismayed; though baffled, he returns to the contest with new arms; prepared alike to seduce or intimidate, to succeed by violence or by fraud.

[p. 12] At so momentous a crisis, which I would willingly consider as the commencement of a happier age, in which righteousness and truth shall flourish, it will not be amiss to reflect on the mischiefs which lurk in the bosom of peace, and which may eventually poison the sources of our national prosperity and grandeur. Of these the most obvious, though perhaps the least formidable in reality, is the infection of vice and infidelity from the renewal of intercourse with the continent. On this head I conceive we have little to apprehend for the sound, or even the reclaimable part of our population. There is indeed but too much reason to fear that the state of religion and morals in a neighbouring country is by no means satisfactory to the friends of piety and virtue. The French Revolution was not an accidental explosion, a burst of momentary passion or frenzy, but a deliberate and premeditated rebellion against authority human and divine: It was the struggle of desperate wickedness to shake off the salutary restraints imposed by Religion and Law on the worst passions of human nature. The conception, and still more the successful accomplishment, of a project thus singular in atrocity, bespeaks an unexampled inveteracy of corruption diffused through the vitals of the community; and is not unnatural to infer, that the evil has derived an accession of extent and malignity from the systematic encouragement of licentiousness by a despotic government; from the destruction of churches; the neglect of public worship; and, above all, from the abolition of the Sabbath, and the blasting influence of an unchristian education on the minds of youth. But the grossness of vice without disguise will be reckoned with disgust by the habitual feelings of virtuous decency **[p. 13]** incorporated with our national character. The common sense of the nation will form a security equally strong against the deadly contagion of irreligious principle. The cause of avowed infidelity has never prospered in this country: Attached by reflection and feeling to the interests of religion and virtue, we smile with contempt at the sophistries and sarcasms of the wretched literati, who, prostituting the powers of a dazzling wit and seductive eloquence to the gratification of public depravity, obtained a celebrity disgraceful and disastrous to themselves and their country, as the retailers of blasphemy, and the panegyrists and advocates of vice.

We are indeed exposed to dangers, and those of no ordinary magnitude. The opposite extremes of defect or excess of religious belief and feeling prevail among us, in a variety of modifications and degrees, to an alarming extent. The partizans of these several errors, disjoined in all other respects by discordancy of principle, sentiment, and ultimate views, are not the less disposed to unite in offensive alliance against the object of their common aversion, the Established Church.

The spirit of disaffection to religious truth, which may justly excite apprehension in this country, is not to be confounded with the gross and crude irreligion of our continental neighbours. A considerable period elapsed, after the establishment of the Reformation in this island, before the enemies of religion were sufficiently numerous to claim distinction as a party, or were emboldened by the tolerance of the age to make a public avowal of their senti- **[p. 14]** ments. In this view, the origin of infidelity among us may perhaps be referred to the middle of the seventeenth century. Commencing about that period, it has since, at different times, and on different occasions, appeared under three distinct forms. It first burst on the astonished world, betraying its native deformity through a thin veil of metaphysical subtleties, and directing its open assaults against the fundamental truths of religion, and the sanctions of morality. But this absurd and audacious impiety was found so revolting to the reason and feeling of mankind, that the unbeliever abandoned a position, which was rendered untenable by popular detestation, and took his stand on the ground of Deism. We must not however imagine that attachment to any specific system of doctrine, or assent to any positive truth, was implied in the name of Deist. The term was adopted as a conventional symbol of union amongst all who agreed in the single principle of denying the truth of Revelation, however widely disjoined in belief and opinion on the subject of natural religion. In the issue of the controversies which followed, the advocates of deistical tendencies were completely unmasked; the fallacy of their arguments, and the pernicious tendency of their doctrines, were clearly and irrefragably demonstrated; the appellation of Deist became a term of reproach; and the licentious freethinker was identified in popular estimation with the professed atheist. The union of unbelievers, as a regular and ostensible party, was dissolved by this discomfiture; it was impossible to act with effect under a character which the reason and piety of the people regarded with contempt and horror; and, owing to this general disposition of the public **[p. 15]** mind, the direct attacks on religious and moral truth were for a long time few and feeble. The faction has again been embodied in modern times, under the less invidious denomination of a Christian sect. As all unbelievers in Revelation were formerly Deists, a considerable proportion of those who are styled Unitarians in the present day have no other title to the name, than their rejection of the principal doctrines which distinguish the Revelation of the Gospel from natural religion. In this statement it is not my intention to wound the feelings of the conscientious Unitarian, who, while he rejects its peculiar dogmas, admits the general truth of Christianity. The charge of infidelity indeed attaches in a certain degree to all who refuse their assent to any material doctrine deducible by the established laws of interpretation from Scripture; and great must be the force of that prejudice, which can overlook the inconsistency of arbitrarily imposing a meaning unwarranted by the usages of language, on a book to which all parties appeal as the standard and rule of faith. But I do not hesitate to aver my conviction, that the profession of Unitarian tenets affords convenient shelter to many, who would be more properly termed Deists, and who by the boldness of their interpolations, omissions, and perversions, by the indecency of their insinuations against the veracity of the inspired writers, by their familiar levity and the awful mysteries of religion, and their disrespectful reflections on the person and actions of their Saviour, are distinguished from real Unitarians, and betray the true secret of the flimsy disguise which they have assumed as a cover from the odium of avowed infidelity. Their position, it must be confessed, has been not unskilfully **[p. 16]** chosen: little ground has been lost in their retreat: the line of separation between the contiguous systems is often indiscernible, and at best faintly marked: and in return for the sacrifice of a name they have obtained a facility of diffusing their pernicious principles with less suspicion. The Unitarian system, it is true, having little to captivate the affections, as disgusting the unsophisticated reason by its obvious contradiction to Scripture, has been hitherto regarded with cool indifference by the mass of the community. Its influence has generally been confined to men of some education, whose thoughts have been little employed on the subject of religion; or who, loving rather to question than to learn, have approached the oracles of divine truth without that humble docility, that prostration of the understanding and will, which are indispensable to proficiency in Christian instruction. On this account the general advancement in knowledge, which ordinarily checks the growth of error, may be considered as favourable to the progress of this sect, which, inspirited and encouraged by opportunity, has long been straining every nerve to increase the numbers of its proselytes. The reflections naturally suggested by the preceding remarks, whilst they are creditable to the religious character of an age in which infidelity is reduced to sue for admittance in the garb of Christianity, afford the consolatory assurance, that, if the minds of our youth are secured from infection, we may easily frustrate the machinations of this enemy by detecting his fallacies, and exhibiting his principles in their true colours.

We now proceed to consider the dangers which threaten the **[p. 17]** peace of the church from an opposite quarter. During the course of the last twenty years the influence of religious sentiment on the people of this country has been increasing with progressive rapidity. The portentous excesses of crime and calamity, which followed the horrible experiment of adopting the principles of unbelief for the general rules of action, awakened the minds of men to serious reflection on their duties. And never was there a period in our history, in which so strong a disposition prevailed to study the truths of Revelation, and to appreciate their value in the direction of human conduct. But, since good is not to be found without an admixture of evil, the irregular action of this feeling has given birth to a multiplicity of errors, which are more extensively received, and more pertinaciously cherished, as the transports of passion and the dreams of enthusiasm have greater attractions for human corruption, than the dull uniformity of sober belief, and the strictness of reasonable obedience. To enumerate the eccentricities of undisciplined affection, to mark the gradations of heresy from simple mistake or absurdity to gross corruption of faith, or mischievous principles of action, would be an endless task. Suffice it to observe, that intemperate effervescence of seal is hardly consistent with the dominion of charity, or the love of truth, in the heart; and that deeper wounds have been inflicted on the church by the madness or folly of enthusiasts and fanatics than by the malice of her most inveterate enemies. I do not affect to dread a renewal of the excess committed by the Donatists of old, or even of the troubles excited by the Puritans in later times. The evil to be reasonably apprehended is a gradual **[p. 18]** diminution of attachment to the national Church, which in its immediate effects would abridge the sphere of her beneficial influence, and might lead in its possible consequences to the subversion of an Establishment, the firmest support, and the noblest ornament of Christianity. That such is the ultimate object, I do not say, of rational and sober dissenters of any denomination; but of that promiscuous multitude of confederated sectaries who have imbibed the spirit of malignant dissent, which in the prosecution of hostility against the established faith forgets its attachment to a particular creed; there is the strongest reason to believe. The views of this dangerous faction are unintentionally seconded by a far more respectable description of men, who rightly conceiving that sound faith and sincere piety are the essentials of pure religion, entertain an indifference to ordinances and forms; overlooking the necessity of permanent fences for the protection of the flock, of regular channels for the distribution of the living waters; and forgetting that a well-constituted Establishment, though it necessarily partakes of human imperfection, affords the best security which can be devised by the wisdom of man, against the vicissitudes of events, alternations of zeal, and the fluctuations of opinion.

2 Howley's Charge of September 1840 as Archbishop of Canterbury

[p. 3] When first I was called to the administration of a great Diocese, the topics on which I was led to address the Clergy assembled on occasions like the present, were mostly of a general nature, of great importance, indeed, but without any particular application to the existing state of the Church, as compared with former times. The Clergy were then engaged in the peaceful exercise of their functions, undisturbed by open hostility; and the only interference in the concerns of the Church, on the part of the Legislature, was confined to its internal improvement, and the better regulation of its discipline. But from the time of my advancement to the still more responsible **[p. 4]** station, which, however unworthy, I now have the honour to fill, a very material change has taken place in this respect. The attention of the Crown and the Parliament has been directed to every part of our social system, and among the number of measurers which have been adopted in consequence, are many which immediately, or remotely, affect the interests of the Church. Of this latter description, the most important, perhaps, are the alterations in the Poor Laws, the new system of Registration, and the relaxation of the Laws relating to Marriage. Whether the inconveniences which have arisen from the working of these measures are only such as must be expected from any great alteration in matters so extensive and complicated, and for which remedies may be suggested by experience; whether, in their effects on society, the good or evil will ultimately be found to preponderate; and whether any of them have been productive of evil, uncompensated by any advantage, it would be a waste of your time to inquire. The Clergy, with that moderation and temper which have always distinguished them as a body, will feel it their duty to obey the laws of their country, to assist in the removal of diffi- **[p. 5]** culties which may obstruct their salutary operation, and in the prevention or mitigation of evils, if any, which they may be calculated to produce.

In my remarks on a measure of the greatest importance, immediately relating to the concerns of the Church, I shall be equally brief. I allude to the Commutation of Tithes, which, after many abortive attempts, has at length been effected in a manner as little liable, perhaps, to objection as could be expected, with the single exception of depriving the tithe-holders of all prospective advantage from the inclosure of waste lands, and thus excluding the Clergy from the share which they would otherwise have had in the growing prosperity of the country. But whether this loss, the extent of which is uncertain, is not more than made up to the clergyman by the facilities given of recovering his dues, without incurring the charge of extortion, or provoking the hostility of his parishioners, and alienating their affections from the Church, deserves to be well considered. Far am I from advising the Clergy to abandon their just claims. The easiness which might, on certain occasions, be laudable, or at worst imprudent, in regard to our rights as individuals **[p. 6]** would be highly reprehensible in respect to the property which we hold in trust for the Church. This applies to the question which has not yet been finally settled, of the assessment of tithes to the parochial rates, and, with still greater force, to the demands of the Dissenters for the abolition of Church rates, – a demand without foundation in justice, which would inflict in its consequences a heavy, perhaps an irreparable, blow on the spiritual interests of the poor. In regard to these and other measures of similar nature and tendency, however inconsistent with our notions of justice or true policy, our opposition will always be regulated, as it has hitherto been, by the principles of Christian charity. We shall insist on nothing but what we deem to be reasonable, and shall never disgrace our profession by intemperate language, by personal invective, or the use of unwarrantable means in the assertion of our rights.

A measure more immediately affecting the internal economy of the Church, is what is commonly termed the Clergy Discipline Act, an Act which affords effectual means of punishing offences which, I am happy to say, are of rare occurrence, and thus vindicating the honour of **[p. 7]** the Church, but will add little to her real discipline. Our dependence in this respect must rest on the character of her ministers, their prudence, their piety, and sense of their duties, their disposition to obey her laws and injunctions, and to submit to lawful authority. The infliction of penalties may operate in the way of example, but it will seldom reclaim a delinquent who has disgraced his profession, or wipe away the blot on his character, which will make his ministrations useless. Yet the powers conferred by this Act cannot be regarded as unimportant, while they afford the means of relieving the Church from the imputation of indifference to the conduct of her ministers, or of removing the offender from the charge of a flock which he is no longer worthy to feed. It were indeed to be wished that a still more expeditious and less expensive mode of proceeding could have been devised, consistently with that tender regard for reputation and property which is required by the principles of our law, and which the Clergy have a right to expect, in common with all their fellow-subjects. There is, however, little reason to think that this law will be frequently acted on, when we regard **[p. 8]** the progressive improvement which has for many years been observable in the attention of the Clergy to their duties, and in the notions entertained by young men who seek ordination, of the responsibility which they take on themselves in entering on the service of the Church. That any of those who engage in our holy profession, with a sincere desire of promoting the honour of God, and bringing their fellow men to salvation, should so far depart from their principles as to fall into scandalous offences, is by no means likely. Even where higher considerations have not due weight, a prudent regard to decency and public opinion will prevent gross violations of the law.

The recommendations of the Church Commissioners, which were already before the public when I last had the satisfaction of meeting you, have at length, after some modification from the wisdom of Parliament, passed into laws. In the changes thus introduced, affecting the condition of the three great classes of the Clergy, the Bishops, the Parochial Clergy and the Chapters of Cathedral and Collegiate Churches, I shall trouble you with but few remarks. The subject has been so fully discussed, the principal features **[p. 9]** of these measures, and even the minutest details, have been so long before the public, that it cannot be necessary to repeat that which must already be known to all who have taken an interest in these matters. My observations will therefore be brief.

The changes effected in respect to Bishoprics have, as far as I can learn, been generally approved. The points which required correction were the unequal allotment of territory into the jurisdiction of the several Bishops, the unequal distribution of revenues, and the necessity arising from hence, of assigning Cathedral preferments, or benefices with cure of souls, to make up the deficiencies of income in the poorer sees. These anomalies have now been removed. The labours of the Bishops have been more fairly apportioned by the union of sees, the division of dioceses, or the transfer of districts from one diocese to another, with regard to the exigency in each particular case. A competent maintenance is provided for every Bishop by taxation of the richer sees. The necessity of commendams being thus done away with, all subordinate preferments will be left to the Clergy; and the Bishop, **[p. 10]** having no other charge to distract his attention, will be able to devote the whole of his time to the care of his diocese, his Parliamentary duties, and the general concerns of the Church. The approach to equality in the revenues of Bishoprics will have the further advantage of diminishing the frequency of translations. Occasions there may be when the power of removing a Bishop from one diocese to another may be exercised with advantage to the Church; it is therefore wisely retained. But, generally speaking, it is better that a Bishop should remain in the station in which he was originally placed, where he has the advantage of local experience, and of that personal influence which is the slow growth of years.

The necessity has long been perceived of strengthening the hands of the spiritual ruler, and increasing the efficiency of the Church in regard to parochial ministrations, more especially by promoting the increase of residence, and thus securing in every parish the presence of a clergyman, and consequently the adequate performance of duties which can never be so fully provided for as by an incumbent living on the spot. By Acts **[p. 11]** which have been lately passed, the extent of non-residence has been subjected to progressive diminution, by reducing the number of exemptions, by limiting the causes of license, by abridging pluralities, and facilitating the erection of glebe-houses. The extent of the subject prevents me from enlarging on particulars, or even enumerating the principal matters which have fallen under the notice of the Legislature. Explanation would indeed be superfluous. It is desirable that every clergyman, however well acquainted with the laws of the Church, should, in all doubtful concerns of importance to himself or his parishioners, apply for instruction to the diocesan before he proceeds to act. I have known instances of excellent clergymen who have lost important advantages, and been involved in serious difficulties, by neglect of this salutary precaution. In reference to all that has been done under this head, I may fairly presume that, on the whole, it is approved by the reason and feelings both of Clergy and Laity, with the exception, perhaps, of those who desire the entire abolition of pluralities, which, in the present state of the Church is impracticable.

[p. 12] I am now led, in the order of things, to a subject of equal importance, on which there has been considerable difference of opinion among wise and good men, – the measures recommended by the Church Commissioners in respect to the Chapters of Cathedrals and Collegiate Churches, which have now received the sanction of Parliament. As the matter is finally settled, discussion of the arguments which have been urged with great force and ability on both sides of the question, could lead to no useful result. The principle in which the opposition to these measures originated, zeal for the Church, suggest the consolatory assurance, that, among those who most disapprove of them, none will be found who will not be disposed to use their utmost endeavours to avert any evils which may possibly arise from the change. If it shall be proved by experience that the efficiency of our Church is increased; that the blessings of her apostolical doctrines, and her pastoral care, are more extensively dispensed to the people; that the sense of the benefits which she imparts, and of the sacrifices to which she has consented, has strengthened her hold on the respect and affection of the county, they will be **[p. 13]** among the first to rejoice at results so different from what they anticipated. If these views should be realized, the Church, when assailed on future occasions, will find her in a strong position. Her defenders will appeal to the improvement in the spiritual condition of the people, which has been effected at her expense; they will show that the funds which remain for the sustentation of these magnificent fabrics, and the maintenance of the Establishments, have been calculated on the lowest scale consistent with the due celebration of the solemn services of religion; and that the rewards of eminent learning and piety have been more largely reduced in number and value than, under circumstance of less pressing necessity, might have been thought desirable. They will protest against the injustice and impolicy of disturbing an arrangement, prepared after careful inquiry and mature deliberation, and confirmed by the author of the State. They will call in the aid of the numerous friends of religion and order to secure the peace of the Church, and protect her from factious violence, or sacrilegious rapacity. Their arguments will make the greater impression, as being evidently founded in truth, **[p. 14]** and our means of resistance will be available in their fullest extent when we have no vulnerable parts to defend. But whatever the issue may be, nothing could be more fatal to the Church than disunion among her ministers. This truth, important at all times, is entitled to particular consideration at the present crisis. From the time of the French Revolution, which, like a dormant volcano, bursting forth on a sudden, spread terror and desolation over Europe, the antagonist powers of good and of evil have been in constant activity, and the period seems to be approaching which will decide the issue of the conflict. We then beheld with dismay and astonishment infidelity avowing its principles, and mustering its hosts for the battle against all that was reverenced as sacred by the Christian world, in the hope of subverting the throne and the altars by the force of arms. At the moment when opposition seemed to be hopeless, the powers which it brought into the field were dispersed and confounded by the hand of an overruling Providence. Far, however, from losing sight of its object, it continued, in the claim that succeeded, to prepare, in darkness and secrecy, for future action; and, **[p. 15]** having recruited its forces, it no longer conceals its hostile designs against our Established Church. On the other hand, a spirit has been raised, which is steadily and energetically working in defence of our sacred Establishment, and of the truth which it is formed to uphold, – a spirit which is gradually extending its influence, and increasing its power ... Under these circumstances, it is very desirable that we should understand our real position, that we should know the strength of our enemies, the support we may expect from our friends, and the means of defence on which we may safely reckon.

It would be unwise to conceal from ourselves that there is a formidable combination against the Church. Among those who would rejoice in her downfall, we may reckon the unbelievers in God and divine revelation, who in principle are hostile to religion, or regard it but as an instrument in the hands of the politician, who may discard it at pleasure, when he finds it inapplicable to his purposes. Of these, some few, perhaps, but only a few, may be favourably disposed towards the Church, in consideration of the benefits derived to the State from her usefulness in the maintenance **[p. 16]** of peace and order. Another division consists of believers in Christ, but prepared by their prejudices or jealousies, their notions of ecclesiastical government, or zeal for their peculiar tenets, to unite even with those whom they most disapprove, in assailing the Established Church. With these may be classed, as concurring in object, though widely differing in principle, the professors of liberal sentiments, who regard all forms of faith as indifferent, and look on all Christian communities, including the Church, as entitled to equal encouragement, or, in other words, to equal neglect. To these must be added the advocates of the voluntary system, who, regardless of the confusion which must ensue from the alienation of the funds by which the teachers of religion have so long been supported, and shutting their eyes to the failure of their favourite plan, wherever from choice or necessity it has unhappily been tried, have nevertheless persuaded themselves that the great mass of the people would be benefited, in respect to spiritual instruction and pastoral care, by the abolition of Church Establishments. The numbers of our adversaries are swelled by the co-operation of irregular bodies, **[p. 17]** whose opinions and purposes are, practically at least, represented by Chartists and Socialists, and who, though in general disclaimed as auxiliaries by the classes above mentioned, would eventually forward their designs. For it cannot be doubted that whatever has a tendency to loosen the obligations of morality, or to weaken the sanctions of religion, or to disunite or confound the several orders of society, must operate against the efficiency, I might say the existence, of an Established Church. Of these several parties, the most violent are perhaps the least to be dreaded. Direct attacks on our sacred institutions would create instant alarm, and unite the great body of the nation in their defence. But who can believe that such a result would be equally certain, if the blessings of religious instruction and worship were withdrawn from the bulk of the community, if our Churches were suffered to fall into ruin for want of the means of repair, if no adequate provision is made for the spiritual necessities of a population daily increasing, if the youth of the country are allowed to grow up in ignorance of the doctrines or practice of Christianity? With assailants so many in number, and possessing the means of **[p. 18]** extending their influence by the use of that powerful engine the press, it would be the height of imprudence in us to rely on the goodness of our cause, without availing ourselves of the means which are with our reach, of defeating their projects. Of the sufficiency of these means, under the blessing of God, we have no reason to doubt. In the very dangers which threaten the Church we find a ground of security. The assaults of which she is the object have excited the sympathy, and quickened the energies of the better part of the people in her defence. Their demonstrations of attachment, and assurance of support, I have the satisfaction of thinking, are not the ebullitions of transient feeling, but the expression of sentiments grounded in principle, and likely to be permanent as the causes in which they originate. The importance and extent of the benefits dispensed by the Church, and which cannot be supplied from any other source, and her legitimate claim to authority in her sacred character, have of late years been more generally recognized than at any former period. The increasing zeal of the Clergy, their attention to their professional duties, and their exemplary forbearance under the insults **[p. 19]** and calumnies which have been heaped upon them, have had their proper effects on the well-disposed portion of the community. Possessing, as they now do, in a more than ordinary degree, the salutary influence on which the success of their ministrations depends, they have only to continue the course which has produced this happy result, in the same Christian spirit, and with increased exertion. A wide field is open before us, presenting objects so vast and so numerous, that, if we had no other reliance than on our own unassisted endeavours, we could not reasonably expect to succeed in attaining them. The Church, at home and abroad, implores our aid; and it is only by answering her call with efforts commensurate to the exigency, that we can enable her to sustain her character, or even place her in security.

In looking at the state of religion at home, the first thing that strikes us is an evil of formidable magnitude, destructive, as far as it extends, of the efficiency of our Church, – the inadequacy of her means for the entire accomplishment of the purposes implied in a National Establishment. The spiritual destitution existing in parts of the kingdom is truly appalling. In these less populous **[p. 20]** counties we can hardly conceive the want of religious ministrations which is felt in the districts where hundreds of thousands of poor and ignorant workmen, collected from all parts of the country, are employed in mines or manufactories, without places of worship for public devotion, and beyond the reach of pastoral care; and the lamentable consequences of this abandonment are seen in turbulence, profaneness, intemperance, and every species of moral depravity. Even here we have to deplore the insufficiency of the Church for the satisfactory discharge of pastoral duties, not only in towns where the numbers are greater, and incentives to vice more abundant, but in extensive rural parishes. But in the places mentioned above, the great disproportion of Churches and Clergymen to the number of inhabitants proves to a certainty, the multitudes must necessarily be left in a state of heathen darkness. I confidently appeal to your judgment and conscience, whether, consistently, I will not say, with charity and Christian principle, but even with common prudence, we can overlook the necessity of remedying an evil which deprives a large portion of the community of the means of grace, and diminishes **[p. 21]** the hope of future improvement by alienating their minds from the Church. But even in places which are amply provided with Churches and pastors, there is reason to fear that, from want of instruction in childhood, there are many who call themselves Christians, yet derive little advantage from these opportunities of learning their duties, and attaining the knowledge of Christ. It is true that, on comparison of past times with the present, we shall see great reason to be thankful to almighty God, who has blessed the exertions of His servants with so large an increase, and at the same time shall perceive the injustice of the reproaches which of late been cast on the Church, as being indifferent or hostile to the general diffusion of knowledge. The number of schools which have been founded in the course of the last thirty years, and principally through the instrumentality of the Clergy, afford decisive testimony in our favour. Considerable progress has been made in the work of education, but still we acknowledge its incompleteness. Not only do the means fall far short of the need, but even where the means are sufficient, they do not fully answer the end. Many children who pass through **[p. 22]** the schools exhibit no fruits of instruction in after-life. This failure is common to the children of all classes, whether educated in the bosom of their families, in classical seminaries, or in parish schools. The causes are in all instances nearly the same, the bad example of parents, evil communications, temptations acting on the passions of inexperienced youth, and the neglect of the ordinances of religion. As far as the poor are concerned, these evils, though they will never cease to exist, may be in a great measure abated by judicious care and attention. It is a part of our pastoral duty, not only to promote the establishment of schools, and provide competent teachers, but to encourage both teachers and children in the performance of the their duties respectively, by frequent inspection. The parents should also be reminded of the obligation that lies on them to attend to the conduct of their children. And a great point would be gained if young persons, after leaving the schools, could be prevailed on to consider attendance at Church as a sacred duty. Sunday schools, for the continued instruction of those who had passed through the infant and national schools, might be rendered conducive **[p. 23]** to this and other useful objects. The system thus completed, would prepare the minds of the young to profit by the instructions of the spiritual rector in more advanced years.

The points on which I have thus cursorily touched are of vital importance to the Church. Her functions will be imperfectly discharged as long as there is any part of the country which does not experience her care; her influence on the generations to come, her perpetuity as a National Establishment, will be greatly endangered, if she suffers her children (for so may the children of the poor be emphatically styled) to grow up in ignorance of faith.

But while the attention of the Christian minister is chiefly directed to the flock assigned to his care, he is no true servant of Christ if he can be indifferent to the fate of the Heathen world, or to the spiritual interests of our countrymen who are widely dispersed through the British dominions in every quarter of the globe. I speak of the two subjects together, because the conversion of the Heathen is closely connected with the prosperity of our Colonial Churches. If the conduct and character of the European population **[p. 24]** in those remote dependencies of our Empire bear evident testimony to the power of Christian principle, the example of their piety and virtue cannot fail to make an impression on the barbarous tribes with whom they are in immediate contact, or maintain commercial intercourse. And we cannot give a more decisive proof of zeal in the service of our Lord, or of charity to our brethren who are scattered abroad, than by furnishing them with the means of working out their salvation, and, at the same time, of holding out the light of the Gospel to the benighted Heathen. Such aid, I am sorry to say, is generally needed. The want of due care to provide spiritual ministrations for the first settlers, the practicability of which is demonstrated by the Romish establishments in the transatlantic dominions of France, Spain and Portugal, is far from creditable to those governments which profess a purer faith. On the culpability of such inattention, or the pleas which may be urged in extenuation, there is no occasion to dwell. A statement of facts will abundantly show that, whatever may be the necessities of the population at home, the destitution prevailing in the Colonies is far more deplorable. In the North **[p. 25]** American provinces, in the boundless tracts of Australia, the expectancies of the Church are limited to a few thousands a year. The lands which, as cultivation increases, might have afforded a permanent maintenance to a numerous body of Clergy have, whether wisely and justly or not, for that is not the question at present, been resumed, or ordered to be sold, whilst, in those and other colonies, the assistance of ministers full double in number to those at present employed is required. Even after all that could be done for the Church by the most liberal government deficiencies would still remain, which could not be supplied without the intervention of voluntary beneficence. Here, then, we perceive, both at home and abroad, an extent of spiritual wants which has an irresistible claim to our charity.

The amount of the aid which may be transmitted to the Colonial Churches from the mother country at this particular time, may probably have the effect of determining whether our Church shall maintain the pre-eminence which is due to its apostolical government, its doctrinal purity, and its connexion with the State, or whether it **[p. 26]** shall maintain a feeble existence amidst the struggles of conflicting sects. If the favourable moment is suffered to pass, the Church of England in the Colonies may be compelled to abandon her claim to the exalted position which she ought to occupy.

If it is urged, in reply, that this is the concern of the State, I am ready to grant that both justice and policy require far greater attention to this only effectual mode of improving the public morals, than has ever yet been bestowed on it by the government of any country. But instead of finding an excuse for inaction in the consideration of what is the duty of others, we must look at things as they are, and endeavour to apply a remedy. In one respect, at least, we have to rejoice, that the neglect or inability of governments has afforded a large scope to the exercise of private beneficence, and multiplied our opportunities of doing the work of the Lord, and obtaining share in the blessedness promised to those who turn many to righteousness.

If, again, the possibility is doubted of meeting at once such immense demands, we may find ample encouragement in the consideration of **[p. 27]** what has already been effected. I well remember the misgivings of others as well as my own, when the system, first tried at Madras, suggested the notion of general education in the principles of the Established Church. But the difficulties vanished successively when the undertaking was commenced in earnest. When the association for building Churches and Chapels was formed, the success of the experiment was regarded as doubtful by many persons. Yet the institution has continued to flourish, and has not only answered its object, by the application of the funds at its disposal, but has given birth to associations for similar purposes, for the employment of additional curates in populous places, and for the relief of the spiritual desolation of the metropolis, by the erection of new Churches. The success of this latter undertaking, under the immediate auspices of the distinguished Diocesan, affords incontrovertible proof of what may be done, by the combination of energy with judgement, in the promotion of a holy cause.

From the facts above stated, and the disposition shown by the public to augment the resources of the older societies connected with the Church, we **[p. 28]** may fairly infer that the fountain of charity is never exhausted, and that every drain on its waters creates a fresh supply. That which exceeds the power of individuals, is often accomplished with ease by combined exertion. This primary law of our nature never acts in stricter accordance with the precepts of the Gospel, than when it leads to joint contributions of talent, labour and wealth, for the advancement of truth and piety. That which is praiseworthy in individuals, is praiseworthy in bodies of men united by the spirit of charity, and acting for no other end. You will already have anticipated my design of recommending to your notice the associations of Clergy and Laity engaged in the support of the Church, and virtually directed by its rulers. If we sincerely desire to impart to all who dwell in the land the benefit of religious instruction and worship, and pastoral care, by assisting the Societies which aid in the building or enlarging of Churches, or in making provision for the maintenance of Additional Curates, we may render a service which far exceeds the reach of our single ability. In like manner, the blessings of religious training may be secured to **[p. 29]** the children of the poor by contributing to the National Society, and to the association established on similar principles in this diocese, which has the strongest pretensions to your support. Nor has the Society for the Propagation of the Gospel less claim to your bounty. Its exertions have of late been extraordinary, and the Churches in many of our foreign possessions would be desolate, if deprived its assistance. These societies are respectively labouring in the advancement of a cause, which has a right to the aid of every true member of our Church; and if they represent the general feeling of churchmen, their operations, considered as national, may in some measure atone for the indifference shown by the State for duties of such infinite importance.

It is proved by experience, that the most effectual method of obtaining the requisite aid is through the agency of local associations. This plan has been adopted in several parts of the kingdom, and, I am happy to add, of this diocese. The example thus set will, I doubt not, be generally followed. And I look forward with the pleasing expectation, that, on my next Visita- **[p. 30]** tion, if my life should be spared so long, I shall find a system established in every parish of regular collections in aid of these societies. There is no reason to fear that such appeals on their behalf would be prejudicial to the local charities; on the contrary, the practice of giving will create habits of bounty: the arguments addressed to the feelings and conscience in favour of these institutions will awaken and cherish in the minds of the people a disposition to honour God with their substance, to compassionate the miseries of the poor.

Before I conclude, I may be allowed to offer a few observations on a subject of the highest importance, not only to the ministers, but to every member of the Church. It is evident beyond contradiction, that unity of purpose and action is conducive to the efficiency of all associations, and that their power is weakened by division. And this is peculiarly true of the Church, a society of divine institution, forming one body, directed by one Spirit, having one hope, and acknowledging one Lord, one faith, one baptism, one God and Father of all. Separation, contention, and strife are directly at variance with the primary notion **[p. 31]** of a Catholic Church, established on principles which imply the co-operation and mutual sympathy of all its members. To these fruitful sources of evil we may trace a great part of the calamities which we have to lament in the present day. If the ministrations of the Church are insufficient at home or abroad; if our places of worship are threatened with ruin for want of repair; if schemes have been wickedly and madly proposed, excluding religious instruction from the schools for the poor, the cause may be found in acrimonious discord which would sacrifice the spiritual interests of the people to the jealousies of rival sects. Among the certain consequences of schism is the dissemination of errors destructive of faith and virtue. The evils of dissent are not fully appreciated by those who look only to the respectable ministers of the orthodox congregations of Dissenters. The name is applied to doctrines and practices of very different kinds; and while it unfortunately belongs to many pious and good men, it serves as a cover to the wildest fanaticism, and the grossest corruptions of morality. In the present condition of things, the utmost we can hope to attain is to draw back such **[p. 32]** of the wanderers as are willing to listen to our arguments, to live in peace with the rest, and to promote the establishment of unity among those who look up to the Church as their common mother. Considering the latitude of opinion in nonessential points allowed within the pale of our Establishment, we may surely adhere to our own persuasions without impeaching the motives of others who differ from us, and may unite forbearance and gentleness with zeal in the pursuit of truth. I would it were possible to extend this great principle of unity to all the Churches of Christendom. The dissensions which separate the Churches of the East and the West, and the corruptions and intolerance which drove the Protestants from the communion of Rome, have been most injurious to the Catholic Church. A reconciliation would, indeed, be desirable. But reunion with Rome has been rendered impossible by the sinister policy of the Council of Trent, which, dreading the result of discussion on many disputed points, made no scruple of multiplying articles of faith, which, however erroneous, can never be disclaimed by that Church till she abandons her pretensions to infallibility. Yet I am **[p. 33]** not without hope that more cordial union may in time be effected among all Protestant Churches; nor do I think it improbable that the gradual admission of light in East may improve the condition of those ancient Churches which have groaned so long under the oppression of infidels, may induce to try their creeds by the standard of Scripture, and dispose them to friendly communications with our own Church.

But whilst we are deeply impressed with the importance of these objects ...[2] and are anxious to **[p. 34]** assist in promoting them, we can never lose sight of our proper and immediate concern, – the care of our own flocks. The extraordinary quantity **[p. 35]** of matter relating to the general interests of the Church has left me little time for adverting to details which form a great part of a clergyman's duty, and affect the efficiency of his ministrations as they are well or ill performed. I must, therefore, confine my observations to a few points. The attention of the Clergy has been of late more carefully turned to the observance of the directions of the rubric, in respect to the Liturgy and offices of the Church; and this laudable regard to order and law cannot fail to be useful, if conducted with sound judgment. The impropriety of performing offices in private houses, which are appointed to be publicly used, is now generally admitted, and I trust we shall speedily see the discontinuance of so irregular a practice. But some allowance may fairly be made to bodily infirmity, and perhaps even to inveterate prejudice or mental weakness. In the correction of irregularities of long standing, much discretion is requisite; and in cases where argument has been found ineffectual, the ultimate object may sometimes be more surely attained by temporary indulgence, than by insisting on immediate compliance with rule.

[p. 36] In the celebration of Divine Service, the introduction of novelties is much to be deprecated; and even the revival of usages which, having grown obsolete, have the appearance of novelties to the ignorant, may occasion dissatisfaction, dissension and controversy. In cases of this nature it may be better to forego even advantageous changes, and wait for the decision of authority, than to open fresh sources of misapprehension or strife by singularity. There is one point, however, of no little importance, in which material benefit would accrue to the public, by a strict observance of the rubric, which prescribes the quality of service required in the Church. A full compliance with its injunctions, in regard to the use of the Liturgy on week-days, is not to be expected in all places; but it is greatly to be regretted that its regulations were ever dispensed with, in respect to the complement of duty on the Lord's Day. I am fully aware that this departure from law, this infringement of the rights of the parishioners, was originally occasioned by necessity, but I am equally certain that it becomes

2 Excursus in text of comments about the ministry of the cathedral at Canterbury.

an abuse which ought not to be tolerated, when the necessity has ceased to exist. The omission of one of the **[p. 37]** services deprives many parishioners of access to the Church, and furnishes others with an excuse to themselves for staying away; it consigns the thoughtless to idleness for at least one portion of the Sabbath, and sends the religious to strange places of worship, with the risk of eventually detaching them from the Church. On the sense of the Legislature upon this subject, expressed by recent enactments, I say nothing. But I leave it to the judgement of those who, without a cogent necessity, omit the morning or evening service, whether they are duly conforming to the laws of the Church, or fulfil the obligations of their office. I would further suggest that, in places where both services are performed with only one sermon, the advantage to the parish would be great, if an encouragement to attendance were held out by the addition of a discourse, a catechetical lecture, or a short exposition of Scripture. The ministers of our Church can never forget that they are the messengers of the Lord to His people, the shepherds of His flock to guide and feed them, the stewards of His household to dispense to their fellow-servants the bread of life; and in order to qualify them for the duties belonging to these several **[p. 38]** characters, they have the promise of His continual presence, and the assistance of His Holy Spirit. Thus appointed and furnished with power, they are subject to an awful responsibility, and would entirely mistake the nature and end of their office if they measured their duty by the compulsory regulations of law, or relaxed their exertions, while anything remained to be done, for the edification of their respective congregations.

Let it not be supposed that any reproach is intended in these observations. I have great reason to be satisfied with the spirit that prevails in the diocese, and the general conduct of the Clergy. In their concern for the interests of the Church, in their readiness to promote education at home and missions abroad, and in the care of their parishes, they have given an unequivocal pledge of continued exertion in the prosecution of those several objects. From the time when I was called to the station which gives me the right of addressing you, I have had the gratification of seeing a gradual diminution of non-residence, an increase in the numbers of ministers, and the quantity of duty performed by them, in the building or enlarging of Churches and Chapels and **[p. 39]** the erection of Glebe-houses in places where there was no fit habitation for a clergyman. And I look forward, not without reason, I trust, to the time when this metropolitan diocese will exhibit a pattern to the rest of the kingdom, as nearly approaching to perfection as can be expected from human infirmities.

I take this opportunity of mentioning, that the measures recommended by the Commissioners, and sanctioned by the Legislature, will give to the diocese a second Archdeaconry with an ample endowment, and thus distribute a burden which must press heavily on any individual, however zealous and active.[3] And this reminds me of the obligations I am under to the Archdeacon for the friendly and effective assistance which I have on all occasions received from him in the superintendence of the diocese. Nor can I conclude without expressing my thanks to the Deans of the several rural deaneries, for their gratuitous discharge of an office, which they have undertaken at my request. Their authority, which has hitherto rested on the voluntary acquiescence of the Clergy, will in future have the sanction of law; and though to my great regret no means have been **[p. 40]** found of remunerating their labours, or even replaying their expenses, I confide in their kindness to their diocesan, and their attachment to the Church, for the continuance of services, which I can pronounce from experience to be highly useful.

Relying on your hearty co-operation in all works of piety and charity, and requesting the benefit of your prayers, I now humbly commend you, my Reverend Brethren, to the guidance of that good Spirit, who alone can supply the will and ability to obey the commandments of our Lord, and give the desired effect to our labours.

3 Letter Commendatory from The Most Rev. The Lord Archbishop of Canterbury, &c., 1841

To the Right Reverend our Brothers in Christ, the Prelates and Bishops of the Ancient and Apostolic Churches in Syria and the countries adjacent, greeting in the Lord:

We, WILLIAM, by Divine Providence, Archbishop of Canterbury, Primate of all England and Metropolitan, most earnestly commend to your brotherly love the Right Rev. Michael Solomon Alexander, Doctor in Divinity, who we, being well assured of his learning and piety, have consecrated to the office of a Bishop in the United Church of England Ireland, according to the ordinances of our holy apostolic Church, and having obtained the consent of our Sovereign Lady the Queen, have sent out to Jerusalem, with authority to exercise spiritual jurisdiction over the Clergy and congregations of our Church, which are now, or which hereafter may be, established in the countries above mentioned. And in order to prevent any misunderstanding in regard to this our purpose, we

3 The Archdeaconry of Maidstone was created in 1841.

think it right to make known to you, that we have charged the said Bishop our Brother not to intermeddle in any way with the jurisdiction of the Prelates or other Ecclesiastical Dignitaries bearing rule in the Churches of the East, but to show them due reverence and honour, and to be ready, on all occasions, and by all the means in his power to promote a mutual interchange of respect, courtesy, and kindness. We have good reason to believe that our Brother is willing, and will feel himself in conscience bound, to follow these our instructions; and we beseech you, in the name of our Lord Jesus Christ, to receive him as a Brother, and to assist him, as opportunity may offer, with your good offices.

We trust that your Holinesses will accept this communication as a testimony of our respect and affection, and of our hearty desire to renew that amicable intercourse with the ancient Churches of the East, which has been suspended for ages, and which, if restored, may have the effect, with the blessing of God, of putting an end to divisions which have brought the most grievous calamities on the Church of Christ.

In this hope, and with sentiments of the highest respect for your Holinesses, we have affixed our archiepiscopal seal to this letter, written with our own hand at our palace of Lambeth, on the twenty-third day of November, in the year of our Lord one thousand eight hundred and forty-one.

4 A Letter addressed to the Clergy and Laity of his Province by William, Lord Archbishop of Canterbury, London, 1845

[p. 3] For a considerable time past my attention has been anxiously turned to the divisions in the Church, occasioned by differences of opinion with respect to the intention of certain rubrical directions in the Liturgy, and diversities of practice in the performance of Divine Service. These questions, relating to matters in themselves indifferent, but deriving importance from their connexion with the maintenance of uniformity and order in the solemn ministrations of the Church, are rendered difficult by the ambiguity of the Rubrics in some instances, and in all, by the doubts which may arise as to the weight which should be allowed to general usage when it varies from the written law. It is partly on these accounts, and partly from uncertainty with respect to the extent of the powers committed to the Archbishop of the Province, in the Preface to the Book of Common Prayer, for the resolution of **[p. 4]** doubts in regard to the contested points, that I have not felt myself justified in expressing an authoritative opinion upon questions occasionally submitted to me on these subjects. I was, indeed, willing to hope that these controversies, like many of much greater importance which have for a season disquieted the Church, would be suffered to die away of themselves, when the arguments on each side had been thoroughly sifted, from the good sense of the parties engaged in them, and the general conviction of their unprofitableness. But having been disappointed in this expectation, and considering the tendency of continued agitation to weaken the sacred bond of affection which ought to unite the Clergy and Laity as members of one body in Christ, I hold it a duty to come forward, in the hope of allaying animosities, and putting a stop to dissensions which are shown by experience to be not only unedifying but mischievous. With this view I would call your attention to a few considerations, which, with persons who are desirous of peace, will, I trust, have their due weight.

It has long been observed that, in the performance of Divine Service in the generality of our **[p. 5]** parochial churches, there has been a deviation, in certain particulars, from the express directions of the Rubric, and that, in some cases, a difference in respect to the sense of the Rubric has led to a diversity in practice. In regard to such points, in themselves non-essential, the most conscientious clergymen have felt themselves justified in treading in the steps of their predecessors; and hence the irregularity (for all departure from rule is irregular), which seems, in some instances at least, to have existed from the beginning, became inveterate. There have, I apprehend, at all times been clergymen who have been distressed by this inconsistency; and of late years it has been regarded by many excellent men as irreconcilable with the obligations which they took upon themselves on their admission into Holy Orders. Under the influence of these scruples, they thought it right to adhere as closely as possible to the letter of the Rubric in their ministrations; whilst others of their brethren, not less conscientious, have been determined by considerations, in their estimation of great weight, to follow the usage which they found established in their respective churches. Under these circumstances a diversity of practice has **[p. 6]** arisen, which is not only inconsistent with the principle of uniformity maintained by the Church, but is sometimes associated in the minds of the people with peculiarities of doctrine, and gives birth to suspicions and jealousies destructive of the confidence which always subsist between the flock and their pastor. To prevent the increase of an evil which might terminate in actual schisms was confessedly most desirable; and the most effectual mode of accomplishing the object, it has been thought, would be found in general conformity to the Rubric. Universal concurrence in this easy and obvious regulation would have combined the several advantages of securing compliance with the law of the Church and the land, of putting a stop to unauthorised innovations, and of excluding party distinctions, in their character decidedly un-christian, from the public worship of God; and I cannot but regret that measures which, with a view to these good purposes, have been recommended by high authorities, should not have been received with unanimous acquiescence, as the means of restoring order and peace, without any departure from the principles of the Church, or offence to the most scrupulous conscience.

[p. 7] At the same time, I am sensible that those who object gave much to allege in their justification. If the written law is against them, they plead an opposite usage, in parochial churches at least, reaching back, perhaps, to the time when the intentions of the lawgiver was best understood, superseding its literal sense, and determining its real meaning; they appeal to the general consent of Bishops, Clergy and Laity, implied in the absence of any effectual interference during so long a period; they object to the sudden revival of rules, which in their opinion are obsolete, and still more, to their rigid enforcement after so long an abeyance. In fairness to them we must allow, that this dislike of alterations in the manner of worship to which they have been accustomed from their infancy, proceeding, as it does, from attachment to the ordinances of the Church, ought not to be visited with unkindly censure; and we can hardly be surprised at any change being regarded with suspicion when so many attempts have been made to introduce innovations which are really objectionable, and tend, as far as they go, to alter the character of our Church. It must also be granted that the intention of the Church is not always clearly dis- **[p. 8]** coverable from the Language of the Rubric, nor determinable with absolute certainty from the records of early practice. In such cases it may with some show of reason be said, that, as the eminent men to whom the several revisions of the Liturgy were successively entrusted, did not see the necessity of seeing directions so precise as to ensure a rigid conformity in every particular, we may be contented to acquiesce in slight deviations from rule, suggested by convenience, and sanctioned by long usage.

Now, whatever may be the force of the arguments on either side, a difference of opinion will probably always exists in regard to the contested points. But all parties will concur in regarding these points as of far less importance than the maintenance of that mutual confidence which, next to support from above, forms the main strength of the Church, producing the harmonious co-operation of its several members, and disposing the people to look up with reverence to their pastor as their spiritual instructor and guide. In whatever degree, or by whatever means, the tie of affection is loosened, a proportionate diminution will follow of that moral influence on which the efficiency of the Clergyman's teaching will always depend.

The case, then, if fairly considered with reference to the existing dissensions, and the results to be expected from their continuance, will show the necessity of mutual forbearance to the peace and the honour, I may even say, to the safety, of the Church. The Laity, it may be hoped, will see the propriety of respecting the consciences of such of the Clergy as have held themselves bound to strict compliance with the express directions of the Rubric, without regard to former disuse; and the Clergy will perceive the expediency of not pressing too harshly, or abruptly, the observance of laws which, having by themselves and their predecessors been long suffered to sleep, have now the appearance of novelty. I am fully alive to the importance of uniformity in the celebration of Divine Service; but I think it would be purchased too dearly at the expense of lasting divisions, – a consequence which, I trust, will be averted by a suspension of the existing disputes. My hope of such an adjustment is grounded on the wisdom, temper, and piety which are engaged **[p. 10]** on both sides of the question. A settlement which would have the sanction of law is at the present moment impossible; and, were it possible, could hardly be attempted with hope of success, till the subsisting excitement has been allayed by time and reflection. But till that time shall arrive, our regard to the spiritual interest of our brethren ought surely to put a stop to contentions, which, besides the offence against charity, engage much time and ability which might be infinitely better applied, and which can afford pleasure to those only who bear ill-will to our Church. The matters in controversy, considered in themselves, are not of vital importance: the service in our Churches has in general been conducted in conformity to the Apostle's direction, with order and decency; and, whether performed with exact regard to the letter of the Rubric, or with the variations established by general usage, will still be decent and orderly. I therefore entreat you to consider, whether the peace of the Church should be hazarded by prolonging an unprofitable controversy, at a time, more especially, when her energies are directed, with such hope of success, to the promotion of religion and morals, and when **[p. 11]** the Clergy and Laity are zealously engaged in united exertions for the erection and endowment of Churches and Schools, and for other pious and beneficial objects, in almost every part of the country.

What I would most earnestly recommend, for the present, is the discontinuance of any proceedings, in either direction, on the controverted questions. In churches where alterations have been introduced with general acquiescence, let things remain as they are; in those which retain the less accurate usage, let no risk of division be incurred by any attempt at change, till some final arrangement can be made with the sanction of the proper authorities. In the case of churches where agitation prevails, and nothing has been definitely settled, it is not possible to lay down any general rule which may be applicable to all circumstances. But is it too much to hope that those who are zealous for the honour of God and the good of his Church, will show, by the temporary surrender of their private opinions, that they are equally zealous in the cause of peace and charity?

[p. 12] On the particular questions which disquiet the public mind, I think it unadvisable to pronounce an opinion. Upon careful examination, I have found reason to think, that some of these questions are more difficult of solution that is commonly imagined, and that the means which occurs at first sight is not always the most correct. And the general question, in respect to what should be conceded to usage in controlling or modifying the written law, seems to me to be open to much doubt. But, if I were ever so fully persuaded in my own mind, I should be unwilling, for reasons already assigned, to pronounce a judgment which, not having legal authority, might be accepted by some and disregarded by others, and might thus increase the confusion which it was designed to remedy. For similar reasons I have not thought it expedient to call the Bishops of my Province together at this time, though it will be my desire, as well as my duty, to seek their advice and assistance when a fit opportunity presents itself. I am, however, fully assured of their general concurrence in deprecating the continuance of discussion, which will undoubtedly multiply strife and contention, **[p. 13]** but which, in the present posture of things, can lead to no beneficial result.

In order to guard against misapprehension, I think it proper to state, that all I have said here is strictly confined to the rubrical questions which have occasioned the present agitation. All change in the performance of the Service, affecting the doctrine of the Church, by alteration, addition, or omission, I regard with unqualified disapprobation. I may further remark, that the danger to the Church would be great, if clergymen, not having the due respect either to episcopal authority or established usage, should interpret the Rubrics for themselves, should introduce or curtail ceremonies at pleasure, or make Divine Service in any ways the means of expressing their own theological opinions or party views. In respect to the Ritual, the Preface to the Book of Common Prayer directs all persons having doubts, or diversely taking anything in the performance of the Church Service, to resort to the Bishop of the diocese for the resolution of such doubts, and the appeasing of diversities. Had due attention been paid, from the first, to this salutary **[p. 14]** rule, the Church might perhaps have been saved from much of the dissension which at various times has divided her members, and grieved and perplexed her rulers, and which, if not speedily checked, may again cause a serious disturbance of her peace. Considering the course I have suggested as offering the only immediate means of averting such a calamity, and at the same time preparing the way for a final arrangement at a convenient season,

I earnestly recommend its adoption, in the hope that, through the blessing of God, it may lay the foundation of lasting peace; 'and to this end' – (I borrow the words of a learned and pious ritualist[4]) – 'to this end may the God of Peace give us all meek hearts, quiet spirits, and devout affections, and free us from all prejudice, that we may have full churches, frequent prayers, and fervent charity; that, uniting in our prayers here, we may all join in His praises hereafter, for the sake of Jesus Christ our Lord.' Amen.

W. Cantuar
Lambeth Palace, Jan. 11, 1845

4 Dean Thomas Comber of Durham (1645–99), *Companion to the Temple* (1672–76).

Section II
Parliamentary Speeches

1 Augmentation of Small Livings, 1831

HL Deb 29 July 1831, vol. 5, cols 515–17

[515] [§] The Archbishop of Canterbury rose, to move the second reading of the Bill for the Augmentation of the Incomes of small Church Livings. The object of the Bill was, to extend the provisions of an Act, of Charles 2nd, entitled, 'An Act for confirming and perpetuating Augmentations made by Ecclesiastical Persons to small Vicarages and Curacies, and for other Purposes.' That Act had been passed with **[516]** a view similar to that which he contemplated, but it had not gone far enough towards effecting its object. It was not his intention, at present, to enter at large on the subject, of appropriations or impropriations, but those who wished to make themselves fully acquainted with it, might consult a letter which had been written to Mr. Percival by Lord Harrowby, which had been recently reprinted, and in which the subject was treated in a full, clear, and lucid manner. He would only observe, that great abuses had prevailed, as to appropriations, from the time of the Conquest to that of the Reformation, and that, instead of being remedied at the Reformation, they had been confirmed and perpetuated. This state of things continued during the reign of Elizabeth. On the accession of James, many attempts had been made to correct these abuses, and at the Restoration an excellent opportunity was presented for that purpose, had it been taken advantage of. The Archbishop of Canterbury and the Bishop of London of that time, had been distinguished for their exertions to get a portion of the revenue of the Church applied to the augmentation of small livings, but they had not been very successful. In the reign of Charles 2nd, an Act was passed to enable impropriators to apply part of their tithes to the augmentation of small livings; and the object of this Bill was, to extend its provisions, and to allow Collegiate Bodies, and Hospitals, and Spiritual Corporations, to apply a portion of their ecclesiastical revenues to the augmentation of small rectories, vicarages, and curacies; and it was proposed, that the incumbents of the richer livings should be empowered, with the consent of the bishop and patron, to assign part of the tithes of their livings to the augmentation of small livings, such assignments to be binding on the successors. He knew, that, if the Bill should pass, there were incumbents of rich livings who were prepared to assign a portion of their tithes in this way, and he was, therefore, warranted in saying, that this measure would do a great deal of good. The condition of the clergy would thus be improved, without any violent revolution of property. But in order to have the provisions of this Bill carried into execution in the safest and most efficient manner, he had taken steps towards instituting an inquiry into the state of Church property. The Bill was no new measure of his. It had **[517]** been proposed some years before among a series of Bills which prepared for the improvement of the state of the Church. He had the satisfaction to state, that he had received encouragement and support in effecting his object of improving the condition of the Church from two successive Administrations. Both the noble Duke opposite and the noble Earl who succeeded, had been equally well disposed to make such improvements in the Church as should be sanctioned by the heads of it. And he had to thank both the noble Duke and his successor for their kindness and courtesy. In conclusion, he had to observe, that this was no concession to unreasonable clamour, but only an improvement which was really called for, and might be safely carried into effect.

2 Pluralities Bill, 1832

HL Deb 23 March 1832, vol. 11, cols 787–95

[**787**] The Archbishop of Canterbury said, that he felt himself called upon to offer a few observations on the objects and prin- **[788]** ciple of the Plurality of Benefices Bill, on moving that their Lordships should then resolve themselves into a Committee to consider that measure. As those objects and that principle had been fully discussed in the last Session of Parliament, he did not consider it necessary, on the second reading of the Bill, to enter into any explanation of its details; but, as a noble Lord, on a former night, had brought forward amendments, which, in point of fact, went to effect an entire alteration of the measure; and as that noble Lord at the same time, accused him of practising a delusion on their Lordships, in vindication of himself, and of the motives by which he was actuated, he begged to be permitted to say a few words upon the present occasion. So far back as the reign of Henry 8th, previous to which the regulation of the Church, as regarded pluralities, was under the canon law, which was opposed to pluralities of all kinds, the first Act was passed on this subject. By

that Act – the 1st Henry 8th – all persons holding benefices valued at 8l. a-year in the King's books, were prevented from holding any other benefice, except by dispensation. A great number of persons, however, who were in possession of certain qualifications, were allowed to hold two benefices; members of the Council were able to hold three, and King's chaplains could hold any number to which it was the pleasure of the Crown to appoint them, without regard to their value. With these exceptions, no person could hold more than one benefice with cure of souls of 8l. a-year. There were other livings under the value of 8l. a-year, which were left in the same state as before, under the canon law, which, though it prohibited pluralities altogether, was so inefficient, that persons could hold any number of livings under 8l. a-year at any distance, under such qualifications as would enable them to hold an ordinary living. Another clause of that Bill permitted deans of cathedrals, and collegiate bodies, to make their own regulations in respect of their own estates, or left them to the operation of the canon law. With these exceptions, and the exception of members of the council, and King's chaplains, who might hold any number of livings, all persons were prohibited from holding two benefices, with cure of souls of the value of 8l. a-year. The Bill which was on the Table provided, that a space of not more than thirty **[789]** miles should intervene between two livings held in plurality, this regulation would have the effect of reducing the present pluralities nearly two-thirds. There was also another important alteration, which, he thought would be considered an improvement, namely, that the office of King's chaplain would not give a title to hold in connexion with it any Church preferment: that office would in future give no advantages beyond those enjoyed without it. It had been found, after the most mature reflection, necessary to make provision for enabling incumbents of the poorer livings to pay their curates. In making that provision, it was necessary to bear in mind that the valuation of livings in the King's books was no sufficient guide in the present day, and the fact he conceived, would afford a sufficient answer to most of the objections that had been urged on that subject; but the conclusive answer which this Bill gave to the chief objection to pluralities was to be found in the enactment that no ecclesiastical person should hold more than two livings, and those only within a distance of thirty miles. It was, he apprehended, no valid objection to this measure, that it did not accomplish that which it did not profess. As to the dignities held in the cathedral churches, he had only to observe that they were of various values, and they could not impose any further restriction upon them than the Bill contained. He was aware that there were anomalies and imperfections in the existing system, and he was far from saying that this Bill would remedy them, or that any Bill could advantageously remove them all, but here they had one most important step taken, and that he hoped, might enable them hereafter to go further in the same path. The noble Lord who had moved the amendments to which he had already adverted, had spoken of this Bill as a delusion, and had declared that it left monstrous abuses remaining which it ought to have remedied. He stated that the bishopric of Winchester, the deanery of Durham, and a variety of other preferments, might be held by one and the same person. He (the Archbishop of Canterbury) admitted that in the present state of the law, these were possibilities which this Bill did not guard against. He confessed that abuses of authority might occur, which, as no rational man had ever committed, so no rational man would ever **[790]** think of guarding against. They did not, in preparing this Bill, calculate all possible contingencies – they did not aim at combating shadows, or fighting with windmills. Again, the House heard a very good speech from the noble Lord against the practice of Bishops holding livings in commendam, but that had nothing to do with the present question; for this Bill professed to deal with pluralities of another class, and with them it did successfully deal. The speech of the noble Lord did not really, for the purposes of the Bill then before them, require much reply, for it was beside the question; but with respect to his Amendments, he would with the permission of their Lordships, go through some of them. The noble Lord, in the first place, proposed to enact that, from and after the passing of the Bill, 'It shall not be lawful for any Archbishop or Bishop actually exercising episcopal jurisdiction, or enjoying the revenues of any diocese, to accept or retain any benefice with the cure of souls, either in commendam or otherwise, or to hold any other dignity or ecclesiastical preferment.' He presumed the word Archbishop was here introduced as a word of course, for it never could for a moment be supposed, that the Archbishop of York or the Archbishop of Canterbury, would hold a benefice in commendam. In fact this was a clause guarding against the abuse of the Royal Prerogative in a case where there was not the least imaginable probability that it would be abused. There was next an amendment to clause 3, which said, 'Provided always, and be it further enacted, that it shall and may be lawful for any Archbishop or Bishop, the revenues of whose diocese do not exceed 3,500l., to hold in commendam any dignity or ecclesiastical preferment without cure of souls, provided the gross annual value thereof, together with the revenues of his diocese, shall not amount to more than 4,000l. annually, and that he shall pay over the surplus, if any, to the Governors of Queen Anne's Bounty, to be by them appropriated, with the sanction of the Archbishop of Canterbury, to the augmentation of bishoprics under the annual value of 3,500l.' He must be allowed to say, and he trusted most of their Lordships would concur with him, if they would only consider the unavoidable expenses which a Bishop must incur

– the expenses he was put to in maintaining more than one re- [**791**] sidence – in visiting the several portions of his diocese from time to time—in subscribing to every charity within his diocese – in relieving the poorer clergy – in educating and establishing his sons, besides making some provision for his family after his death – that was fixing the revenue of a Bishop too low. He was aware that it had been said, that the income which the noble Lord fixed for a Bishop was as much as a Judge generally had, but it should be recollected that a Judge stood in a very different situation from that of a Bishop. When one of the parochial clergy became a Bishop, he found himself transferred from a situation in which his income scarcely equalled his necessary and proper expenditure; but what was the fact with respect to a Judge? He was transferred to a situation of less labour perhaps – of more dignity certainly; his former position being one not entailing much expense, and giving facilities for the accumulation of a fortune: whereas the situation of a Bishop was widely different; he was from the outset surrounded with circumstances calculated to create pecuniary embarrassment. The expenses of his entrance upon his sacred duties were in themselves of no small amount, and even though he should exercise all the economy that was consistent with the feelings of a liberal mind, he would still find it extremely difficult to maintain those appearances which his situation required. From his own experience, and the evidence of facts, he could affirm, that, if the incomes of the Bishops were to be regulated according to the rules laid down by the noble Lord, much of the usefulness and dignity of their station in the Church would be at an end. With respect to livings in commendam, he begged to mention one consideration, while he was upon the subject, which was not altogether unworthy of attention – it was, that those livings might in some sort, be said to possess the advantages of two rectors, for Bishops always paid their curates larger salaries than other holders of benefices. He considered that the whole of this enactment directed against livings in commendam, was unnecessary, and it might prove mischievous. There was no case in which a living happened to be held in commendam in which, if it were necessary to separate it, the separation might not be effected without the aid of this enactment; and further, he did not see that [**792**] any of the amendments would have the effect of preventing unnecessary translations. The third Amendment proposed by the noble Lord was as follows: – 'And be it further enacted that if any spiritual person having a deanery, prebend, or canonry, or any precentorship, treasurership, subdeanery, chancellorship, or any wardenship, or fellowship in any cathedral or collegiate church; or any dignity, benefice, or ecclesiastical preferment, either with or without, any cure of souls, shall after the passing of this Act, accept, or be admitted to any other deanery, prebend, or canonry, precentorship, treasurership, subdeanery, wardenship, or fellowship, in any cathedral or collegiate church, or any other dignity, benefice, or ecclesiastical preferment, either with, or without cure of souls; then, and immediately after such acceptance or admission, the first deanery, prebend, or canonry, precentorship, treasurership, sub-deanery, chancellorship, wardenship, or fellowship in any cathedral or collegiate church, or other dignity, benefice, or ecclesiastical preferment, either with, or without cure of souls, shall be ipso facto void.' On this Amendment it was needless to say much: it spoke for itself; and it was one, the adoption of which, he thought, but few of their Lordships would be disposed to agree to. One of the most extraordinary propositions ever made to that House, was contained in the proposed Amendment to clause 9, the object of which was, to give power to the Archbishop of Canterbury, in certain cases, to grant license or dispensation for holding two benefices, whose joint value did not exceed the amounts therein specified; and then this proposed amendment said, that such person who shall have obtained the degree of Doctor of Divinity with a certificate from the Archbishop of Canterbury, and solemn declaration inserted in the testimonial thereof, that the same was not conferred from partiality or affection, entreaty or interest, but purely and solely from a conviction of the graduate's pious zeal, theological knowledge, and pastoral aptness to accept and hold such benefice, provided the population of one of such benefices shall not exceed 500 souls, and the joint annual value of such two benefices, &c. No noble Lord could imagine that the Archbishop of Canterbury had the means of granting those certificates upon his own knowledge. In all such cases he must **[793]** rely upon the testimonies supplied to him by others. He trusted he had never shown a disposition to shrink from any burthen, duty, or reasonable responsibility, belonging to his situation; and he did persuade himself that, in objecting to this it would not be thought that he was departing from that which had ever been his practice; but it was a duty which he owed not merely to himself, but to his successors, to protest against such a clause. Under this Amendment the Archbishop of Canterbury would be required not only to judge of the knowledge, but of the intellectual, moral, and even physical, qualifications, of the persons presenting themselves as candidates. This was almost impossible; and, if possible, it would not be useful. Their Lordships must also see, that the provision which the noble Lord would make for the parochial clergy, or rather the minimum to which he would reduce them, was quite inconsistent with the maintenance of a family, or with their comfortable and respectable living. With any observations on this topic it was not necessary to trouble the House, as the plan proposed conduced neither to the real object of the Bill, nor to the diminution of pluralities. The proposed Amendment to Clause 11, was this – 'And he it further enacted, that, from and after the passing of this Act, every Archbishop and Bishop shall, on or before the 1st day of July in every year, make to the Archbishop of Canterbury, to be by him transmitted, together with the like return from himself to his Majesty in Council, on or before the 25th day of March, a return of the gross annual revenues or emoluments of his diocese, from whatever source derived, during the succeeding year; and also specifying the name and value of any dignitary, benefice, or ecclesiastical preferment, held therewith; and that every other spiritual person shall make a like return of the name, and true and full value of any dignity, benefice, or ecclesiastical preferment, held by him to the Bishop of the diocese in which it is situated, to be by him transmitted to the King in Council, on or before the aforesaid 25th day of March.' He would appeal to the noble Lord, whether such a clause as this ought to be introduced into the Bill – supposing such a measure to be advantageous (and he, for one, should not object to ascertain the value of all emoluments possessed by dignitaries of the **[794]** Church) it ought rather to form the subject of a separate substantive Bill, than to be thus introduced into a measure which had another object in view. He repeated that he was most anxious to have the amount of Church property ascertained, for there had been gross and scandalous exaggerations on the subject; and he had no doubt that the proposal contained in the noble Lord's Amendment would soon be acted on; but this mode of doing it appeared in the highest degree exceptionable, for it could not fail to lead to frauds in a variety of ways. A discretionary power was given to the Archbishop of Canterbury, as to granting or withholding dispensations; and of course he would take, in every case, the value of the benefice, as well as all other circumstances, into consideration; but it would be quite impossible for the Legislature to adopt any principle, if the living were under the value of 8l., of making value the criterion, without having some documents before it. He was most desirous that such an inquiry should be instituted, in order to show the gross misstatements that were disseminated, through the medium, chiefly of cheap pamphlets, but they were reiterated at public meetings, by persons who did, and ought to know better. This mode of proceeding, he verily believed, was adopted in order to place the Church in an invidious point of view. It was asserted in some of these pamphlets, and had been repeated at certain meetings, that the revenues of the Church were 9,000,000l. per annum; but whenever a return of the ecclesiastical revenues should be made, they who had put forth, and those who had believed such exaggerations, would look at that return with no small degree of surprise, and would find how egregiously they had been deceived. The Church had nothing to fear from inquiry; and he had every reason to hope that means would be taken to ascertain what its revenues actually were. The mode which the noble Lord had suggested of annual returns, was not the best that could be desired for that purpose, because such returns would be attended with great inconvenience, and they would be extremely difficult to make out correctly, even by those who wished to act most honestly. He would spare their Lordships from going into the other parts of the Bill, and would only refer to the clause which took away from their Lordships the privilege of appointing chaplains. **[795]** He trusted their Lordships would believe that he was the last man to wish to interfere unnecessarily with their privileges; or to bear hard upon any members of the clergy. As the value, however, of such appointments was merely imaginary, he had no doubt their Lordships would willingly resign such privileges for the good of the Church. As for himself, so far as the Bill was concerned, he had encountered so much opposition that he was almost disheartened. In attempting to please everybody as far as possible, he had stirred up opponents on all sides, without forwarding his object. This was the third Session the Bill had been before Parliament. He would, however, conclude, by moving that their Lordships go into Committee, where they might deal with the Bill as they thought best.

3 Reform of Parliament (England) Bill, 1831

HL Deb 7 October 1831, vol. 8, cols 302–04

[302] The Archbishop of Canterbury said, it was his intention to have addressed their Lordships at an earlier hour this evening, and if he had had an opportunity of doing so, he would, as he greatly desired to have entered into a full statement of the reasons which imposed upon him the painful necessity of opposing a measure which came before that House with the strong recommendation of his Majesty's Government, and which had been carried by a majority of the House of Commons. But having been disappointed in that wish, he hoped, after the splendid display of argument and of eloquence which they had heard in the course of the Debate, that he should be considered as acting most properly, both to their Lordships and to himself, if he trespassed on their attention as briefly as possible at that very late hour. He meant to confine himself to a few words, and he would not trouble the House even with these, if he did not deem it necessary, in justice to himself, to state his opinions and feeling on the general subject of Reform. Most sincerely as he admired our happy Constitution, still he did not carry his veneration so far as not to allow that it had its defects and anomalies; neither had he such a strong predilection for things as they were as not to think that improvement was desirable and might be effected. Whatever abuse or corruption had crept [303] into the Constitution, by neglect or by vicious practice, he was anxious to correct by safe and constitutional remedies. To a Reform synonymous with the extermination of abuses, and the restoration of the excellencies of the Constitution, he professed himself a sincere friend, and amongst the right reverend Prelates who sat on the bench near him, he did not believe there was a single individual who did not concur with him in that sentiment. He had heard, with great satisfaction, in the course of this Debate, the opinions delivered by noble Lords in opposition to this Bill, because they had declared that their opposition was directed, not against the principle of the Bill, or the general principle of Reform, and they had expressed their willingness to accede to a measure of gradual, temperate, and safe Reform. In that sentiment he entirely concurred with them. He could not help indulging a hope, that the result of this discussion might be an union of men of all parties, having the same great object in view – the good of their country, and that, thus uniting, they would prepare some measure for the consideration of Parliament, so cautiously worded as to tranquillize the fears of those who dreaded agitation, and, at the same time, sufficiently efficient to satisfy the friends of the Constitution, who, while they desired to have its excellencies preserved and its blemishes removed, were unwilling to try an experiment so extensive as that which was now proposed. Some persons might think that a notion of this kind was chimerical and futile. He was not of that opinion; he thought that, on each side, feelings and prejudices might be sacrificed; and in proportion to those sacrifices – in proportion as the question was relieved from the asperities and difficulties which surrounded it – in that proportion would those who adopted that wise and temperate course command and receive the gratitude of the country. He would only add, in conclusion, that, if it were their Lordships' pleasure to pass this Bill, he should sincerely rejoice, and no man more so, than himself, if the apprehensions which he entertained of its effects should turn out to be groundless. If, on the other hand, their Lordships threw out this measure, and popular violence, which he did not expect, should unfortunately follow, he would be content to bear his share in the general calamity; but, in either case, he should have this consolation, [304] during the few remaining years he had to live, that in the course which he had taken, he was actuated by no sinister motives, but that he had opposed the Bill because he thought that it was mischievous in its tendency, and would be extremely dangerous to the fabric of the Constitution.

4 Education Bill, 1839

HL Deb 05 July 1839, vol. 48, cols 1234–55

[1234] The Archbishop of Canterbury said, that he had had the honour of presenting several petitions to their Lordships' House this evening, all of which had been directed against the plan proposed by the Government in relation to the scheme of education, and against the appointment of a committee of the Privy Council to carry out that measure; and praying the House to avert the evil by which the Church was threatened by the adoption of such a course. In the general sentiments expressed in those petitions he entirely concurred, although he entertained a full sense that that concurrence of opinion placed him in a situation extremely distressing to himself – he meant that of being in opposition to her Majesty's Government. He had never found himself in such a position, without the greatest pain and concern, and he could assure their Lordships, that nothing but the paramount importance of his duty could have determined him to place himself in that position, which was in many respects unbecoming; but, at the same time, he felt that standing in the situation in which he stood, invested as he was, to a great degree, with the important charge of the Church, the guardianship of which, as well as of the moral and religious interests of the country, in a great measure, devolved upon him, he could not, consistently with the obligations under which he was placed, decline coming forward upon this occasion. If, however, so far as his own personal feelings were concerned, he was disposed to decline the duty, he could not have resisted the call which was made on him by the voice, he would not say of the clergy, but of all the friends of the Church, and not only of all the friends of the Church, but also by a very numerous body of dissenters. The clergy, who were always the objects of attack upon these occasions, might possibly be reputed to be acting from interested motives, but could that charge, by any possibility, be supported, when it was seen that a body, dissenting from the Church, a body most highly respectable in itself, most anxious for religious freedom, and entirely devoid of political bias, had come forward on this occasion, and could it be supposed that the Church had no regard for the interests **[1235]** of religion, and would sacrifice the real interests of the people to political considerations? With respect to those who were friends of the Church, it would be seen that this was a matter which affected the true foundation, not only of the Church, but of religion itself. It was a question as to the manner in which the people should be educated – whether they should receive their education on the sound principles of the Church, or whether the door should be thrown open to the instillation of principles of every sect, however wild or extravagant. Much had been said against the clergy upon this occasion, and he presumed that they were attacked as distinguished from the Church, because they were supposed to be the most vulnerable. It was said, that the clergy wished to keep the people in ignorance, that they were actuated by bigotry, and that they put forward pretensions to the exclusive education of the people. There was, however, no foundation for any such objections. If they were guilty of any crime, it was not that they were adverse to the diffusion of knowledge, but that they wished to extend it further than it seemed proper that the people should have it, and that to knowledge of affairs relating to the world – to mere secular knowledge, they would add the sanction of religion. With regard to the accusation of bigotry, he presumed that that meant nothing more than a decided attachment to that religion which they considered the best, and to that charge certainly they were inclined to plead guilty, and he thought that there was no man in his senses but would give them credit for feelings of that kind. As to their arrogating to themselves the education of the people, all that they desired was, that the education of the children of the parents among their flocks who were attached to the Church might not be taken out of their hands, that there might be no interference with them in the performance of their duty with the young as well as the old, so that the children of their flocks might be educated in the same principles, and in the same faith and doctrines of religion, which they would afterwards hear preached in Church. In considering this charge more particularly, their Lordships would perhaps allow him to say a few words in reference to the history of the education of the poor of this country. It certainly might appear surprising to those who were not acquainted with the state of things in **[1236]** those ages, that very little was done at the time of the Reformation for the education of the poor. The ignorance which up to that time had pervaded the country, and the evils which had resulted from it, had made the greatest impression upon the minds of all men, and the ignorance which was then most particularly desired to be removed was that of the higher classes, and many schools were therefore established immediately after the Reformation, which were, however, in the nature of grammar schools, and were meant for the instruction of the higher classes in languages, in order that they might be recovered from the ignorance which existed among them. It was not, however, until the end of the seventeenth century, in 1685, that the first charity school was erected in this great town for the education of the poor. That school was established by the friends of the Church. Subsequently, at the beginning of the eighteenth century, the want of education among the poor began to press on the minds of the friends of the Church, and at that time societies, composed exclusively of the clergy, were formed, and they in the course of a few years extended the scheme, which subsequently continued to flourish to the great advantage of this town. The schools had since increased in number, but that was the work of the Church; it was the work of the Society for Promoting Christian Knowledge; and while at first the number of persons instructed amounted to only 400 or 500, and had subsequently increased to 700, it was now so much extended that a selection of them only could obtain room in St. Paul's Cathedral at the annual celebration. Under the authority of this Society, about 1,500 schools had been established in England and Wales, and they were instituted on the principles of the Established Church, and not on the principle of dissent. What was done then was very inadequate, and when the population increased, the want of education in this country was found to be so great, as to make the friends of religion despair. It seemed impossible to devise remedies for the defects in the existing system, for nothing material had been done by the friends of the Church; and at that time throughout the country there was such a want of education, and there was such a mass of uneducated people, that the most sanguine persons would have been disheartened, About that time, however, a **[1237]** new system was established. He meant that which was first instituted by Dr. Bell, which was formed on the model of a school which he had seen in the East Indies, and which was afterwards adopted by Mr. Lancaster, and was now indiscriminately used, so far as the mechanism was concerned, as the Madras or Lancasterian system, for they were both the same, and gave an opportunity to the Society to extend their labours for the education of the poor. The House was aware, what was the state of the country at that time, and in seeing the change which had taken place in the course of thirty years since those schools had been first established, would be able to judge of the great obligations under which the country rested to this Society, and how much they were entitled to it for its labours. The Society at first proceeded to the accomplishment of their object by promoting the erection of new schools 'throughout the country, and establishing a central school in London. In their report, they said, that they found themselves in connection with almost every diocese in England and Wales, and that by means of their funds, amounting to 120,000l., they had aided in procuring the establishment of new schools in 1,553 places. The number of schools formerly established, was 6,778, and the scholars amounted to upwards of 597,000; while in 1837, the number of schools was 17,341, while the scholars were a million and eighty-seven. Now, when the House heard these facts stated, the accuracy of which there was no reason to doubt, he thought that they might admit that the charge against the clergy, that they desired to keep the people without education, was totally without foundation. But then they were charged also with bigotry. Was it, however, to be expected – could the country with any show of reason expect – that they could act in opposition to their own principles and to the principles of that Church of which they were members? When they professed that their religion was pure in its doctrines, true in its constitution, sound in its morals, and was calculated in every respect to supply the spiritual wants of the poorer classes, could they endeavour to promote the education of children on principles of religion opposite to those which they themselves professed? He must say, that although they might be exclusive in their principles, and although they might confine the education **[1238]** and the instruction which they delivered to that which was according to the doctrines and precepts of their own Church, they were otherwise by no means exclusive, for they admitted children of every description into their schools – no one was excluded; but at the same time he must admit that they insisted that they should all be instructed in the principles of the Established Church. He conceived, that they were right in adopting this course, and that it could not be said that they were wrong; the boon had been most thankfully accepted by many Dissenters, and in reality might be accepted by all Dissenters, who were usually called orthodox. So far as the catechism and the commandments were concerned, there was nothing in them which was offensive to any Dissenter, and he could see no reason why the most conscientious Dissenter who held these doctrines should not allow his children to go to the schools; for, in truth, the only exception which could be urged was in some words used in the catechism. With regard to attending public worship, they were not compelled to follow the tenets of the Established Church, provided their parents took them to any other place. He knew that this was the regulation which existed, for at this moment there was a school established in Westminster at which there were upwards of forty Roman Catholic children, but in reference to them he saw no difficulty; because if ever there had been any expressions in the liturgy opposed to the Roman Catholic faith, they had been expunged by the good sense of those who reviewed it in after times. He trusted that he had sufficiently explained the opinion of the clergy. Their schools were open to the children of Dissenters, and they went as far as could be possibly considered proper. He trusted, therefore, that by what he had said he had absolved the Church and the friends of the Church in this country from the charge of having any desire to keep the people in ignorance, of having any aversion to the diffusion of knowledge, of being actuated by bigotry to their QWU [own?] principles; firm attachment they had, but bigotry they had none; and of having acted with any unfairness towards the Dissenters. It appeared with respect to what the Church had done – it appeared from public returns made in the year 1833 – that the exertion of the Church and of the friends of the Church, **[1239]** in the promotion of education exceeded those of the dissenters in a degree which he was almost afraid to mention. If he took the lowest calculation that he had seen, made by an eminent person, it would seem, that the state of education furnished by the Church was twenty to one when compared with the education afforded by dissenters. But, in making that statement, he must observe, that the dissenters were not so much without education, because many of their children were educated in the schools of the Established Church; and so far they swelled the number of the scholars in those schools. Still there had been a very great deficiency in the amount of education, and even now there was a great deficiency in the education of the people. He had seen different statements and calculations upon this point, but the results were so uncertain that he would not trouble their Lordships with them. Whatever was said, however, these calculations showed, that there was a great deficiency in the amount of education in this country. No one more deplored this deficiency than the friends of the Church, and than the persons who conducted the society of which he had been speaking, and which might be considered the great organ of education in the hands of the Church, although there were many schools in the hands of the Church which were not connected with that society. They had been labouring to supply that want, and to introduce schools more extensively. In the course of the year 1838, and during the present year, they had been making great exertions – exertions which, he trusted, had been attended with a considerable degree of success; there was every prospect of it; and the friends of the Church had come forward in a manner that did the highest credit to their zeal and their expectations; although liable to all the imperfections which belonged to everything human, they would, he hoped, be realized in a high degree. It was proposed to establish a diocesan society; it was proposed, that teachers should be trained, for the want of proper schoolmasters had been extensively felt; it was proposed to establish a training school in every diocese, and he trusted that the best effects would follow. It was proposed, also, under the superintendence of the bishop and chapter of each diocese, to establish schools in every parish, or in **[1240]** every district where they could be conveniently founded. These schools were to be under the charge of the minister of the parish, and they would give to the whole agricultural population the benefits of religious and moral instruction. It was proposed likewise to establish a system of superintendence to secure the efficiency of the schools, and the uniformity of their proceedings. And, in a short time, he hoped, that the schools would be so far founded, that every clergyman – every good clergyman did it now – but he hoped soon that every clergyman would consider it as much his duty to promote a school in his parish as he did now to perform his duty in his Church. At the present time, if a clergyman neglected the duty of his church – if he absented himself from his parish, or failed in the performance of his duty – he was a marked character among his friends; and he (the Archbishop of Canterbury) trusted, that the time was not far distant when the same would be said of any neglect of the clergyman's school duty, and that every one of the clergy would deem it proper to promote the establishment of a school where there was none, and to superintend it if there was one. Now, considering the relation in which the Church stood to the State – considering the number of its members – considering the purity of its doctrines – considering the excellence of the moral and religious feelings which it tended to promote, and considering its obedience to the laws of the Government and of the State – he did not think that it was asking too much if it looked up to the Government of this country to assist it in promoting education. He thought that the claim could hardly be resisted. And at the same time the Government ought to have so much confidence in the Church as to intrust it with the management of the education of its own children, under the conditions he had before stated; or, at least, that the Government would abstain from all interference with religious teaching. He thought, that if the Government granted relief or assistance, it had a right to ensure the efficiency of its grant, and that wherever there was a grant of public money, the public had a right to see how it was applied. He was certain, however, that if the Government received an assurance that the schools were conducted properly with respect to secular learning, they might leave the religious instruction **[1241]** to the care of the members of the Church. In claiming thus much, was there any assumption – was there any arrogance – was there any desire to take into the hands of the Church all the education of the country? The Church had never advanced any pretension of that kind. He did not say, that injudicious language might not have been occasionally used upon this subject; but he appealed in confirmation of his statement to the conduct of the clergy in general. A grant of 20,00l. had been lately most laudably and most liberally made by the Government to schools connected with the National Society and with the Lancasterian Society. Had the clergy complained of the share of the Lancasterian Society? The National Society had taken their share, not only without complaint, but thankfully; they had never inquired what proportion was given to the other body, and they had been satisfied with the plan as a temporary expedient. Such it was stated to be. When Lord Althorp introduced it, he said that he brought it forward as an experiment. It had succeeded – it had been usefully applied, and he had never heard that the conductors of the Lancasterian schools were dissatisfied with the share they had received. It was considered by all as an experiment, as a temporary expedient; it was thought that a permanent system would be established in conformity with the expectations held out, and that the whole system of national education would be definitely settled. It was conceived also by the clergy that this system would be referred to the whole Parliament, and both societies had the greatest confidence that the wisdom of Parliament would distribute the fund faithfully, and with a due care for the claims of the various parties that might be entitled to consideration. He was satisfied, then, that it was hardly surprising, if they viewed the present state of things with suspicion and jealousy, and to that he attributed the great sensation in the country respecting the minutes of the Privy Council. It was considered that these minutes laid the foundation for a permanent system, without any application to Parliament. The country saw that these minutes established a board composed exclusively of her Majesty's Ministers, that the board was invested with large discretionary powers, and that it was disposed to introduce many innovations, not effected by any act of legislation, but by a mode of **[1242]** proceeding entirely excluding one branch of the Legislature excluding their Lordships' House from interfering, or from expressing any opinion on a matter of such great importance to the interests of the people. These apprehensions were greatly increased, because it was impossible not to look at the wild and extravagant schemes of education entertained in various quarters. They had seen a system of education proposed, from which religious instruction was entirely excluded. They had also seen a system of general education proposed, from which all creeds and catechisms were banished, and which would prevent the friends of the Church of England from educating their children according to their own views and their own persuasion of what was right. They had seen also, that it had been proposed to carry a scheme into execution for establishing what was falsely called a liberal system of education, without the intervention of Parliament. Let it not be conceived, however, from what he had said, or from the extract which he would read, that he was implicating the Committee, or that he was ascribing to them any participation in the design; but he meant only to show, that it was the plan of some persons. It was contained in the publication of a large society connected with education. The purport of the extract was, that All hope of amending the present system of education was to be abandoned in the nicely balanced state of parties; it would be some years before such a measure as the people had a right to demand would be passed by the House of Lords, but a bill was not a sine qua non. Ministers had the power in their own hands, by a simple vote of the House of Commons, of extending the schools, and of commencing a reform of those already established. It only required the establishment of a board of education, with the same powers of granting educational assistance as was given to the Lords of the Treasury. 20,000l. had been voted for erecting school-houses, but they served only to deceive the public into the belief that education was advancing, when it was really making but little progress. Let there be model and normal schools for the training of qualified teachers; let the central board not only determine the building of the schools, but superintend the training, and the ground would be laid for further improvement. The power of withholding pecuniary assistance would induce the schools which were mismanaged to be placed under the board. The plan was simple and feasible. An individual might waste a whole life in arguing with schoolmasters and schoolmistresses, and in **[1243]** reasoning with governors, without changing the system in above half-a-dozen schools; but a central board would, in a short time, produce a change which would appear to be the effect of magic. He hoped that he was not so far misunderstood as to charge the Committee of the Privy Council with any design of this nature. He had read the extract to show what power, in the estimation of some persons who wished to introduce a system of education which would entirely overthrow the National Church, would be in the hands of the Committee. If the persons who had written this had framed the Minute in Council, he could not see how it could have been framed more in accordance with their wishes; although, assuredly, if they had selected persons to execute the plan, they would not have selected the President of the Council and his colleagues to carry the scheme into execution. Such was the power which was lodged in the Committee, and which would officially pass to their successors, and if the plan were placed under other agencies. He would now take up the papers laid before their Lordships, with the view of showing that he had not in the slightest degree exaggerated the power thus conveyed to the Committee of the Privy Council, and which it was not possible to conceal might be used if the power were lodged in unsafe hands. In doing this he felt it necessary to go into the history of the education grants which had proceeded from the Government. He found from the papers laid before the House what was stated by Lord Althorp, the Chancellor of the Exchequer, when he moved that 20,000l. should be granted for the purpose of education. The terms of the resolution were exactly as he found them in the Treasury minute, from which he would read. He found that after the Lords of the Treasury had read the Act of the last Session, by which a sum of 20,000l. is granted to his Majesty to be issued in aid of private subscriptions for the erection of schools for the education of the children of the poorer classes in Great Britain, it was stated, The Chancellor of the Exchequer feeling it absolutely necessary that certain fixed rules should be laid down by the Treasury for their guidance in this matter, so as to render this sum most generally useful for the purposes contemplated by the grant, submitted the arrangements for the consideration of the board. That arrangement with which he need **[1244]** not trouble their Lordships in detail, provided, amongst other things – That no portion of this sum be applied to any purpose whatever except for the erection of new school-houses; and that in the definition of a school-house the residence for masters or attendants be not included; that no application be entertained unless a sum be raised by private contribution equal at the least to one-half of the total estimated expenditure; and that no application be complied with unless upon the consideration of such a report, either from the National School Society, or the British and Foreign School Society, as shall satisfy this board that the case is one deserving of attention, and there is a reasonable expectation that the school may be permanently supported. Now, they saw what were the resolutions proposed by the Chancellor of the Exchequer of that day, and which were liberally complied with by the Lords of the Treasury in the application of the grants. The Lords of the Treasury were by this minute absolved from all necessity; they were directed to apply the money between the two societies, who were in communication with all parties in the country, and who were able to say what schools were entitled to the grant, and there could be no misapplication whilst the board acted upon that principle. The next year the Lords of the Treasury resumed the consideration of the subject, and reported the number of schools which had been built during the first year – there were sixty-two schools erected, having 12,191 scholars, at a total expense of 19,380l., the amount of 8,000l. and upwards having been appropriated towards that sum by the Lords of the Treasury. So far it appeared that the grants were of great advantage, even if they went no further than establishing sixty-two schools. And on their minute the Lords of the Treasury entered this: – My Lords have the satisfaction of perceiving that there exists throughout Great Britain the utmost anxiety that the funds provided by Parliament for the purposes of education should be made generally useful, and that private charity and liberality so far from being checked, have been greatly stimulated and encouraged by reason of the public assistance afforded on the principles laid down in their minute of the 30th August, 1833. It was truly said that these grants had greatly stimulated the exertions of private benefaction. But at this time the number of applications for schools had increased to that degree that the Lords of the Treasury were obliged to lay down a restriction, and **[1245]** to confine the grants to schools that should accommodate 400 scholars and upwards, and accordingly they applied the grants to the schools in connection with the National Society, and with the British and Foreign School Society, upon that principle, for upon that principle alone would they be enabled to make the sum meet the demands. The number of scholars to be accommodated in the schools then applying for assistance in connection with the National Society was 10,674, and in connection with the British and Foreign School Society 7,500: and the Lords of the Treasury were so much satisfied with the distribution thus made, that they recommended a further grant of 20,000l. These grants were made in succeeding years, and were applied on the same principle; and on the 5th July, 1838, the Chancellor of the Exchequer submitted to the board 'The expediency of procuring and laying before Parliament more specific and detailed information than had been as yet obtained with respect to the schools, towards the erection of which grants had been made by the public. For this purpose it appeared to him that the National, and British and Foreign School Society, should be invited to direct an inspection to be made of the several schools which they had recommended to this board, and for the erection of which grants had been appropriated out of the parliamentary votes.' Another suggestion at the same time which the Chancellor of the Exchequer recommended was the erection of a 'model school,' to which, as considered by itself, there could be no objection, but would meet with general approbation. The Chancellor of the Exchequer suggested 'That in considering the number of new schools which had been assisted by the parliamentary grant, as well as the schools which were previously in existence, it appeared to him that the erection of model schools for the instruction of teachers by both societies would greatly tend to add to the efficiency of their several establishments; and that it was therefore expedient that the respective committees should be called upon, if they concurred in this opinion, to take steps for such purpose. Towards this object public aid might advantageously be directed; provided a suitable plan for carrying these intentions into effect were submitted to the Treasury, and approved of;' but then 'it was provided that the principle of private contribution, already laid down and carried into **[1246]** effect by previous minutes of this board, should be strictly adhered to.' And the Chancellor of the Exchequer proceeded to recommend, that 'these two important and pressing questions should without delay be brought under the notice of the National and British and Foreign School Societies, in order that their opinion might be expressed, and if those opinions were favourable to these proposals, that they should be carried into early and practical effect.' He knew that there was no occasion to proceed further with this than to point out to their Lordships that, on the 5th July, 1838, it was the opinion of the Chancellor of the Exchequer that the principle of private contributions should be adhered to, and that reference should be made to the National Society and to the British and Foreign School Society, with respect to the erection of a model school. He now came to another era. He would not delay the House by referring to the papers relating to the letter addressed by the Secretary of State for the Home Department to the Lords of the Treasury, or of their answer thereto, because he understood that the plan suggested had been superseded by the subsequent proceedings. The order appointing the Committee of Privy Council, however, superseded the Board of Treasury. He did not know that the Committee of Privy Council would not answer as well as the Lords of the Treasury, who had so much on their hands. But he must say that the Committee of Privy Council was empowered to do a little more than the Lords of the Treasury. The Board of the Treasury could only receive applications from two societies, and determine upon them, and three or four of the members of the Board had sufficient occupation to prevent their having time to examine the different claims made to the two societies. The Lords of the Treasury had been superseded, and an appointment had been made of a Committee of the Privy Council, consisting exclusively of her Majesty's Ministers. That selection had been made without any regard to the fitness of the Members; he did not say that they were unfit; the selection was made without any regard to their fitness, but merely on account of the official situation which they held; and if the noble Lords retired tomorrow, their successors coming to the same places would take upon themselves **[1247]** this duty. When he considered that this was the foundation of a permanent scheme, it was singular that neither of the two Archbishops nor the one Bishop belonging to the Church, who were members of the Privy Council, should have been appointed. It might have been expected that the Government would have consulted such of the Bishops as were members of the Privy Council, and the only reason he knew why they were not consulted was, that their consent to the scheme never would have been obtained. But that was not a reason to satisfy the country, and it never would be. When these eminent persons were appointed, they drew up certain minutes. On the 13th of April, 1839, a scheme for the future guidance of the Committee was read. In the first place they proposed to found a school, in which candidates for the office of teacher in schools for the poorer classes might acquire the knowledge necessary to the exercise of their future profession, and might be practised in the most approved methods of religious and moral training and instruction. This school was to include a model school, in which children of all ages from three to fourteen might be taught and trained in sufficient numbers to form an infant school, as well as schools for children above seven. If a model school meant anything, it of course meant a model for all the schools throughout the country. Then came a most remarkable article. It related to religious instruction which was brought very prominently forward; and certainly the country would hear of nothing respecting national education in which religious instruction was not provided for. The subject, therefore, was in itself very properly brought forward; but as to the mode in which religious instruction was to be given, he could not say so much. Religious instruction, it seemed, was to be considered as general and special. He really did not know how to explain this.

There was, he recollected, a passage in one of the reports on prisons complaining that convicts in gaols were not instructed in the truths of natural and revealed religion. Now, he supposed that general instruction referred to natural religion, and that revealed religion was what was meant by special. [A noble Lord 'No.'] The noble Lord said 'no.' He would not say it was; but that was the most natural interpretation he could put upon the language. He **[1248]** wished the noble Lord would state what was meant by general instruction in the truths of revealed religion? What was it but the teaching of the peculiar truths of religion. In fact the whole of Christianity consisted of peculiar truths – truths, many of which were certainly contested by various denominations of Christians, but which must be acknowledged by those who would be esteemed as orthodox in the faith taught in the primitive ages of Christianity. He would not, however, go into an examination of what those truths were; but this he would say, that there was no such thing as instruction in Christianity without instruction in those peculiar truths. But to revert again to the minute of the Committee: – Periods were to be set apart for such peculiar doctrinal instruction as might be required for the religious training of the children. He had read, not many months ago, a report that in some parts of Germany, the attempt at combining religious instruction of different creeds with secular instruction, in the same school, had been abandoned, it being found impossible to conduct such a plan with satisfaction to any party. Different schools had been since established for the different persuasions of Catholics and Protestants, and the reason assigned for this appeared to be a very sound one; namely, that it was wrong to teach one set of children certain doctrines as true in one part of the schoolroom, and another set of children in another corner of the room that those doctrines were false. In a German publication, which he believed had not yet been translated into the English language, he had read a report of a person who had been sent to inspect the style and system of education adopted in different parts of Germany and France. The writer stated, that in some of the German states they had schools which comprehended children of all denominations, and even Jews; but that the persons intrusted with the care of those schools had protested strongly against such a measure, and that the inconvenience arising from it had been such, that alterations had been made in many instances. Their Lordships must at once feel how great would be the confusion introduced into the schools proposed to be established here if religious teachers of various denominations were to be admitted. The chaplain, who according to the scheme was to be appointed to **[1249]** conduct the religious instruction of children whose parents or guardians belonged to the Established Church would find it very difficult to maintain his authority if the parent or natural guardian of any other child were to be permitted to secure the attendance of the licensed minister of his own persuasion, at the period appointed for special religious instruction, in order to give such instruction apart. What confusion, too, would such a system produce in the minds of the children themselves! It was essential to the teaching of religion, that it should be taught with authority. Teachers did not appeal to the reason of the child, but taught him on authority. They said, such and such is the truth; such and such is the law of God; such and such is the rule of morality; and the child received it, as children receive all instruction, implicitly. If he were, at the same time told, that there are six or eight different opinions upon those truths, laws, and rules, to what can it possibly lead but to scepticism; to a rejection of all religion, or to an indifference to any? It must end in a rejection of the spiritual doctrines of religion from a conviction, that they are not true, and in a rejection of its moral precepts when it suits the convenience of the learner to suppose they are without any sanction. It was very true, that this scheme was not adopted. These resolutions of the Committee of Council were superseded by the report of the 1st of June, which was presented to and approved by her Majesty in Council. He had, however, felt it right to make these observations upon the original scheme preparatory to any remarks he should feel it his duty to make on the Order in Council, dated the 3rd of June, approving of the report of the Education Committee, dated the 1st of June. He did not think the opinions of the Members of the committee, as expressed in the scheme they first laid down, were at all superseded by the subsequent report and Order in Council. The Order in Council set forth the report of the committee in these terms: – 'The Lords of the Committee recommend, that the sum of ten thousand pounds, granted by Parliament in 1835, towards the erection of normal or model schools, be given in equal proportions to the National Society and the British and Foreign School Society. That the remainder of the subsequent grants of the years 1837 and 1838, yet unappro- **[1250]** priated, and any grant that may be voted in the present year, be chiefly applied in aid of, subscriptions for building, and, in particular cases, for the support of schools connected with those societies; but that the rule hitherto adopted, of making a grant to those places where the largest proportion is subscribed, be not invariably adhered to, should application be made from very poor and populous districts, where subscriptions to a sufficient amount cannot be obtained.' It might be very proper to make grants without adhering to the rule about the proportion of the contribution; but this point was stated so loosely, that there was no guarantee whatever for the propriety of those grants in particular cases. For 'The Committee do not feel themselves precluded from making grants in particular cases which shall appear to them to call for the aid of Government, although the applications may not come from either of the two mentioned societies.' By this the restriction which originally accompanied the grant was entirely removed; and certainly relieved the Lords of the Treasury from any responsibility in making these grants, giving the committee a discretionary power. The committee then repeated their opinion: 'The Committee are of opinion, that the most useful application of any sums voted by Parliament would consist in the employment of those moneys in the establishment of a normal school, under the direction of the State, and not placed under the management of a voluntary society.' (Thus these two societies were completely lost sight of.) But the Committee state 'That they have experienced so much difficulty in reconciling conflicting views respecting the provisions which they are desirous to make in furtherance of your Majesty's wish, that the children and teachers instructed in this school should be duly trained in the principles of the Christian religion, while the rights of conscience should be respected, that it is not in the power of the Committee to mature a plan for the accomplishment of this design without further consideration, and they therefore postpone taking any steps for this purpose until greater concurrence of opinion is found to prevail.' He would appeal to their Lordships, whether a very large and undefined discretion was not thus left to the committee, which he did not say would be abused, but which might be very grossly abused. He could not, when considering the extent of this discretionary power, wonder that **[1251]** the established clergy, the great portion of the Protestant Dissenters, and indeed all who had the interest of religion at heart, should feel alarmed at this enormous power being given to the committee, more especially when they connected it with what followed; for 'The Committee recommend that no further grant be made now or hereafter for the establishment or support of normal schools, or of any other schools, unless the right of inspection be retained, in order to secure a conformity to the regulations and discipline established in the several schools, with such improvements as may from time to time be suggested by the committee.' A great portion of the people of this country were of opinion (and he must say he agreed with them), that a power was thus conferred upon the committee which ought not to be entrusted in the hands of any number of men, and certainly not to men who were exclusively members of her Majesty's Government. What security had they that, in process of time, these grants would not be made from political motives, or in favour of prejudices and predilections? They knew not how many circumstances might arise to affect the minds of the successors of the present committee. He concurred in these apprehensions and fears, which became stronger when he considered the whole of the scheme – when he recollected with what deliberate intention their Lordships had been excluded from having the slightest concern in the regulation of a matter so immediately bearing upon the best interests of the people, upon their religious education, and their moral training. Was not a subject of this kind proper for Parliamentary discussion? Was it fit that it should be disposed of by only one branch of the Legislature? Were their Lordships, many of whom had particularly directed their attention to the subject, and all of whom were qualified to judge of it, were they to be shut out from all participation in regulations of this description? Was it consistent with the respect which was due to this branch of the Legislature? Was it consistent with the respect due to the Lords spiritual and temporal, that the only assembly in which the Church had a voice should not be heard at all upon such an important subject? He did not mean to say, that the influence of the Church was not great elsewhere; but at the same time their **[1252]** Lordships' House was the only place in which the Church was represented at all by her ministers. He was sure that their Lordships, whatever might be their political sentiments, would agree with him in this; that the moral and religious instruction of the great mass of the people of this country was a subject peculiarly belonging to the clergy of the Established Church; that the Sovereign was the head of the Church, and bound by the most sacred obligations to the maintenance of its authority; that all the advisers of the Sovereign were under the same obligation not to advise her Majesty to anything that could be prejudicial to the Church, and that, if they did so, they would be acting in violation of a most sacred duty, and most unconstitutionally; and he would further add, considering the connection of the Church with the State, they would also be acting with the greatest impolicy with respect to the true interests of the people, whom they would hardly venture to say, could be better instructed than by the ministers of the Established Church. If (said the most rev. Prelate) the Church does not teach the true doctrines of our holy religion – if it does not inculcate the purest morals – if it does not insist upon obedience to the laws and the authorities of the country – upon loyalty to the Sovereign and the performance of every Christian duty – I say, my Lords, it is utterly unworthy of your support. Look to some other source of moral and religious instruction, and cast away a Church which is so grossly deficient in its duty, or fails in attaining that object, for the attainment of which all religious establishments are formed. Again, I say, if such be the case, let us look elsewhere: But since that cannot be said, it is, I assert, the duty of the Crown – it is the duty of the Government, to advise no measures which shall be to the prejudice of the Church. I do not mean prejudicially interfering with its temporalities, but which shall diminish its salutary influence over the people; and that, in the distribution of the public money for the encouragement of religion, their first object ought to be to maintain and extend the religion of the State; that religion, which, by the instruction it imparts, combines the great majority of the people of this country with the vast establishment which is responsible to the State for the proper performance of its duties. When public money was granted **[1253]** for religious purposes, that, I say, ought to be the primary object of the Government. He did not mean to say that all assistance should be withheld from the dissenters. But whatever was done with respect to religious instruction, ought to be free from all party or political considerations; and those sums which were given, not to the just claims of the Dissenters, but in such a shape as to promote dissent, were not given consistently with the support which the State was bound to give to the Established Church of this country. He conceived that making such grants had a tendency to promote religious dissent, which was in itself a great evil, and cherished much misunderstanding among the people, and who must understand one another better before they could agree in their religious tenets. At the same time, he did not wish to be understood to say, that a certain degree of consideration was not due to the Dissenters. He had a great respect for those who religiously dissented. For political dissent, he must say, he had no respect whatever. Its objects were not religious. But, while he said that due consideration ought to be paid to the claims of the dissenters, he still maintained, that the distribution of those funds, and the management of all other matters connected with the very important subject of the religious instruction of the people ought to be decided by the united voice of Parliament, that no measure ought to be resorted to that excluded their Lordships from a share in the deliberations; and that he was convinced the people of this country would look with more confidence at any measure having the support of their Lordships, than to that which was only supported by one branch of the Legislature, a branch of which he was not inclined to speak with disrepect, and which was, perhaps, in its character, the most popular branch of the Legislature. The most reverend Prelate then concluded by moving the first of the following resolutions, stating, that after the first was carried, he should move the others seriatim, 'That this House has had under its consideration the various documents which have been presented by her Majesty's commands respecting public education, including those which refer to the application of public money in former years in aid of the building of school-houses in connection with the National Society and the British and Foreign School **[1254]** Society; and also the letters of the Secretary of State and the President of the Council the 4th, 6th, and 9th of February respectively; the Order in Council of the 10th of April, appointing a Committee of Council; the minutes of proceedings of that Committee of the 13th of April; and the report of the same Committee of the 3rd of June.' '2. That it appears, from the documents last mentioned, that a Committee of Council has been appointed, consisting exclusively of Members of her Majesty's Government, for the purpose of considering all matters affecting the education of the people, and of superintending the application of any sums which may be voted by Parliament for that purpose.' 'That on the 13th of April last it was proposed by such Committee to establish a model school, which might serve as an example for other schools, and a normal school, in which a body of schoolmasters might be formed competent to assume the management of similar institutions in all parts of the country.' '3. It appears, by the report of the Committee, approved by her Majesty in Council on the 3rd of June, that the Committee is empowered to retain the right of inspection, in order to secure a conformity with such regulations as they may approve of for the management and discipline of all schools to which aid may be granted; and to make grants of public money to any schools which may appear to them to require such aid, irrespectively to the religious doctrines which may be inculcated in such schools.' '4. That it appears to this House, that the powers thus intrusted to the Committee of Council are so important in their bearing upon the moral and religious education of the people of this country, and upon the proper duties and functions of the Established Church, and at the same time so capable of progressive and indefinite extension, that they ought not to be committed to any public authority without the consent of Parliament.' '5. That it appears to this House, that the particular scheme of education set forth in the Minutes of the Committee of Council of the 13th April is open to grave objection with reference to the arrangements made for the religious instruction of children, to the use within the school of any other than the authorised version of the Scriptures, and to many other important details; and although it is stated in the report of the Committee of Council of the 3rd of June, that it is not in the power of the Committee to mature a plan for the formation of a normal school without further consideration, and that they therefore postpone taking any steps for the purpose until greater concurrence of opinion is found to prevail, yet the report gives no assurance that the scheme approved by the Committee on the 13th of April may not be hereafter carried into execution at the discretion of the Committee.' '6. That, under these circumstances, this **[1255]** House considers itself bound by the obligations of public duty to present an humble address to her Majesty, conveying to her Majesty the resolutions into which it has entered, and humbly praying, that her Majesty will be graciously pleased to give directions that no steps shall be taken with respect to the establishment or foundation of any plan for the general education of the people of this country without giving to this House, as one branch of the Legislature, an opportunity of fully considering a measure of such deep importance to the highest interests of the community.'

Index

Printed in Great Britain
by Amazon

61670284R00111